Translated Texts for Historians

This series is designed to meet the needs of students of ancient and medieval history and others who wish to broaden their study by reading source material, but whose knowledge of Latin or Greek is not sufficient to allow them to do so in the original language. Many important Late Imperial and Dark Age texts are currently unavailable in translation and it is hoped that TTH will help to fill this gap and to complement the secondary literature in English which already exists. The series relates principally to the period 300–800 AD and includes Late Imperial, Greek, Byzantine and Syriac texts as well as source books illustrating a particular period or theme. Each volume is a self-contained scholarly translation with an introductory essay on the text and its author and notes on the text indicating major problems of interpretation, including textual difficulties.

D0911148

Front cover: the figure of Megalopsychia from a mosaic in the Yakto villa at Daphne, near Antioch, cf. Libanius, *Or.* 11.138 with note. From D. Levi, *Antioch Mosaic Pavements*, Princeton 1947.

A full list of published titles in the Translated Texts for Historians series is available on request. The most recently published are shown below.

For full details of Translated Texts for Historians, including prices and ordering information, please write to the following:
All countries, except the USA and Canada: Liverpool University Press, 4 Cambridge Street, Liverpool, L69 7ZU, UK (*Tel* +44–[0]151–794 2233, *Fax* +44–[0]151–794 2235, *Email* J.M.Smith@liv.ac.uk, http://www.liverpool-unipress.co.uk). **USA and Canada:** University of Pennsylvania Press, 4200 Pine Street, Philadelphia, PA 19104–6097, USA (*Tel* +1–215–898–6264, *Fax* +1–215–898–0404).

Translated Texts for Historians
Volume 34

Antioch as a Centre of Hellenic Culture as Observed by Libanius

translated with an introduction by A. F. Norman

Liverpool
University
Press

First published 2000
Liverpool University Press
4 Cambridge Street
Liverpool, L69 7ZU

British Library Cataloguing-in-Publication Data
A British Library CIP Record is available
ISBN 0–85323–595–3

Set in Monotype Times by
Wilmaset Ltd, Birkenhead, Wirral
Printed in the European Union by
Bell and Bain Ltd, Glasgow

FOR BEN
without whose help this would never have been seen

TABLE OF CONTENTS

EDITOR'S NOTE

I would like to express thanks to the following people for their different important contributions to this volume. John Matthews brought this unpublished material to the attention of the Editorial Board of Translated Texts for Historians and arranged for the typing of the two long speeches, 11 and 62. Ben Norman produced a typescript of the remaining speeches after revision by his grandfather, Professor A.F. Norman, and provided an invaluable communication line with Professor Norman in the later stages of preparation. Regine May did extensive typographical and copy-editing work to produce the final integrated manuscript, and also compiled the index. We are very sad that Professor Norman did not live to see this volume, over which he took great pains.

The map of Antioch is based an that in the translation of *The Chronicle of John Malalas* by Elizabeth Jeffreys, Michael Jeffreys and Roger Scott (Byzantia Australiensia 4, Melbourne 1986), 309. It in turn was redrawn from the map in G. Downey, *A History of Antioch in Syria* (Princeton 1961), plate 11. Translated Texts for Historians is grateful both to the Australian Association of Byzantine Studies and to Princeton University Press for permission to use this map.

Mary Whitby
June 2000

GENERAL INTRODUCTION

It is characteristic of the man that by far the greater part of the information concerning Libanius is to be recovered from his own works. The most material account he gives is that of *Oration* 1, originally composed and delivered in A.D. 374, which was intended as a moralizing essay on Fortune, with his own career to that time as his point of reference, in the same way that twenty years before he had taken the career of his rival Acacius to illustrate his essay on Genius. To this purely sophistic essay there was added in chronological sequence over the next twenty years a series of occasional supplements, seemingly unpublished and unrevised, so that the whole work becomes an old man's journal and consolation. The resultant rather shapeless oration, which bears the convenient, if inaccurate, title of the *Life* or the *Autobiography*, thus provides the chronological framework to which the mass of information contained in his other works can be referred. These works, discounting purely scholastic exercises and declamations, consist of the surviving orations, public and private, over 60 in number and covering a period of more than 40 years, together with more than 1,500 letters, the vast majority of which are concentrated in the years A.D. 355–65 and A.D. 388–93.

Thus we know that he was born in A.D. 314 in Antioch of a good municipal family which was just recovering from the disastrous punishment inflicted upon it by the intemperate wrath of the emperor Diocletian ten years before. Fatherless at the age of ten and with his uncles as guardians thereafter, he was brought up in the traditional Greek education of grammar and rhetoric, normal for his age and standing, but by the age of fifteen he had undergone his own conversion and, quite untypically and against the wishes of his family who envisaged a more worldly career for him, he was firmly set upon a career in rhetoric. In A.D. 336, with family opposition at last overcome, he set out to complete his studies in Athens, at an age more mature than that of the average student. There he remained for four years, a brilliant but awkward student, impatient of the professorial incompetence he found there, and priggishly non-conformist. By the end of A.D. 340 he had turned his back on Athens to try his luck as a private teacher in the new capital of Constantinople, with its parvenu society. His success was meteoric, but came at the cost of professional intrigues and rivalries which he did nothing to avoid. Nor was he popular with certain members of the imperial administration, and a combination of rivals and officials forced his withdrawal from the capital on the occasion of the riots of A.D. 342. Within two years, however, he was settled as municipal sophist in Nicomedia where he stayed happily for five years, forming firm and influential friendships although officialdom looked upon him askance because of his visible adherence to the old religion, and barred the young Julian from associating directly with him, despite the fame of his oratory. This continued to flourish and in A.D. 349, after the delivery of his panegyric on the reigning emperors (*Or.* 59), his repute was such that he was recalled by imperial mandate to take up the official chair at Constantinople. Return he must, however reluctantly, and there he remained, thoroughly miserable and only too eager to get away from a place and people he disliked and despised.

Even so, in A.D. 352/3 he refused the prestigious offer of the chair of rhetoric at Athens, for, prompted by his uncle, he was already hankering after a return home to Antioch. A successful vacation visit and lecture tour followed in the summer of A.D. 353, when, buoyed up with promise of his cousin's hand in marriage and with the half-promise of his old teacher Zenobius to vacate the sophistic chair in his favour, he returned to Constantinople to pull strings to secure his release from his post in the capital. This he succeeded in doing with the plea of ill-health, and in A.D. 354 he secured his leave of absence, much to the relief of his rivals. In the spring of that year, he returned home for good, to find that his plans had gone all awry. His fiancée was dead; Zenobius had changed his mind and retracted his half-promise; Antioch was in throes of riots and disturbances, egged on by the excesses of the Caesar Gallus, who had arrested the whole city council, his uncle included. Most of these difficulties, however, were soon resolved. The councillors were released almost immediately; Gallus was soon removed in disgrace, to be replaced by Strategius as prefect, a good friend of Libanius; Zenobius died within months, and Libanius duly took his place as sophist of the city, whereupon he embarked on a period of extraordinary literary activity. With the support of his uncle, a leading light in the council, and the good will of the prefect, whom he was to reward with a famous panegyric, his position was consolidated against all rivalries at home, and his fame abroad was enhanced by orations like the *Antiochikos*. Above all, his correspondence files were organized to maximum advantage for the first time to ensure the widespread promotion of his prestige; only in his personal life was there something left to be desired. Ill-health, the excuse by which he had gained his leave of absence from Constantinople, now became a reality, and he was to experience chronic visitations of gout and migraine, which he faithfully records for the next fifteen years. Moreover, in place of his dead fiancée, he now took in concubinage a slave woman, by whom he had the one illegitimate son Arabius, later called Cimon, whose legal status was to cause him so much worry in later life. The woman herself remains unmentioned in his writings until after her death in A.D. 390, when she is described as 'worth many a servant to me' (*Or.* 1.278).

His correspondence and the *Autobiography* combine to give this picture of extraordinary dedication to his art in these early years in Antioch. Overwork, illness and his valetudinarian tendencies, however, take their toll, and in A.D. 359, following the deaths in close succession of some of his closest friends, his mother and his uncle, his mentor and most influential supporter, these induce a deep depression verging upon nervous breakdown, a reaction which he would again suffer at times of crisis in later life, as at the death of Julian, for instance. Simultaneously, it was a time of growing political tensions between Constantius and Julian, and there was a hardening of official attitude against him as a known acquaintance of Julian. In A.D. 360 he had to contend with a hostile and bigotedly Christian prefect, Elpidius, who promptly administered the snub of halving his official salary. Antioch, pro-Constantian in sentiment and with a large and active Christian element, seems to have followed this lead. At any rate, Libanius' assistant teachers now found themselves in financial straits also, and he has to approach the council on their behalf (*Or.* 31), with what results remains unclear.

From this dejection he was rescued by Julian's bloodless accession to the position of sole Augustus. He could not but welcome unreservedly most aspects of policy of the new régime, for the social, religious and educational principles of the new ruler matched his own, except that he was never a proponent of the extremes of reactionary paganism as practised by the new emperor and his neo-Platonist entourage. Indeed, Julian's first year was bittersweet for Libanius. He had the felicity of seeing all the ideals which he had so long advocated being put into action, yet he was expected to be mouthpiece of a city which was slow and resentful in its acknowledgement of the new emperor. In addition, there were personal considerations which gave him cause for hesitation.

He belonged to a family which had twice to its cost experienced the petu-
lance of princes, and several members of it had given offence to Gallus
and even to Julian himself (cf. Amm. Marc. 22.9.16f.; Lib. *Ep.* 679).
Caution was therefore to be the watchword.

Such hesitations were removed upon Julian's arrival in Antioch in
July A.D. 362 *en route* for his Persian campaign. Libanius was warmly
welcomed and received into the emperor's intimate circle. This short
period forms the high-water mark of his sophistic achievements. He
could at last imagine himself in his ideal role, comparable with that of
his illustrious predecessors of the Antonine age, sophist of his city, and
expressing himself with the independence for which he had yearned
before his ideal emperor. It was, to him, a meeting of minds on the intellectual plane, with the common ground to be found in Hellenic eloquence
and devotion to the old religion, from which it was inseparable. To be
sure, he never subscribed to the mysteries of neo-Platonist thaumaturgy,
to which Julian, more of a mystic, was increasingly devoted, and he used
his independence to temper the heavy-handedness of religious extremism
displayed by some of Julian's officials with counsels of prudence and
toleration. He had friends among the Christians, even in his own family,
and friendship and adherence to the law he places higher than official
bigotry in the application of the new religious policies (e.g. *Epp.* 757,
763, 819). In his personal relations he retained his independence: he was
non-conformist enough to refuse the honorary office offered him by
Julian (*Or.* 2.8; Eunap. *V.S.* 495f.), but for all that he could not escape
the imputation of using his new-found influence for mere self-advance-
ment, a charge which he indignantly denies, both then and later (*Epp.*
797, 1154; *Orr.* 1.123; 2.8; 51.30).

This harmony was soon marred. The populace of Antioch, vocal,
volatile yet obstinately devoted to Constantius' memory in opposition
to the reforming zeal of the new emperor, soon became at odds with
him, and tempers were further exacerbated by the onset of famine, so
much so that Libanius found himself obliged to act as mediator between
his city and the emperor, whom it had offended so deeply as to cause
him to vent his bile upon it in the satirical *Misopogon*. Neither his
personal intercessions nor the orations he sent on after Julian's departure
(*Orr.* 15; 16), succeeded in healing the breach, and the quarrel remained
unresolved until Julian's death, or, as Libanius was to repeat, his
murder, later in the year. The news was welcomed with such transports
of delight in Antioch as to cause the greatest anguish for him, and to

bring on another breakdown. However, he displayed resilience and consistency enough to produce his two great orations in Julian's memory (*Orr.* 17; 18), during the next two years, even in the face of such popular revulsion. The sophist of the city now saw a complete reversal of his role: now he was morally obliged to justify his dead emperor's memory before a hostile and ungrateful public, and this he proceeded faithfully to do, with the result that for the rest of his life he was even more of a marked man, suspected as an actual or potential malcontent.

The period following Julian's death is the most hazardous of Libanius' life. He became the target for assassination attempts under Jovian, and many of his friends were actively involved in the revolt of Procopius in A.D. 365. Indeed from that year his correspondence files vanish altogether, and even for the years A.D. 363–5, they are in such disorder that it may be conjectured that a hurried withdrawal of any possibly incriminating items has taken place as an act of prudent self-censorship. Thereafter through the reign of Valens he lived dangerously, in growing obscurity and official disfavour. Twice, and only by the skin of his teeth, did he escape charges for treason based upon correspondence, but the letters were found in the archives of the recipients, not his own. For him the keeping of correspondence files in such unhappy times was something he refrained from doing until he was finally free from any accusation of treason, in A.D. 388. Similarly with his orations. The only oration which he certainly composed under Valens is the original *Autobiography* of A.D. 374 (and even that has been sanitized, as is indicated by the later recapitulations of the period in *Or.* 1.156–81, written in A.D. 382), together with now lost addresses to his old friend, the prefect Modestus. An attempted panegyric on Valens was frustrated by the schemes of hostile courtiers. Such enforced silence could not but be galling for him, and the only redeeming feature is the intermission from his illness which he records as occurring in A.D. 370 and lasting until A.D. 386, when it recurred more seriously than before.

After Valens' death at Adrianople in A.D. 378, he finally emerges from this obscurity and before the new and as yet untried Theodosius published a call for the restoration of Julian's memory and ideals, setting himself up as the mouthpiece of a pagan revival in the East, as Symmachus was to be in the West (*Or.* 24). But his influence was much more restricted than before, and Theodosius soon showed himself in his true colours as a committed orthodox Christian. He certainly composed orations for the Olympia of A.D. 380 and 384, but they

remained undelivered (*Or.* 1.184, 222). Nor were there many opportunities for panegyrics in the grand manner that he would have desired:
only two are recorded in six years (ibid. 179ff., 232), yet, paradoxically
enough, he enjoyed sufficient favour with the higher officials to be
awarded an honorary title of office in A.D. 383 as a reward for long
service to education. It was at the local level that his influence had
waned. Criticism began to surface about his personal and professional
conduct as early as A.D. 381/2 (*Orr.* 2; 62), not from his rivals, as he
might have expected, but from lay persons, and this came as a shock to
him. His repeated complaints about the encroachments of the studies of
Latin and law upon his own Hellenic system were beginning to cause a
reaction against him in the social strata upon which he depended, and in
turn his reactions were the more bitter. With advancing age he had developed an unhappy knack of upsetting people who mattered, and a combination of generous humanity towards the oppressed and a stiff-necked
and self-righteous vanity caused him to give offence to the *honorati*, the
magnates among the city council, to an ever more influential Christian
community, in which he lived, and to a succession of resident governors,
Icarius, Proclus, Eustathius, Eutropius for instance, with whom his relations began fair and ended foul, often because of some real or imaginary
fault rooted in minor disagreements about his professional attitude.

He may indeed act as patron to the oppressed bakers in time of
famine, but the Christians have already organized corporate relief
works which are more effective, and his protests about social injustice,
whether directed against religious vandalism (*Or.* 30), brutal prison
conditions (*Or.* 45), forced labour (*Or.* 50), or protection rackets
(*Or.* 47), though thoroughly justified in the face of a rapacious and
corrupt administration, serve only to marginalize his position. Even the
much-vaunted *Orations on the Statues* (*Orr.* 19–23) lose their immediacy
and effect as compared with Chrysostom's *Homilies*, for only one
(*Or.* 23) is at all contemporary with the events, the rest being composed
to be read by the recipients rather than actually delivered to them, and
for Libanius an unspoken panegyric missed its mark. However, the
unkindest cut of all was the increasing disaffection among both pupils
and parents, which demonstrated his growing insecurity, exaggerated
by the recurrence of his old ailments and by his allegations of magic practised against him, so that he can quite matter-of-factly speak of his
'enemies', whereas in *Oration* 62 he had taken issue only with a single
individual.

In his final years it was the impact of his domestic problems upon his professional life that gave him the greatest concern. His success in elevating the status of his bastard son Cimon to legitimacy and succession to his fortune made the lad a ripe candidate for curial service, which they both interpreted, probably correctly, as victimization, and with his growing unpopularity among councillors and governors this victimization also extended to his professional associates – Eusebius and Thalassius. Hence the tirades of *Orations* 42 and 54, and the turn-around in attitude towards the council from being one of support to one of bitter opposition (*Orr.* 48–9). Criticism against him, his family or his professional system became tantamount to sacrilege, and after Cimon's death in A.D. 391 he became a frustrated and embittered old invalid, one of whose last recorded comments is the curse on false friends which ends his *Autobiography*.

Bentley in his *Phalaris* described Libanius as a recluse pedant. Nothing is further from the truth. From the nature of his profession and his standing in it, the acceptance of the kinship between his Hellenic education and the old religion as an article of faith, coupled with his conception of rhetoric as the performance of public service – all combined to ensure that he would consistently express these ideals to the world at large and his own community in particular, come what may. He could and did, therefore, in all sincerity claim that attacks upon his educational system were both sacrilegious and anti-social. Not averse to change in itself when it was right, he refused to subscribe to the notion of change for the sake of change, nor to give up the principles with which his training had imbued him. But this, from the nature of the models he had set for himself, the second-century sophists and Aelius Aristides in particular, harked back to that time when sophists expressed themselves with independence upon social, moral and religious questions before emperors and officials who treated them as equals. In *Oration* 2 he prided himself that his conduct had earned him the epithet 'charming'. But, except for the brief and blissful interlude with Julian, he could rarely attain that ideal, and with the sudden and drastic changes of his own time, his charm rapidly became unpopularity with sections of society that really mattered to him. In his latter years he still had a devoted, though reduced, following, but these were small fry. Growing impotence resulted in frustration and disappointment, in both professional and personal life, so that he appears as vain, self-righteous and cantankerous, a far cry from that personal attraction that his talents had earned him in his prime. Even the 'reform' speeches, in which he shows himself to be enlightened and humane in his attempts to lead public opinion, earned him few friends owing to vested interests, and they fell short of the great display speeches with their purity of style and exquisite refinement, which had earned for him the soubriquet of 'Demosthenes the Second'.

SELECT BIBLIOGRAPHY

Works of Reference

R. Foerster (ed.), Libanius, *Opera*, 12 vols., Leipzig 1903–27, repr. Hildesheim 1963.

A.H.M. Jones, J. Martindale and J. Morris (eds.), *Prosopography of the Later Roman Empire*, I, Cambridge, 1971.

E.L von Leutsch and F.G. Schneidewin (eds.), *Corpus Paroemiographorum Graecorum*, Göttingen 1818–39, repr. Amsterdam 1965.

J.P. Migne, *Patrologiae cursus completus, series Graeca*, Paris 1857–66.

T. Mommsen (ed.) *Codex Theodosianus*, Berlin 1905, repr. 1954.

C. Müller, *Fragmenta Historicorum Graecorum*, 5 vols., Paris 1841–70.

Pauly-Wissowa (eds.), *Realencyclopaedie der classischen Alterthumswissenschaft*, Stuttgart 1894.

J.J. Reiske (ed.), *Libanii Sophistae Orationes et Declamationes*, 4 vols., Altenburg 1791.

O. Seeck (ed.), *Die Briefe des Libanius zeitlich geordnet*, Leipzig 1906, repr. Hildesheim 1967.

J.C. Wolf (ed.), Libanius, *Epistulae*, Amsterdam 1738.

Translations and Commentaries

G. Downey (trans., comm.), 'Libanius' *Oration in Praise of Antioch'*, (*Or.* XI), *Proceedings of the American Philosophical Society* 103.5 (1959), 652–86.

G. Fatouros and T. Krischer (eds.), Libanios, *Briefe*, Munich 1980.

G. Fatouros and T. Krischer (trans., comm.), Libanios, *Antiochikos* (*Oration XI*), Vienna and Berlin 1992.

A.J. Festugière, *Antioche païenne et chrétienne*, Paris 1959 (contains translation of *Or.* 11.196ff., with archaeological commentary by R. Martin, also translations of *Orr.* 34–6; 3; 55; 58).

L. Harmand (ed., trans., comm.), Libanius, *Discours sur les patronages*, (*Or.* 47), Paris 1955.

J. Martin (ed., trans., comm.), Libanios, *Discours* II (= *Or.* 2–10), Paris 1988.

J. Martin and P. Petit (eds., trans., comm.), Libanios, *Autobiographie* (*Discours* 1), Paris 1979.

A.F. Norman (ed., trans., comm.), Libanius, *Selected Orations* I (= *Orr.* 13–18; 24), Loeb Classical Library, London and Cambridge, Mass. 1969.

A.F. Norman (ed., trans., comm.), Libanius, *Selected Orations* II (= *Orr.* 2; 30; 33; 45; 19–23; 47–50), Loeb Classical Library, London and Cambridge, Mass. 1971.

A.F. Norman (ed., trans., comm.), Libanius, *Autobiography and Selected Letters*, 2 vols., Loeb Classical Library, London and Cambridge, Mass. 1992.

P. Wolf (trans.), Libanios, *Autobiographische Schriften* (*Orr.* I–V), Zurich and Stuttgart 1967.

Historical Sources

Ammianus Marcellinus, *Histories*, ed. by J.C. Rolfe, 3 vols., Loeb Classical Library, London and Cambridge, Mass. 1935–39.

Codex Theodosianus, trans. by C. Pharr, Princeton 1952.

Eunapius, *Lives of the Philosophers and Sophists*, ed., trans., comm. by W.C. Wright, Loeb Classical Library, London and Cambridge, Mass. 1922.

Julian, *Works*, ed., trans., comm. by W.C. Wright, 3 vols., Loeb Classical Library, London and Cambridge, Mass. 1913–23.

Julian, *Oeuvres complètes*, ed., trans., comm. by J. Bidez, G. Rochefort and C. Lacombrade, 2 vols. in 4, Paris 1932–64.

Julian, *Epistulae, Leges, Fragmenta*, ed. J. Bidez and F. Cumont, Paris 1922.

Malalas, *Chronica*, in Migne, *PG* 97; ed. L. Dindorf, Corpus Scriptorum Historiae Byzantinae, Bonn 1831.

The Chronicle of John Malalas, trans. by E. and M. Jeffreys and R. Scott, Melbourne 1986.

Socrates, *Historia Ecclesiastica*, in Migne, *PG* 67; ed. G.C. Hansen, Griechische Christliche Schriftsteller, Berlin 1995.

Themistius, *Orationes*, ed. H. Schenkl, G. Downey, A.F. Norman, 3 vols., Leipzig 1965–74.

Themistius, *Orationes*, ed. W. Dindorf, Leipzig 1832.

Zosimus, *Historiae*, ed., trans., comm. by F. Paschoud, 3 vols., Paris 1970–89.

Selected Modern Literature

Antioch-on-the-Orontes, Princeton Excavations, 5 vols., Princeton 1934–48.

G.W. Bowersock, *Julian the Apostate*, London and Cambridge, Mass. 1978.

P. Brown, *Power and Persuasion in Late Antiquity: Towards a Christian Empire*, Madison, Wisconsin 1992.

R. Browning, *The Emperor Julian*, London 1975.

Av. Cameron, 'Education and Literary Culture', in *The Cambridge Ancient History*, XIII, eds. Av. Cameron and P. Garnsey, Cambridge 1998, ch. 22.

G. Dagron, 'L'Empire romain d'orient au IVᵉ siècle et les traditions politiques de l'Hellénisme: le témoignage de Themistios', *Travaux et mémoires* 3 (1968), 1–242.

G. Downey, *A History of Antioch in Syria*, Princeton 1961.

G. Fatouros and T. Krischer, *Libanios*, Wege der Forschung, vol. 621, Darmstadt 1983. Contains among other articles on Libanius, the following:

G. Downey, 'The Olympic Games of Antioch in the Fourth Century A.D.', 1939.

J.W.H.G. Liebeschuetz, 'The Syriarch in the Fourth Century', 1959.

P. Petit, 'Zur Datierung des "Antiochikos" (*Or.* 11) des Libanios', 1981.

P. Petit, 'Die Senatoren von Konstantinopel im Werk des Libanios', 1957 (= transl. of P. Petit, 'Les Senateurs de Constantinople dans l'oeuvre de Libanios', 1957).

F. Schemmel, 'Der Sophist Libanios als Schüler und Lehrer', 1907.

A.J. Festugière, *Antioche païenne et chrétienne*, Paris 1959.

A.H.M. Jones, *The Later Roman Empire*, 3 vols., Oxford 1964.

A.H.M. Jones, *Cities of the Eastern Roman Empire*, 2nd ed., Oxford 1971.

R. Kaster, *Guardians of Language: The Grammarian and Society in Late Antiquity*. Berkeley, Los Angeles and London, 1988.

Doro Levi, *Antioch Mosaic Pavements*, vol. I Text, vol. II Plates, Princeton 1947.

J.W.H.G. Liebeschuetz, *Antioch*, Oxford 1972.

H.I. Marrou, *A History of Education in Antiquity* (trans. G. Lamb), London 1956.

J. Matthews, *The Roman Empire of Ammianus*, London 1989.

Ch.R. Morey, *Mosaics of Antioch*, London 1938.

P. Petit, *Libanius et la vie municipale à Antioche au IVe siècle après J.C.*, Paris 1955.

P. Petit, *Les Etudiants de Libanius*, Paris 1956.

D.A. Russell, *Libanius: Imaginary Speeches*, London 1996.

A. Schenk von Stauffenberg, *Die römische Kaisergeschichte bei Malalas*, Stuttgart 1931.

B. Schouler, *La Tradition hellénique chez Libanios*, 2 vols., Lille 1983.

O. Seeck, *Geschichte des Untergangs der antiken Welt*, Berlin 1897–1921, repr. Darmstadt 1967.

G.R. Sievers, *Das Leben des Libanius*, Berlin 1868, repr. Amsterdam 1969.

J.H.W. Walden, *The Universities of Ancient Greece*, New York 1912, repr. 1970.

P. Wolf, *Vom Schulwesen der Spätantike: Studien zu Libanius*, Baden Baden 1952.

ABBREVIATIONS

BLZG	O. Seeck (ed.), *Die Briefe des Libanius zeitlich geordnet*
BZ	*Byzantinische Zeitschrift*
Cod. Th.	T. Mommsen (ed.), *Codex Theodosianus*
Corp. Par. Gr.	E.L. von Leutsch and F.G. Schneiderwin (eds.), *Corpus Paroemigographorum Graecorum*
FHG	C. Müller, *Fragmenta Historicum Graecorum*
Foerster	R. Foerster (ed.), Libanius, *Opera*
JHS	*Journal of Hellenic Studies*
JRS	*Journal of Roman Studies*
PG	J.P. Migne, *Patrologiae cursus completus, series Graeca*
PLRE	A.H.M. Jones, J. Martindale and J. Morris (eds.), *Prosopography of the Later Roman Empire*
RE	Pauly-Wissowa (eds.), *Realencyclopaedie der classischen Alterthumswissenschaft*
Reiske	J.J. Reiske (ed.), *Libanii Sophistae Orationes et Declamationes*
TaPhA	Transactions of the American Philological Association

For standard abbreviations for ancient works, see L.S.J. Lampe and G.W.H. Lampe, *A Patristic Greek Lexicon*, Oxford 1961.

PART I

IN THE REIGN OF CONSTANTIUS

ORATIONS 11 AND 31

ORATION 11: THE ANTIOCHIKOS:
IN PRAISE OF ANTIOCH*

INTRODUCTION

Debate concerning the date and purpose of this speech, as to whether it really was an Olympic oration and whether its date of composition was A.D. 356 or A.D. 360, was finally resolved by Paul Petit in his article *Zur Datierung des Antiochikos* (1981). The core of his argument lies in the brief but compelling citation from *Ep.* 36 (Foerster), dated to A.D. 358/9, which had been ignored or misinterpreted since the time of Sievers (1868), viz:

> A fourth speech comes your way, that in praise of our city. This, at the Olympia anyway, was heard according to the dictates of custom, by our city. This gathering is something which the majority of people avoid by scattering to their own home-towns.

The date of this letter rules out the later date for the composition of the speech, and its explicit statement that it was delivered on the occasion of the Olympia, coupled with his introduction to the speech itself where he affirms that this was his first venture into that field, points decisively to the festival of A.D. 356, the first Olympia to be celebrated since his return home in A.D. 354. Libanius is thus taking the first opportunity of fulfilling his debt to his native city and of proclaiming the virtues of the old religious institutions which had marked its rise to become one of the great centres of the Hellenistic and Greco-Roman world.

The letter, however, adds some more mundane considerations. Whatever its importance to Libanius and his fellow pagan intellectuals, the delivery of such ceremonial orations was evidently regarded as being a relatively minor part of the festival. It appears to be relegated towards the final days, certainly to those when the major attractions – the formal opening, the races and athletic contests and the shows – were over, and the spectators were ready to disperse. It appears that such an oration sped them on their way; the majority of them simply had no time for such oratory. It may also

---

* Foerster (I, 412–535), Reiske (I, 275–365)

be suspected that, considering the subject matter of such an oration, there was some antipathy towards it on the part of visitors from other Syrian cities. Antiochene pride, as expressed by such an enthusiast as Libanius, might well be too much for resentful neighbours to stomach.

For Libanius, and for pagan intellectuals generally, the Games of A.D. 356 by happy coincidence followed closely upon the elevation of Julian to the rank of Caesar in the winter previous, and among the pagan underground it was fairly common knowledge as to where his religious sympathies now really lay, even though he and they were under constant observation by Constantius' secret police. While this elevation can in no way be interpreted as causing Libanius to develop as he did his chosen theme of the patronage of the old gods for Antioch's success and to proclaim it so openly, there is little doubt that for him and his like-minded fellows the event gave a ray of hope after their recent experiences, and the sanctity of the occasion gave him the opportunity of expressing that uplift of spirit to better advantage. Thus his insistence upon the harmony between the ancient and the modern (§10f.) and upon the rôle of the gods in the creation of the city (e.g. §52) reinforces that same sense of spiritual uplift and transmits it to his own time, enabling him to round off the whole with a recitation of the glories of Daphne, where the festival reached its climax, and a reminder that twice within living memory emperors had acknowledged its sanctity by the prestigious act of assuming presidency of the Games.

The particular type of epideictic oratory to which this oration belongs – that of the laudation of a specific city – had a long and respected history in the tradition of Greek rhetoric, so much so that it formed part of the formal studies of theorists like Menander Rhetor with his rules and hints for the formulation and sequence of ideas, which Libanius duly observes. Beginning with funeral speeches, that of Pericles in Thucydides Book 2 *par excellence*, whose words are echoed by Libanius in the first and last paragraphs of this speech, it was the ideal vehicle whereby a city's achievements as a civilizing power could be expressed in elevated moral terms of universal application so beloved of later moralizing sophists. In this respect the classical orator Isocrates and, for Libanius in particular, the second-century sophist Aristides, in their Panathenaic orations expanded the concept into that of a pan-Hellenic culture, where the criterion of a true Hellene is to be found not in race, but in language and education. This was an ideal which the Hellenistic and Greco-Roman world could, and did, enthusiastically adopt, and rhetoric was the instrument whereby all men of education, be they a Themistius from backward Paphlagonia, a Libanius from cosmopolitan Antioch or a Synesius from furthest Cyrenaica, could, whatever their final careers, find their true roots. Moreover, since so much of the content was of religious origin, it was inevitable that in this wider Hellenistic world, the old gods of Greek myth should be identified with the local genius of the place. Hence it was natural for Libanius, whose own conversion to rhetoric was of a quasi-religious nature, that, in a speech on his own city on a religious occasion like the Olympia, he too should go back to first beginnings to reveal the divine favour which had sustained it to become what it was, the acknowledged metropolis of Asia. That was something the new capital could never do, and for him the rôle played by protecting deities of the city is thus crucial not only for its past history but also for the manifold activities of everyday life, the virtues of its council, the discipline of its commons and the business in its streets, culminating in the glories of Daphne and its festival.

Such being his theme, he must exercise great care in the choice and presentation of his material, and Libanius is as instructive in what he omits as in what he presents. His practice in panegyric which he is jokingly to outline in *Ep.* 19.7ff. to Anatolius (translated in Norman (1992), I, 487ff.), is here applied in enthusiastic sincerity. Thus, any failings of the first Seleucids are glossed over, their successes emphasized; the end of the dynasty is ignored, and Antioch's acceptance of Roman sovereignty ascribed to divine will in truly Homeric guise. The virtues of his contemporary councillors, upon which they obviously prided themselves, are paraded for their delectation, though in a manner too materialistic for Julian's taste, as was to be revealed in the *Misopogon*. The discipline of his commons conveniently ignores the late disturbances under Gallus, and there is no hint in his picture of the industrious Antiochenes of that army of the poor to which Chrysostom bears witness. It is only natural that for him in such an oration the presence and influence of an intrusive religion like Christianity should not be apparent, but the totality with which it is ignored becomes the more startling, granted its long history and development in his community. So it is that there is no mention of the Great Church, begun by Constantine and so recently dedicated by Constantius. There is no room here for so alien a topic. Instead, there is concentration throughout on the Greekness of the society and on the old religion with which that Greekness is inextricably linked, with two other emperors cited as the champions of its major festival.

The message of Libanius throughout is designed to attract the attention of the élite and the educated in the community and, by implication, of their fellows throughout the cities of the East. Nor can it be said that his statements, however rosy the colours in which they are presented, are without foundation. His audience was contemporary with what he has to say of the Antioch of his day, and he must be seen to be telling a tale grounded in fact and in their own experience, even though by the laudatory nature of his chosen vehicle he may be colouring it to their tastes according to the rules of panegyric, already mentioned. Thus, when he speaks of the council as being the nerve-centre of the city he bears witness to the intense concentration of the imperial administration upon the welfare of the councils as expressed in its mass of legislation on the subject, however ham-fistedly it was applied. The idealized picture of the city council acting in paternal fashion towards the commons, which in its turn follows them with filial discipline, embodies the whole concept of the institution of patronage as the basis of society, which it was. Even the deference of the governors towards the council and its readiness to speak its mind towards them has some basis in contemporary fact, once it is remembered that the prefect Strategius, then in office, had been appointed with the specific mission of restoring Antioch to order after Gallus' recent excesses by use of a policy of conciliation; and the account of the warmth of relationship between citizens and emperor is confirmed by Julian's statement (*Or.* 1.40d) that Antioch adopted the honorary title of Constantia in his honour.

On a more material plane Libanius reveals himself as an accurate commentator, as is only to be expected since his audience had the evidence before their own eyes, or indeed were themselves often responsible for its maintenance or construction. The evidence of archaeology, for instance, confirms him in his statements about the general topography of the city, the water supply, even such details as the fact that the front doors of houses abut on the main street. From the slightly later date of the Yakto mosaic comes confirmation that the baths or shops and stalls, and their wares, were everywhere such as he describes them. In fact, as regards the veracity of some of his statements, it seems that sometimes it is forgotten that his audience were in a position to know the facts as well as he did. Thus some moderns point out that the axis of the main street runs not from east to west as he states, but from northeast to southwest. Libanius was however engaged on an oration, not a town planning survey. His audience knew well enough that the Beroean gate was in the east of the city and the Daphnean in the west, and one may reasonably conclude that his picture of Antioch is, granted the purple patches, a tolerably accurate one.

That it was a vivid one which expressed the mood and aspirations of his audience cannot be doubted. To some outside observers of his day the parade of curial virtues as enunciated by Libanius might seem merely meretricious, as it did to Julian, and the behaviour of his councillors that of ostentatious arrogance, which is the picture of Libanius' friend Letoius given by Theodoret (*Historia Religiosa* 14), but in their own eyes it was a fitting acknowledgement of their status. Otherwise it is difficult to account for the appearance on Antiochene mosaics of the personification of such virtues, most notably that of *megalopsychia*, that greatness of spirit upon which he is so eloquent and which becomes the hallmark of his ideal council. His clientèle chose not merely to hear about such congenial topics but actually to live among pictorial representations of them. This in itself is testimony to Libanius' achievement in capturing the spirit of the community of which he was so proud to be a member.

Available editions are those of Foerster (I, 412–535) and of Reiske (I, 275–365), though with more difficulty. Translations and commentaries (cf. Bibliography) are those of Downey (1959); A.J. Festugière (1959), translation into French of §§196–271 (pp. 23–37), with very good archaeological commentary by R. Martin (pp. 38–61); Fatouros and Krischer (1992), with introduction, translation and exhaustive commentary, in German.

Indispensable aids to study are: Downey (1961), excellent for the topographical history of Antioch; Liebeschuetz (1972), a very sound study of fourth-century Antioch; Petit (1955), a profound, detailed and provoking study.

Those who have access to a specialist library could with advantage cross-refer to the excavation reports and the books of Doro Levi (1947) and Morey (1938) noted in the Bibliography.

THE ANTIOCHIKOS: IN PRAISE OF ANTIOCH

(1) With good reason we could both be reproved – I, whose life has been spent in oratory, and you, my audience.[1] Against you the complaint would be that you looked upon my performances on other topics with

---

1 A startling introduction, designed to develop *captatio benevolentiae*.

the utmost complaisance, that you encouraged me to undertake some of
them, and yet that you neglected to give me this one mandate – a composition in praise of our city. Against me the complaint would be that I,
who have more compositions to my name than any man alive,[2] both in
panegyric or exhortation, as well as competitions of various forms, yet
am speechless with regard to the praise of my own native city. **(2)** On
second thoughts, you are not to be blamed for not seeking any pane-
gyrist, for though it is all very fine to hear one's own praises sung, it is
perhaps not in good taste to solicit it. I, however, am clearly open to the
charge, because, for all that I should have paid my debts of honour on
the spot, I have delayed doing so until now; I have never stopped talking
in the city on any other subject, and yet have delayed my speech in
honour of the city. It is just as if you minister to others before your
mother's very eyes, and yet neglect her. **(3)** Moreover, it also is illogical
for a man to agree that he has his skill from you, and yet not to use it on
behalf of the donors; or to demonstrate his superiority in the meetings
in the square, and yet not to publish these demonstrations in book form.[3]

(4) Though there are such abundant opportunities for any who wishes
to reprove me for my silence, yet I have a certain amount of justification
for it. I have made no speech, admitted; but the reason is not that I had
always resolved to make no speech. My mind was made up to speak, but
I hoped somehow that my abilities would improve as time went on, and
that the passage of time would make some addition to my skill. **(5)** Thus
it was in an attitude of respect and not of idleness, and in the desire to
give finer honour, not entirely to avoid honouring the city, that I have
been silent up to now, and have done nothing more to satisfy the audience; my excuse for not having spoken before will be that I never intended
this to be so.

---

2 Besides earlier compositions, which include *Oration* 59 (the Panegyric on Constantius
and Constans), the *Hypotheses* of the orations of Demosthenes, and an unknown number of
declamations, his literary output since his return to Antioch had been enormous. In addition to declamations, he had delivered panegyrics on Gallus Caesar (*Or.* 1.97), on Zenobius
(*Or.* 1.105) followed by a monody on him, an address of welcome to the prefect Strategius
(*Ep.* 405), and an address 'On Genius', with his rival Acacius as its theme (*Ep.* 405, Eunap.
VS 17.2). A list is to be found in Foerster (XI, 617ff.).

3 Libanius, however, is very reluctant to publish his orations, as shown by the pressure
that Julian has to apply to get *Oration* 13 published and to receive *Oration* 14 from him
(*Epp.* 760, 758); also Strategius' strenuous efforts to get the widest circulation for Libanius'
panegyric on him (*Or.* 1.111).

(6) Now, it is a commonplace among panegyrists that they should allege that their abilities fall far short of the subject at issue,[4] and that they beg pardon of the audience if, despite their desire to approach their ideal, they fall short of it for all their efforts. Now such a line I think is exactly suitable for me, but not at all suitable for the rest who have launched upon such a project. (7) For if they were not natives of the city, there was no necessity for a speech; if they delivered their oration skilfully, they would give pleasure, but if they did not, they would not be thought to fail to render the tribute. But when a man has it in his power whether to speak or not, he deserves praise if he makes a good job of it, but if he fails, he deserves no pardon either. (8) If a man originally had not the slightest need of entreaties, and then later of his own free will should fall into such a need, he could have no reasonable ground for entreaty. I, on the other hand, am forced into the oration by the just demands of my native city, and I am faced with the dilemma, that I must either speak as best I may from my present resources or else be thought an undutiful citizen. On every count, therefore, I should readily be pardoned. (9) For instance, if I had sufficient wealth to fulfil the office of choregus,[5] it would perhaps be all right that I should fulfil my duty in that manner, and not choose the risk of an oration: however, since Fortune has deprived me of the opportunity of such service,[6] and since I must obviously make some personal offering to the city, my tardiness in speaking is ground for pardon for my modest silence.

(10) Now, many of the audience here present see the present fortune of the city, and are completely ignorant of its past glory: they admire the present and, unaware of the existence of a glorious past, they think that

4 A Periclean notion (cf. Thuc. 2.35) from the Funeral Speech, as are also the commonplace of §10, and the conclusion to this oration.

5 The notions and the vocabulary are developed from those of classical Athens, where the rich citizen at his own expense furnished a chorus for a play entered in a state festival. The *locus classicus* is Lysias, *Or.* 21.1ff. In the later Roman Empire, however, it becomes a euphemism for the performance of duties (*munera*) imposed compulsorily upon the city councillors by the imperial administration, which an Attic purist like Libanius described as 'liturgies'.

6 As related in the *Autobiography*, he had in his teens turned his back on a career as decurion to pursue that of sophist, and thereby obtained the sophistic immunity from liturgies which he now enjoyed. In addition, however, his family fortunes had been drastically reduced by the confiscation of his grandfather's property after the revolt of Eugenius in A.D. 303. These were never restored – not even by Julian, cf. *Orr.* 1.125; 51.30. *Ep.* 1154; note 79 below.

I will deal immediately with its size and its present abundance, as if I too agreed that the city has achieved pre-eminence in its later institutions but was inferior in those earlier. **(11)** I must first speak of those sections of the past which demand mention, and then of the present, so that there may be an obvious harmony between the present and past institutions, both because we owe what we have to our predecessors, and because our present fame has risen from no baser origins.

(12) However, before I give an account of the first inhabitants of the land, I must recount the nature of the countryside and climate, its position with regard to the sea, the water supply, and the food supply, and in general, all the wealth of material to be found here. The land is of greater antiquity than the people who inhabit it; so any panegyric must be about the land before it deals with the inhabitants.

(13) Now, the first and foremost cause of praise for a city is the fertility of the land, as in the case of a ship, it is when all the other portions fit to the keel. So we must examine this point first of all. **(14)** My attitude, I must confess, will not be like that of others, who force themselves to demonstrate that the place whose praises they sing, whichever it may be, is the centre of the world.[7] First of all, if any one has this advantage, and the additional advantage of beauty also, then it belongs to one city only, since it is impossible for the rest to be central. Thus, their speeches are, for the most part, nonsense. **(15)** Again, if to be the centre involved some general superiority, there would be some sense in their eager rivalry on this account. However, if there is no comparison as regards fertility between Egypt and rocky Delphi, what need is there to show that the city whose praises are sung is central, in preference to showing that it is beautiful?

(16) Yet this I can say of my native city – that it is the fairest thing in the fairest land under heaven. It is, of course, generally agreed that the land upon which the sun shines as he first rises,[8] is the best in the world. **(17)** This was once a prize which caused contention among kings; whoever got it, was correspondingly the greater. Its name coming to the notice of all men, brings some pleasure, and fills their souls with joy, no

---

7 Centrality was an ideal situation for both classical and later thinkers and writers, cf. Plato, *Laws* 745b; Aristides, *Or.* 13.99. For the claims of Delphi to be the *omphalos* (navel), Pindar, *Pyth.* 4.4f.

8 A rhetorical commonplace as laid down with detailed rules by Menander Rhet. 3.345. Syrian notions of the sun-god reached their peak under the Emperor Elagabalus a century before.

less than dreams, with their visions of gardens, gladden the sleepers.[9] **(18)** So the first fruits of all that the East possesses, come to us. For to some the Earth gives one thing but not another, or else it gives produce of all kinds, and yet, through extremes of climate, trouble persists, or again, if this trouble of extremes be removed, it weakens its general kindliness also by drought. **(19)** We, however, have all things which vie with each other – the earth, the streams and the temperate climate. The land, for instance, is as level as the sea; it is deep, fertile and friable; it yields easily to the ploughshare, and it surpasses the desires of the farmers in its kindliness; it is good for sowing and planting alike and it is well adapted for crops of either kind. In summer, it has tall trees, and corn stalks, taller than trees are elsewhere. It has corn in abundance, and beauty in super-abundance. **(20)** There is no lack of anything which, if present, would be an improvement. If you mention Dionysus, he revels in our midst; if Athena, the earth is luxuriant with her olives.[10] So wine in plenty is exported to our neighbours, and a still greater quantity of olive oil is transported to all quarters in merchant ships. **(21)** Demeter loved our land so much more than Sicily that while Hephaestus put only one golden furrow on his shield, she has made a large portion of our land golden in colour with the corn, the like of which you can find nowhere else, the gift of her who really is the golden goddess.[11] **(22)** We have hills, either in our own territory or around it; some bisect the plain, others, with a broad sweep enclose the entrance or bar it in at the outer limits. Some of them differ in appearance from the level plains, for they are raised aloft, yet they vie in fertility with the lands at their feet. Farmers work there, in land no less desirable, driving their ploughs to the summits. In short, whatever the level plain alone produces elsewhere, here is produced by the mountain districts also; whatever the mountain districts usually provide elsewhere, here is provided by the plains also. **(23)** It has not been divided up to grow either plants or seed. You can

9 Cf. Artemidorus, *Oneirocritica* 2.25, 4.11. Libanius firmly believed in dreams and their interpretation for good or ill, e.g. *Or.* 1.67, 245.

10 Owing to deforestation and climatic change Syria has lost much of the timber, oil and wine production for which it was famous in antiquity, as in Pliny, *N.H.* For Libanius these deities favour Antioch not only by their products but by their presence in the temples erected in their honour.

11 Sicily, the granary of Rome in the later Republic, as in Cicero, *Verrines*: it was also the location of the mythical rape of Persephone, hence Demeter, and of the working of the shield of Achilles by Hephaestus, Homer, *Iliad* 18.478ff. 'Golden' Demeter, ibid. 5.500.

see in one and the same place, trees growing and corn beneath them. In fact, though it shows these crops separately, it produces them all together, for their part of our domain is rich in barley and in wine, and partakes in everything. **(24)** The fact that the hill districts do not lag behind the plains in fertility prevents our land from falling an easy victim to famine, for, in the freakishness of the weather, harm is not done in both areas at once.[12] Any deficiency in the plain is often advantageous to the uplands; conversely, any harm which affects the upland areas may not appear on the plains. Thus we can for the most part find a secure livelihood through the prosperity of either the whole country, or at least half of it. **(25)** The more infertile of the mountain districts make their contributions in other ways. Either from their quarries, they provide stone for the city walls, or timber for roofing and other purposes, and besides this, kindling wood for baking ovens and baths, whereby we are enabled to survive and live at ease. **(26)** Flocks of sheep and goats make their contribution to human welfare: no part of the land is cast off as useless, as for instance happens with a mutilated body, but it either gives a generous return for the toil spent upon it or it presents its gifts spontaneously.

(27) Besides, who could enumerate the streams which irrigate the land? – whether they be great or small, perennial or seasonal, they are all equally beneficial, whether they have their source in the mountains, or rise in the plain, whether they unite with each other, or flow into the lake, or into the sea?

(28) Indeed, our springs and the abundance we have of them is really our hall-mark. No one would be so confident or proud in the possession of the Nymphs' fountains.[13]

(29) Such then is our land, and on its behalf The Hours do their careful dance,[14] not disturbing our joy in it by any unpleasantness from them. For winter does not greedily snatch at the season of spring nor take upon itself the joy we have in the spring: nor does summer, in the same way, stretch towards winter and encroach upon autumn. Each

12 Antioch was however to experience famine in the reigns of Julian and, more severely, of Theodosius, A.D. 362/3 and 382/5: cf. *Or.* 1.126, 206ff., 226ff.

13 'Nymphs', for Libanius, are above all water deities – the providers of springs and fountains (*Nymphaea*).

14 'The dance of the Hours', i.e. of the Seasons, cf. Homer, *Hymn to Apollo* 192ff. It is pictorially represented in mosaic at Daphne, cf. Levi (1947), I, 85ff., illustrated ibid., II, Plates xiii, b–e.

season remains within its own limits, and detaches for itself an equal portion of the year, and departs on the approach of its successor. To crown all, the seasons which cause such bodily discomfort from their excesses of cold or heat, by tempering their excesses wish to appear mild in character. **(30)** I am sure that they have, so to speak, covenanted with each other to share in each other's power. Winter, by its mild and equable character, seems to demonstrate that it has a share somehow in summer: summer in its turn receives from winter enough to prevent distress arising from heat. **(31)** Winter provides the Earth with its fill of rain, and takes away the cold. Summer sends up the corn and brings it on with its warm breezes which protect both our bodies and the ears of corn from the bane of heat. So we alone can enjoy the season, whichever it may be, and can welcome its successor with gladness because each one contains some mixture of charms.[15] **(32)** Of the rest of mankind, the greater part either complain bitterly of the whole cycle of the seasons, or else enjoy some good and some bad; in this they are in exactly the same position as those who pass from a state of peace into one of war, whenever the good season runs its course and departs, and even before they can enjoy it properly the bad season encompasses them about. They lament the departure of their good season when they cannot enjoy it, and they dread the onset of the other. They are compelled either to run with sweat and wallow around the waterholes, or else, isolated by the snow, to spend their time in bed just as if they were invalids. **(33)** We alone enjoy a climate where the season, whichever it be, is pleasant, and the one to come no less so. The one which has showered blessings upon us goes upon its way, and another approaches bringing equal blessings in its train. We are just like travellers who are sent cheerfully upon our way with a succession of shady springs and halts from beginning to end.

(34) Such is the climate we enjoy: with regard to the sea our position is such that if we did not enjoy it, I would have considered it to be to our disadvantage. We are neither at several days' distance from the sea nor situated upon the actual coast. **(35)** The harm which would be inflicted upon the city in either case, I will now attempt to demonstrate in brief. In fact, everyone is aware how harmful it would be to be entirely

---

15 The description of the 'Mediterranean' climate in Syria (warm wet winters, November–March, and hot dry summers, April–October) in this almost lyrical account stems from ideas of Plato, e.g. *Critias* 108e ff., but has its confirmation in the experience of both speaker and audience.

without access to the sea: you would not be far wrong in calling a city thus situated blind in one eye,[16] but to assert that there is some advantage in not lying on the sea coast demands some explanation. **(36)** First then, the cities on the coast must of necessity fear the inundations caused by the sea,[17] and their confidence must be undermined by the example of those places which have been covered by the sea. **(37)** Secondly, there are those who take joy in their power to gaze over the surface of sea, to see the merchant ships plying their trade and to hear the bosun's orders. Yet it is responsible for as much sorrow as joy: when the surf is driven by the waves, the vessels sink before the very eyes of those who lately rejoiced, the orders to the sailors change to groans and the town is filled with talk of the shipwreck. **(38)** However, the greatest cause of misfortune is that a seaport town must necessarily be full of nautical vulgarity, base clamour, ribald cries and all the rest which can defile and destroy the morals of towns. It will receive sailors who put in from abroad, and will itself have its complement of sailors. Then, the defect of the part spreads throughout the whole population. **(39)** Now our situation allows us to enjoy the benefits of the sea and yet offers security from the troubles which arise from it: so we stand outside the range of harm along with the inhabitants of the hinterland, while with the inhabitants of the seaboard we harvest the sea. **(40)** From the inland people we differ in the abundance of supplies, from dwellers of the coast, in the decency of our conduct. Whatever is a credit to both of these classes, we too possess; whatever is to their discredit, we avoid. So while they are partly superior and partly inferior to each other, we are on the winning side with both of them and on the losing side with neither. **(41)** We are thus far enough from harbour to keep us free from the evils which the sea can cause, and near enough to share in its advantages. The intervening distance is 120 stades, so that a well-girt man setting off from the coast at sunrise will carry goods from there and arrive here by noon.[18]

(42) So much, then, for the nature of the land, the mixed climate and the situation with regard to the sea. Next I should give an account of the noble descent of the inhabitants of the land, both the original inhabitants,

16 Cf. Aristotle, *Rhet.* 1411a4 f., citing the metaphor of Leptines that the destruction of Athens would leave Greece with only one eye.

17 By tidal waves caused by earthquakes, cf. Amm. Marc. 17.7 (a digression on the earthquake at Nicomedia in A.D. 358, with echoes of Plato, *Critias* 108e ff.).

18 The port is Seleucia Pieria. The distance agrees with that of Strabo, 16.2.5 (p.751). Cf. Downey (1961), 63, note 63 for a brief discussion of variants.

their successors and those who succeeded them also, and I should show everyone that it was a fine land with fine people in it – as, for example, a well found ship has a good crew. **(43)** Yet though my speech may seem too long for the occasion, I shall deal with only a fraction of the subject. The fact is that there is such a mass of past history that, even if I pass much of it over in silence, my oration still cannot help appearing too long. Thus, the history books will confine themselves to a circumstantial narration,[19] while I must speak as befits the present occasion.

(44) Inachus was the son of Earth and the father of Io. With Io Zeus fell in love and was united. Hera found out about it, and turned the girl into a cow, but Zeus persisted in the association. Hera, on finding this out too, harried the cow with a gad fly, so that she roamed over both continents. **(45)** Inachus then, in search of his daughter and unable to find her, however much he desired to do so, launched his ships, and put aboard as the crew the Argives mentioned in the story with Triptolemus as commander of the whole enterprise, and sent them out to seek his vanished daughter.[20] **(46)** They sailed every sea, through every strait, past every headland; they disembarked at the islands, scoured the coastal regions and even penetrated far inland on the mainland, finally resolved to die rather than fail in their quest. **(47)** When they arrived at our land, too, they disembarked at night, marched up the mountain to the few scattered inhabitants, and went round the houses, knocking at the doors and asking for Io. They were well received and conceived a

19 For the literary sources available to Libanius, cf. Downey (1961), 36ff., with list and discussion. He probably had access to material from the histories of Posidonius and Nicolaus of Damascus, as well as the *Deipnosophistae* of Athenaeus. Strabo (l.c.) also taps the same sources. Malalas (*Chron.* 443) also cites the *Acta* of the city, a local history of Antioch containing material with which Libanius was almost certainly acquainted. Libanius concentrates on the influence of the divine throughout, beginning with the religious connections between Antiochene cults and the earliest Greek mythology, before passing on to their influences upon historical but non-Greek characters, and finally to acknowledged Greek and Macedonian influences.

20 The Io legend is most famously treated by the Greek tragedians, especially Aeschylus, *P.V.* 700ff., *Suppl.* 540. The story of her wanderings in Syria and Egypt was current by Herodotus' time, cf. 1.1, 2.41. Strabo also deals with her in his account of the foundation of Antioch (16.2.5). Malalas (*Chron.* 28ff.) gives variations, including Io's death in Syria. Episodes figure in Antiochene mosaics, cf. Levi (1947), I, 75ff, II, Plates xii, a.1. The story of Triptolemus and his wandering in search of her provides Libanius and the local historians before him with the most respectable justification of their claim to connect the material of the earliest Greek mythology with the earliest settlements around Antioch by the names Ione (Iopolis in Malalas), and the cult of Zeus Nemeius or Epicarpius (§51).

liking for the land, and thus made it the end of their travels. Their zeal for the search was replaced by their desire to stay, and giving up the object of their quest, they attached more importance to this wonderful land than to the purpose of their expedition. **(48)** This was not so much neglect of Io as neglect of their native land, for Inachus, in sending them out, had given them orders to return with the maiden or not to return at all. Thus when they gave up the search, they of their own free will severed their connection with their homeland. **(49)** Now if they had reached the ends of the earth, with no more land left for them to search, and had decided to stay there, the cause would lie in necessity, not in their liking for the district. However, since there was so much land yet unexplored in which they could hope to find her, if they preferred to stay rather than to entertain more hopes, by this resolution they obviously preferred an alien land to their own. Such a spell had the district cast upon them. **(50)** And as soon as they reached the land, they were utterly possessed by it. Their affection for their own country gave way before the admiration for the country that held them. For myself, I would not expect Homer, who flourished at a later period, to say that there is nothing more sweet for men than their own native land and to contradict this decision of the Argives, for often a better place seizes upon men's imagination and casts out the memory of the land which bore them. **(51)** Now this Triptolemus, who had led the search for the Argive maiden, settled the people under his command, founded a city at the mountain's foot and gave the name of Zeus Nemeius to the temple in the city, and of Ione to the city itself, deriving the name from that of Inachus' daughter. Though they gave up the search for her and built their city, they honoured her with the name they gave the town. As they cultivated the land and reaped its fruits, they changed the name Nemeius to that of Epicarpius. **(52)** Thus Triptolemus after laying the first foundations of the city, departed and henceforth was accounted one of the heroes, because of the honours paid him. Then the god, by whose approval the city was begun, wished it to grow from the best stock, and urged Casus,[21] a fine man, to come here from Crete; of course the flower of the Cretans followed in his train. **(53)** When they arrived, they found the Argives more kindly disposed than the people they had left at home, for Minos bore a grudge against them and expelled them, while the Argives welcomed them

21 The myth of Casus and the Cretans links the region of Antioch, through the name of Mount Casius, with the Minos legend, as well as the cult of Zeus Casius.

gladly and granted them a share in the city, the land and all they had. Casus too knew how to return a favour so well as to receive one. He perceived that the institutions of Triptolemus had been for the most part changed so he restored them and founded Casiotis. (54) Then with deeper insight, he tried to obtain for the city the goodwill of the Cypriots and he married the daughter of Salamenus, lord of Cyprus. A fleet accompanied the maiden on her voyage and formed a naval escort for the bride,[22] but as soon as they made the acquaintance of our land, they turned their backs upon their island and became a part of our city. (55) Now evidence that Casus was renowned for his ability can be found in the fact that the ruler of such a great island gladly welcomed such a union; evidence for Casus' mild government lies in the fact that the bride's escort chose his protection instead of the things dearest to them. (56) It is said that some of the Heraclidae[23] too, in the wanderings upon which they were driven by Eurystheus, along with numbers of the Eleans, scorned the whole of Europe and the rest of Asia and here found rest from toil; here they settled and made Heracleia an extension of the city. (57) Note then that the best and noblest from all these sources flowed together here, as though to a place divinely appointed to receive men worthy of admiration. These roots united their several virtues in us alone – the ancient lineage of the Argives, the law-abiding nature of the Cretans, the royal ancestry of Cyprus and the divine descent from Heracles. (58) Those whom we have received from Athens, and any other Greek sources which are intermingled with us, I shall mention when the progress of my narrative reaches the proper occasion for the topic.

(59) Now, however, I must recount how even under the Persian empire the place was long revered.[24] Indeed, it was respected even by the gods of

22 According to Malalas (*Chron.* 201) her name was Amyce – the name of the plain near Antioch.

23 The Heraclidae, banished by Eurystheus from Argos, were settled according to Athenian legend at Marathon, but their story was embroidered with numerous variants later. One of these was that they, with a band of Eleans, founded the city of Heracleia, the later Daphne. The influence of the Seleucid founders, Macedonians claiming descent from Heracles, is to be seen in the currency of this legend. For Heracles on mosaics at Daphne cf. Levi (1947), I, 21ff., II Tables iv b, xxx b, etc.

24 Libanius proceeds to connect divine aetiological stories referring to a period before the foundation of Antioch with various non-Greek rulers. Thus Cambyses' Egyptian campaign of 525 B.C. is connected with the temple of Artemis at Meroe, a suburb east of the city (for which temple, its repair and the boxing contests held there cf. *Or.* 5.42ff.). The temple was allegedly built by the almost legendary queen Semiramis, who, as a historical figure,

the Persians, and before them by the Assyrians. When Cambyses was conducting his expedition against Egypt, he had his wife Meroe with him. They encamped in the place to which the lady has given her name, and she went to sacrifice in the temple of Artemis which Semiramis, queen of Assyria, had built for the goddess. **(60)** She noticed that the roof had become unsafe with age, and she asked Cambyses to repair the fault. He then added to the walls and made the temple more lofty, and also made an enclosure big enough to contain the celebrations of a festival, to which he gave his wife's name. She offered a demesne to the goddess and set women to supervise it, filling the temple with Persian luxuries, and dedications of thrones, beds and bows all of solid gold. **(61)** When this had been completed, it occurred to the inhabitants of Ione to go down to Cambyses. As soon as the deputation delivered their message, he summoned them to him and asked them who they were and in what circumstances they occupied his land. **(62)** Upon finding out their origin and the reasons for their journey, he marvelled at their desire to meet him in preference to remaining unnoticed as he passed on his way; he behaved not as though he had the right to demand thanks of them for occupying his land, but as though he himself owed them thanks for dwelling in it. The evidence is in the fact that he gave them presents and allowed them to depart as if they were his benefactors. **(63)** So let any who will, talk of the ferocity and madness of Cambyses,[25] for it will appear more than ever clear that our ancestors lived with the help and under the protection of the gods. That he, who behaved harshly to everyone and took pleasure in cruelty, rose superior to his own character at the sight of them, and was not stirred to anger against Greeks who dwelt upon the king's land, was of course due to the gods who granted them safe conduct all the way to his headquarters; they ensured that, by the removal of their fear, they should be full of confidence, and, by calming his temper, that he should not be exasperated. **(64)** What need is there then for me to turn my back on the obvious and to speak from inference? The place was beloved of the gods from the start. The great god of the Persians, under whose protection they campaign and whose name in Persian is Mithras,[26] stood over Cambyses in his dreams

---

was queen and later regent of Assyria, c. 800 B.C. Cambyses' wife, Meroe, after whom the suburb is said to be named, repaired it.

25 E.g. Herod. 3.30ff.

26 Text corrupt. The suggestion of Foerster (crit. note) is here translated.

and addressed him, telling him to leave the place and not to proceed with his Egyptian expedition. He foretold also that there would be a city in the place, founded by the Macedonians. **(65)** Cambyses was grateful to the god, and somewhere near the temple of Artemis, he set up a temple to her brother. And so our district received the god of the Persians as a loving inhabitant and an oracle of the future. Cambyses' attitude with regard to the prophecy was not influenced at all by envy as usually happens.

(66) Now, those who sing the praises of Athens and Corinth invent battles of the gods around the cities; for Corinth there was the battle of the Sun against the ruler of the sea,[27] for Attica there was that of Athena against the same god.[28] They almost dissolve the harmony of the universe in their impudent tales of battles of the gods with their irreligious praises of their cities. In thus insulting the divine, they do the favours of devotion, but they do not realize that by this one falsehood they destroy the credit of the rest of their eulogies. **(67)** We are the darlings of the gods, and without any warfare between them, either, – nor is it right to say so. Thus those cities of Greece and we both have our claims to fame, but in their case it would have been better left unsaid; here no one would have dared to say it. **(68)** The inhabitants of Ione then, generation after generation, behaving justly towards each other, gained their livelihood from the soil and bestowed upon the gods their proper due; in all happiness they inhabited a Greek city in the midst of heathendom. They had and maintained their manners pure in the midst of such an evil in just such a way as the most convincing story about the Alpheius has it. The Alpheius, you remember, led his stream from the Peloponnese to Sicily through the midst of the sea and yet untouched by the sea.[29] **(69)** Our city indeed did not grow to greatness of size and population all at once, and this was a good thing, in my opinion. The expansion awaited a more favourable occasion. For a time, while it was detrimental for her to be any larger, she existed in a lesser role and remained rather small. **(70)** How does this come about? If it had reached its maximum extent while the Persians still possessed Asia, with their wealth of treasure, strength in war and universal repute, we would of necessity have been ordered by our leaders

27 Cf. *Or.* 14.28; Pausan. 2.1.6.

28 Cf. Herod. 8.55; most famously illustrated on the west pediment of the Parthenon.

29 The river god Alpheius fell in love with the water nymph Arethusa, and pursued her from the Peloponnese across the Ionian Sea to Syracuse, without contamination by sea water: cf. Strabo 6.2.4 (p. 270f.), Pausan. 5.7.2.

to share in their campaigns, and we would have had the alternative to obey and go campaigning, or to refuse and fight the Persians, one city alone against such a mighty empire. The first course would have been discreditable, the second unsafe. **(71)** As it turned out, however, our city did not expand out of due season, but it held such a situation that it was absolved from acting in any way distasteful to it and from suffering any harm: it advanced to greatness only when it was time for it to rule, just as the children of noble family are unnoticed in a tyranny because of their youth, and reach their prime when the tyranny is ended.

(72) Thus, after the battle of Issus,[30] and the flight of Darius, when Alexander had part of Asia in his hands and desired to hold the rest, and thought little of what he had conquered as he fixed his gaze upon the ends of the earth, he came to this country. Here he pitched his camp near the fountain which now, by his agency,[31] has got the appearance of a temple, but which then was merely a beautiful spring: here he cared for his body after his labours, and drank the cold, clear, sweet water of the spring. **(73)** The pleasure he had from the drink reminded Alexander of his mother's breast, and he exclaimed to his companions that the water possessed all the qualities of his mother's milk, and so he gave the fountain his mother's name. Now, when Darius was campaigning against the Scyths, he thought the River Tearus in Thrace[32] was the finest of all rivers, and so he set up a pillar with the inscription that the Tearus was the finest river of them all. Alexander, however, did not single out our fountain with any intention of instituting a competition about its waters, – he likened it to Olympias' milk – such was the pleasure he found in its waters. **(74)** Hence he immediately beautified the place by building a fountain and anything else he could considering his rapid passage upon urgent business. He also began the foundation of a city,[33] as if he had found a

30 The battle of Issus, 333 B.C., where Darius was defeated by Alexander. Although Alexander went south along the Syrian coast after the battle, there is no other evidence that he actually visited the location of Antioch except for Malalas, *Chron.* 234. It is not, however, impossible.

31 The Antiochenes evidently claimed him as one of their own, because of the name of the fountain Olympias, cf. infra §250. An epigram (*Anth. Pal.* 9.699) on the naming of it by Alexander refers to such a claim.

32 For the Scythian campaign of Darius I (c. 512 B.C.) and the river Tearus, cf. Herod. 4.90.

33 Libanius here is the only authority to claim Alexander as a potential founder of the city, a deduction from the names of the spring, of the cult of Zeus Bottiaeus (Bottius, Malal. *Chron.* 193), and of Emathia (on Mt Silpius). As the Scholiast (*ad loc.*) notes, these were the

place which could match his own exalted character. **(75)** He experienced two desires – one for our country, the other for the acquisition of the remainder of the world; one tended to make him stay, the other urged him to go on, and so he was torn between settling the place and prosecuting his campaign. He let neither stand in the way of the other, for he did not allow himself to undo his whole enterprise because of the city, nor, in fulfilling his mission, did he let the desire he had for forming a city be quenched. He retained both ambitions, and gave the city a start and directed his forces against Phoenicia. **(76)** The start which he gave to the settlement was the institution by Alexander of the worship of Zeus Bottiaeus, and the naming of the citadel by the name of his own country, Emathia. This, in my opinion, was the token of Alexander's decision to choose our city, when his wars were over, instead of his homeland. **(77)** Such then was the prelude to the foundation of the city; the reputed son of Zeus[34] was reckoned as one of our founders and gave evidence to the report by his actions. Then he soon was taken up to his father and was unable to complete his ambition. His successor, or rather of his many successors the one true heir to his position, our city found in Seleucus,[35] who gained the throne by his strength of character once and again later. **(78)** For he made those whom he assisted stronger than their enemies, but once he had raised them to this level they began to conspire against him. He was saved from the snare which surrounded him, and once again became an object of admiration for the assistance he rendered others. These he found were amenable, and in his turn he reaped the reward of gratitude – the recovery of all from which he had been wrongfully expelled. **(79)** For Seleucus, by his courage and ability, became hipparch under Perdiccas, and when Perdiccas had been killed in Egypt, he was invited by the Macedonians to assume his position. He did so and became satrap of Babylonia.[36] **(80)** He went as ally to Antigonus who

---

names of a city and a district of Macedonia, thus perfectly adaptable to a foundation story of Antioch in a panegyric oration.

34 For Alexander's divine origins cf. Plut. *Alex.* 2f.; W.W. Tarn, *Alexander the Great*, Cambridge 1948, 670ff. Libanius seems somewhat sceptical, as is Dio Chrysostom, *Or.* 4.19ff.

35 For the history of Seleucus I Nicator and the other Diadochi, cf. E.R. Bevan, *The House of Seleucus*, London 1902, I.

36 In 320 B.C., cf. E.R. Bevan, *The House of Seleucus*, London 1902, I, 28f. For the confused in-fighting between the Diadochi and the career of Seleucus between 320 and 300 B.C. the best narrative source is Diodorus Siculus, Bks. 18–20.

was at war with Eumenes, whom he helped to destroy, but he did not apparently realize that in helping Antigonus he was helping a rogue. Antigonus had been raised to eminence through him, and yet conceived a grudge against his benefactor and plotted his death. Then – as if in a play – some god stretched his protecting hand over him, for from the same family arose plots for his death and the means of his salvation.[37] **(81)** Just as Ariadne, in admiration of the handsome Theseus brought the youth safe from the labyrinth with her length of cord, so Demetrius, son of Antigonus, in admiration of Seleucus' noble qualities, advised him of his father's treachery by means of a message which he wrote in the dust with the butt of his spear, and unnoticed by the others present informed him of what was impending. **(82)** Then Seleucus showed the endurance of a Euagoras,[38] and a little later increased his power. He retired before this crisis and made his way to Egypt where he confirmed Ptolemy in the possession of his kingdom, not by the provision of a numerous army but by his own physical and mental powers. When he had secured Ptolemy's position he persuaded him to restore him, and with a force of infantry and cavalry, about 1,000 of both, he expelled his enemies from Babylonia and recovered his kingdom, his wife, children and former prestige. **(83)** Thinking that, though he had thus recovered his own, Antigonus should be punished for the plot against him, he made war against him, and, in an engagement in Phrygia, defeated and slew him.[39] Thus in open battle he exacted vengeance, as a man of honour, for the treachery against him which as a god-fearing man he had avoided. **(84)** After the death of Antigonus, the possessions of the vanquished fell to the victor and the empire of Seleucus took as its frontiers both Babylonia and boundaries of Egypt. Now at last it was the time for our city's greatness to come to

37 Antigonus the One-Eyed (Monophthalmus) drove him out of the satrapy of Babylonia and he retired to Egypt in 316 B.C., where he assisted Ptolemy against Antigonus' son, Demetrius Poliorcetes, in the campaign of 312 B.C., before recovering Babylonia (Diod. Sic. 19.12ff.).

38 Ruler of Salamis in Cyprus, exiled 415 B.C., restored 411 B.C., cf. Isocr. *Euag.* 26ff. The allusion links the Cyprian elements of Antiochene pre-history and those of the Cypriote rulers with those of the Macedonian founder himself.

39 At the battle of Ipsus, 301 B.C. Antioch was founded in 300 B.C., immediately after the foundation of Seleuceia Pieria which was probably intended by Seleucus as his new capital instead of Seleuceia-on-Tigris. Malalas' account of the foundation of Antioch (*Chron.* 198ff.) gives more details of the two foundations, only reporting Seleucus' activities in Seleuceia, which Libanius has here edited out, evidently as incompatible with his panegyric on Antioch, later to become the acknowledged capital.

pass, as previously it had happened with its first beginnings. **(85)** And everything came to pass by the hand of god. There was a city named after Antigonus, founded by him,[40] separated from the site of the present city by a distance of forty stades. After his victory, Seleucus began to sacrifice there, and the ox had been slain and the altars had received their customary dues, and already the fire, licking round the offerings, was blazing fiercely. **(86)** Then Zeus[41] sent to the altar from his sceptre his own eagle, the bird which was his companion and friend. The eagle darted down into the midst of the flames, snatched up the thigh-meat as it was burning and began to carry it off. **(87)** Everyone's gaze and attention were fixed upon this occurrence, which was clearly done by the will of heaven. Seleucus despatched his son on horseback to follow the flight of the bird on the ground, and to direct his horse according to the direction it took, for he wanted to know what the eagle would do with the flesh it had taken. **(88)** He was guided by its flight to Emathia, as he rode gazing upwards. There the eagle lighted upon the altar of Zeus Bottiaeus, which Alexander had set up at the time when he was so delighted with the fountain, and deposited it there. Everyone, even those not versed in such lore, agreed that Zeus' intention was to recommend that the place should become the site for a city. Thus the impetus which Alexander had given to the foundation, and the beginnings he had made, reached completion[42] and the king of heaven by means of this omen became our founder. **(89)** Then Seleucus collected all the skilful builders, all the labourers and gleaming marble for the task. Timber was felled for roofing, and money poured out for building. **(90)** In drawing out the limits of the city, he had elephants stationed around the area at places where he intended towers to be, and he marked the length and breadth of the colonnades and streets by a trail of flour[43] which ships then at anchor on the river had brought up. **(91)** And so the city rose rapidly, and rapidly it was filled, for the inhabitants of Ione came down to dwell in it – Argives, Cretans and

40 Antigonia, founded by Antigonus in his occupation of Syria c. 307 B.C., cf. Malal. *Chron.* 199, Diod. 20.47, lay 5 miles upstream from Antioch. The story of its destruction may indicate simply its degradation from city to village status, since it reappears again in 51 B.C. (Dio Cassius 40.29). However, transfers of population, particularly those resulting in increased Hellenic representation in the new foundations, were regular.

41 Zeus and Apollo together were the founders and patrons of the Seleucids, cf. M. Rostovtzeff, 'Progonoi', *JHS* 55 (1935), 56–66.

42 Cf. §74 above; the alleged foundation by Alexander on the site of Antioch.

43 A similar story is told about the foundation of Alexandria, Amm. Marc. 22.16.7.

the Heraclidae, who were, I am sure, Seleucus' kinsfolk by virtue of descent from Temenus long before.[44] Also such of Seleucus' own soldiers who chose to settle there, swelled its numbers. **(92)** Antigonia, the memorial of his enemy, he had demolished and he transferred its population here, among them some Athenians. The people thus transferred were at first afraid that they would share in the anger he felt against Antigonus, but when they realized that their change had been for the better, they dedicated a bronze statue in honour of Seleucus, adding bull's horns to his head – Io's token.[45] **(93)** And thus the city was named by Seleucus, the name being that of his father Antiochus.[46] Seleucus built it, but it preserved his father's memory, for he credited the most notable of his achievements to the member of his family whom he considered most notable.

(94) Seleucus settled this much renowned suburb of Daphne[47] too, to be the temple's portion, and granted the place to the god once he found the legend to be a fact.[48] The story is that Apollo fell in love with Daphne but could not win her, and began to pursue her: she, because of her prayer, was changed into a tree, and he then used his love to form his crown. **(95)** So runs the tale. The truth of it was revealed to Seleucus while he was hunting. He was on horseback and with his hounds in pursuit of his quarry, and when he came by the tree which once had been the maiden, his horse shied and stamped upon the ground with its hoof, and a golden arrowhead appeared from the earth. **(96)** This was

---

44 Temenus, a Heraclid, legendary ancestor of the kings of Macedon.

45 Seleucus had, at a feast of Alexander's, killed an escaped bull with his bare hands; hence his statues bore horns; so Appian, *Syr.* 57. Libanius adds the final touch for his Antiochene audience, reminding them of Io's horns.

46 Which Antiochus? – father or son of Seleucus? The best Mss. read 'father', cf. Strabo 13.4.2, Appian, *Syr.* 57.; others 'son', cf. Julian, *Misop.* 347a, Sozom. *H.E.* 5.19, Malal. *Chron.* 200.19. More recently, Foerster (III, xxxiv f.) changed his mind, preferring 'son' to the 'father' which appears in his text. However, the Syrian tetrapolis founded by Seleucus has cities named after himself (Seleuceia), his wife (Apamea), his mother (Laodicea) and almost certainly, therefore, he intended Antioch to be named after his father, whatever Libanius wrote, cf. Downey (1961), Excursus 1.

47 So renowned that Antioch was differentiated from other foundations of the name by the title Antioch Epidaphne, Plin. *N.H.* 5.18, a transliteration of the Greek ἡ ἐπὶ Δάφνῃ, cf. Strabo 6.2.4 (p. 749).

48 Cf. Foerster VIII, 44f. Pausanias (8.20.2) notes this as a variant legend to that current in Greece. For the temple of Apollo in Daphne (and its destruction by fire in A.D. 362), cf. Amm. Marc. 22.13.

engraved with the name of its owner Phoebus. In grief at the maiden's transformation, I presume, he had thrown down his arrows and the head of one of them had come off and lay hidden in the ground, and was kept as a warning to Seleucus to revere the place and to think it – as it was – the temple of Apollo. **(97)** Now the sudden appearance of the fountain on Helicon[49] was a miracle, so they say, resulting from Pegasus striking the rock with his hoof. This event here is all the more miraculous for it is so much more plausible for a fountain than for an arrow-head to appear. **(98)** Seleucus had no sooner picked this up than he saw a snake coming face to face with him and hissing with uplifted head. As he approached, the snake gazed calmly at him and vanished. This appearance of the snake in addition to the objects which appeared from the earth, was even more convincing proof that the god haunted the spot. An enclosure was marked out forthwith, with trees and temples therein and very soon the grove flourished and was protected by solemn imprecations. **(99)** Daphne was Seleucus' pride and joy, for besides the apparitions he had actually seen, he was also guided by an oracle which he had received from Miletus to cheer him in a time of despondency.[50] This promised him his future greatness and bade him, when he became ruler of Syria, to dedicate Daphne. **(100)** After thus fulfilling all his religious obligations and with this auspicious commencement, he built upon foundations which gave expectations of success, namely divine favour and our city; he tamed the wilderness and made the best of his land teeming with towns. It was certainly with no idea of luxurious ease that he founded our city; it was to be a source of other cities, in such numbers that wayfarers were served by cities, not inns.[51] **(101)** While other kings take pride in the destruction of existing towns, his glory has been that he made cities rise which had not before existed. He sited so many of them over the land that there were enough of them to be named after

49 The fountain Hippocrene. A festival of the Muses was held on Helicon, Pausan. 9.31.3.

50 The Seleucids were devotees of the oracle of Apollo at Didyma, near Miletus. Libanius' story of the oracle's comforting words is confirmed by Appian, *Syr.* 56, and by Diod. 19.90.4 (where he is addressed as 'King', dated to 312 B.C.). The Seleucid era certainly begins in that year, and Daphne becomes sacred to Apollo, with his statue by Bryaxis adorning the temple Seleucus dedicated.

51 Appian, *Syr.* 57 lists as his foundations 16 Antiochs, 5 Laodiceas, 3 Apameas, together with city names of Macedonia (e.g. Beroea, Edessa) and of Greece (e.g. Chalcis, Larissa). The most notable foundation named after himself was Seleuceia-on-Tigris.

Macedonian cities and also to have names derived from the titles of his
relations. There were several with the same name, derived from some
family name either of his male or female line. **(102)** Moreover, if you
wish to make a comparison with the Athenians and Milesians who are
agreed to have despatched more colonies than anyone else, he would
clearly appear as the founder of more cities than they were, so excelling
them in the size of each one that any single one was worth ten of theirs.
As you enter Phoenicia, you can see cities of his; as you enter Syria here
you can see cities of his even greater in number and size. **(103)** This fine
practice he extended as far as the Euphrates and the Tigris: he girt Babylonia about with cities, and settled them even in Persia. In short, no
place fit to receive a city he left without one, but he continued his work
of hellenizing the natives.[52] **(104)** Yet though he founded many cities
after ours, it cannot be said that he preferred any other to it. Here he
established his capital himself, and gave it its due in other respects, as
though he built the others to be handmaids to our city, and never saw a
more fitting place for his palace.

(105) So in the midst of such achievements he lived and died,[53] and his
inheritance passed to men not inferior to him. All his descendants were
fine men, sons of fine fathers; the sons emulated their fathers in ordinary
matters and in the love which they had for our city. **(106)** As I view their
achievements, and, as from some vantage point, gaze upon the nobility
of each of them, it seems to me that silence is not the proper reward for
their abilities, nor is the recital of them practicable. Silence would denigrate our leaders and their renown; the recital would be too great to be
done by any save many orators and the greatest possible band of sophists. **(107)** What way then can be found in such an impasse? Some I must
mention, others I must neglect – or rather, I must not concentrate upon
the entire achievements of some of them but give a representative selec-
tion. I must insist of the others that they were in no way inferior to those
whom I mention, and I must bid my audience check my narrative by
reference to the works of history.

(108) Now Antiochus, son of Seleucus, fought no wars, for every

---

52 He was also enabled to demobilize his veterans with due reward.

53 Seleucus was killed by Ptolemy Ceraunus in 281/0 B.C., after the defeat of Lysima-
chus at Corupedion. His remains were brought back to Syria for burial in a shrine at Seleuceia Pieria. Libanius, for the edification of his Antiochene audience, avoids any mention of
the original importance of Seleuceia as Seleucus' chosen capital in the West.

enemy cowered in fear.[54] He came to a prosperous old age and bequeathed to his son a kingdom no less than the one he had received. His son[55] too kept the peace, for there was no need for him to do otherwise. In his time there was a remarkable instance of our city's high renown. **(109)** He married into the family of Ptolemy, king of Egypt. Ptolemy came here, and was filled with admiration for the beauty of the statue of Artemis. He wanted it to belong to his own kingdom and so went off with it. There the goddess was worshipped but she longed to return to our city. Thus she harassed with illness the wife of Ptolemy and told her in her dreams why she did so. She was then sent back by those who had removed her, and was restored to her ancient temple, and in view of this fact, her name was changed and she was addressed as Eleusinia.

(110) Moreover in this same reign yet another portent occurred both similar to and yet different from this first. The similarity lies in the fact that it deals with the divine; the difference is that it involved the importation of a deity from abroad. I will explain my meaning. **(111)** In Cyprus, the gods who honoured Cyprus by dwelling there from time immemorial, conceived a desire for our country and were spurred on to change their abode. Thus they made it necessary for our city to consult the oracle at Delphi, and persuaded Apollo that there was only one way of appeasing their wrath – the removal of these gods who dwelt in Cyprus, to Antioch. **(112)** So the king sent to the island envoys by whose agency he hoped that this could be contrived. They could neither remove them openly nor escape detection if they tried to steal them, so they had resort to the following device. They said that they wished to make exact copies of the statues of the gods there. This they were permitted to do, and they industriously polished away day and night, but the priests kept retiring to rest. The copies were so accurately wrought by the craftsmen that they took down the originals, setting the copies in their place, and

---

54 Libanius exaggerates. Antiochus I Soter (died 261 B.C.) had to contend with the encroachments of Pergamum and with the inroads of the Gauls into Asia Minor (hence his cognomen Soter (Saviour)), and also with pressure from the Ptolemies for Palestine (the so-called First Syrian War).

55 Antiochus II Theos engaged in more hostilities with Ptolemy Philadelphus, whose wife Arsinoe is the one mentioned in §109. These were ended by his marriage with Ptolemy's daughter, Berenice, but at the cost of putting away his existing wife Laodice and their issue, the cause of a series of bloody dynastic feuds over the next generation, whereby Seleucid power was sadly weakened. Libanius tactfully ignores all this unsuitable information, concentrating instead upon the instances of divine favours bestowed on Antioch.

put them aboard their vessels under the very eyes of the Cypriots and brought home the originals as if they were the newly made copies, and left behind those copies with all the appearance of the originals. **(113)** This was, to be sure, not due to the skill of the artificers but to the desire of the gods to depart; thus they had endowed the craftsmen with superhuman skill. Now what can be so glorious in the acquisition of fresh territory, or the capture of enemies, as the fact that the gods should think it fitting that they should dwell here?

(114) Another occurrence also, not unlike this, which happened in the following reign points to the same conclusion. Isis, the horned goddess of Egypt, left Memphis to come and dwell here. She induced Seleucus, fourth in descent from Seleucus,[56] to send for her, and indeed Ptolemy to present the goddess willingly, and so ships were fitted out and the statue was transported here. **(115)** Our city was a dwelling-place of the gods, so that if we so desired, we could set up in opposition even to Olympus, for the residence of the gods there is a poets' tale, while the proof of their sojourn here is the evidence of our senses. **(116)** Fresh occurrences came about with the lapse of time; for instance when the sway of Rome became supreme, the presence of the gods remained in the city's possession, and they experienced, in relation to Zeus Cassius, something of the same kind as Ptolemy had done with Artemis. They removed his statue,[57] but he hurled his bolts upon everything and harassed them to ensure his return, and he made them change their minds. **(117)** Thus both gods from abroad made plain their desire to come to us, and our own gods refused to be removed elsewhere. By their beauty they acquired our love, and as they affected others, so were they affected by us. They were attracted by us, their lovers, and in turn they developed an attachment to the land they loved. Such was the affection for their land, which possessed our native gods, and such the eagerness of foreign deities to belong to us.

(118) I have dwelt at some length upon this recital about the gods for there can be no greater subject of praise either of us or of any other people. However, if it be thought that the grandest recital is that of

---

56 Seleucus II Callinicus (246–226 B.C.) lost the Seleucid lands in Asia Minor and in the East. The divine support for Antioch is used to veil such secular reverses, even if the story is not an invention of Libanius himself to account for the growing popularity of the cult of Isis.

57 As proconsul of Syria in 51/0 B.C. L. Calpurnius Bibulus sent to Rome two statues of Zeus Ceraunius and Athena, set up by Seleucus I. Libanius evidently confuses Ceraunius with Casius (or Cassius). The story is referred to by Malal. *Chron.* 212.

deeds of martial prowess, our ancestors, as they marched out to war, had many a trophy set up over many an enemy, as was the way of warfare in those days. **(119)** There is no need to dwell overlong upon details, but Antiochus the Great,[58] so called from the greatness of his projects and power, considered it was a paltry business merely to preserve his possessions, and so he devised additions to them. Thus he provided this also, the newer portion of the city, hardly inferior to the old city, bounded by the river. He introduced Greeks – Aetolians, Cretans and Euboeans – and he provided full security by means of fortifications. **(120)** And in the same way as he increased the area of the city, so he tried to extend the frontiers of his empire, as it were fitting the jacket to the increased girth of the wearer. He got colonists enough to attain all his ambitions he hoped and handled them by the rule of fear or of law. Then he pursued the course he had decided upon, even making fresh acquisitions – for some of his adherents came over of their own free will and the rest were schooled by their defeats not to rise against him. **(121)** And it was in such a manner that he made his expedition to Ionia, and showed by his words and deeds that he was the Great Antiochus,[59] that the name he bore was no idle compliment, but that he deserved this title because of his own mighty deeds. These resulted in increased revenue for us, and the city was beautified with the spoils of war. She cared for her subjects, routed her opponents and then became even to those last as some kindly deity, for she excelled the Persian system of government both in might and in the quality of her leadership.

(122) After him, another Antiochus[60] ascended the throne. He was at once a man of peace and a man of war. He rejoiced in peace provided that he was not provoked; in war he was courageous, if ever there was

58 Antiochus III the Great won his title by his successes in recovering revolted Seleucid territories in the East and in Asia Minor. There, however, he encountered the Romans and was utterly defeated at Magnesia, 189 B.C. By the Peace of Apamea (188 B.C.) he was forced to abandon Asia Minor entirely and to pay an indemnity of 1000 talents a year – a disaster which Libanius ignores. Instead he concentrates upon his development of Antioch into the island formed by the Orontes, and upon the influx of new Greek settlers. These can only have been veteran settlements or Greek refugees fleeing from reprisals at home.

59 A statement true enough for the career of Antiochus before his invasion of Greece and his final defeat, no hint of which occurs in a panegyric.

60 Antiochus IV Epiphanes, who follows the short reign of Seleucus IV Philopator, here unmentioned. Libanius' commendations, though not entirely undeserved, disguise the famous incident with Popillius Laenas, which confirmed his client status in Roman eyes, cf. Livy 45.11; App. *Syr.* 66.

need for it. He did not because of the allurements of peace give ground to those who wronged him, nor did he despise peace because of his victories. He knew, as well as any man, how to take up arms at the right moment, and how to lay them down again. **(123)** When the brigands in the Taurus had organized themselves, and were ravaging Cilicia to their hearts' content and besides everything else were ruining the common intercourse of the world, he smote them more fiercely than ever Minos, from the Cyclades, smote the Carians. By so doing, he allowed the cities to associate with each other, and by removing the threat of fear, he opened up the routes for merchants. In return for this, a statue of him taming a bronze bull was created by the grateful peoples, the beast indicating the mountains of the same name.[61]

(124) Although I could speak at length about the rest of the kings, to avoid boring you by the length of my speech, as I have said, I will confine myself to this statement – that just as they inherited their names from generation to generation, so did they inherit their ability of character;[62] some in time of peace watched over the city; others in time of war made its name glorious: all had the one same object, to hand down to their successor the city greater than it was when they inherited it. **(125)** One built a temple of Minos, another of Demeter, another of Heracles, and so on. One constructed a theatre, another the city hall, another levelled the roads, others brought water by aqueducts, either from the suburbs to the city or from the springs which abound in the old city to the new city.[63] Temple after temple was built, and the greater part of the city consisted of temples, for it was all the same thing; the adornment and protection of the city was bound up with the provision of shrines of

61 The statue of the bull, a gift of the Cilicians with punning reference to Mt Taurus, probably gave its name to the Taurian Gate in the city, cf. Downey (1961), 619f. 'To their hearts' content', lit. 'plundering the Mysians', proverbially a weak and defenceless folk. For Minos, cf. Thuc. 1.4.

62 Libanius here treats in passing the last century of the declining Seleucid monarchy (163–63 B.C.). Although some of the names listed in §126 appear as epithets applied to later kings (e.g. Demetrius I Soter, Antiochus VII Callinicus, Seleucus VI and Antiochus XI Epiphanes) he concentrates upon the first and most forceful members of the dynasty from Antiochus I Soter to Antiochus IV Epiphanes (281–163 B.C.).

63 The temple of Minos is only mentioned here. For that of Demeter cf. *Or.* 15.79; Jul. *Misop.* 346b; of Heracles, Malalas, *Chron.* 246. On the theatre cf. Downey (1961), 72. The City Hall (*Bouleuterion*) was, according to Malalas, *Chron.* 205, built by Antiochus IV Epiphanes, in his new quarter of the city, Epiphania. On the water supply of Antioch, cf. §240ff. infra; Martin in Festugière (1959), 54ff.

the gods. **(126)** In fact, it would be easier to count the waves of the sea than to try to embrace in any narrative the additions with which each of them magnified our city. Hence I shall not deal with impossibilities, but I shall call as evidence for each man's character the name he enjoyed. One was called 'Soter', another 'Theos', another 'Callinicus', another 'the Great', another 'Philopator', another 'Epiphanes'. There is not one who could be seen but to have some evidence of this kind. **(127)** Yet, if it rebounds to the credit of Athens that one of her politicians went by the name of 'the Just', and another by some other such title,[64] much more creditable is it for our city that the kings should be seen to deserve such titles of address – not merely one or two of them, but all of them in succession and in such numbers.

(128) We have also experienced not merely the best of kings but also the best of queens.[65] They left their looms and overcame the limitations of their sex in their relations with the city. They showed consistent foresight, more appropriate to men, some by the assistance they provided in respect of the laws of burial, others by adorning the gods with temples and the city with honour – as though they dwelt with their husbands not merely for the procreation of children, but for the imitation of their conduct towards the city.

(129) Thus, whilst heaven was resolved to govern Asia according to the will of the Macedonians, this city was, as it were, the citadel of their empire, and in all good fortune they dwelt here and adorned her with works from all the world. However, when by the will of heaven, their empire fell and the world was girt with the golden chain of Rome, so to speak, the city quickly perceived the divine will and accepted the change without disturbance. Even if she had opposed it, it was destined that she should be their subject, and so she acceded to them peacefully, and made the future free from bitterness, providing no excuse for rancour.[66]

64 Aristides, 'the Just', cf. Plut. *Arist.* 7.1–2; Phocion 'the Good', Plut. *Phoc.* 10.4.

65 Apame, wife of Nicator, seems to merit this commendation, but the early queens, with the exception of Berenice and Laodice, the feuding wives of Antiochus II Theos, whose influence on the fortunes of the dynasty was baneful, seem to have been quite anonymous. Libanius, in good rhetorical style, makes a virtue of this anonymity, emphasizing the universally accepted truism that a woman's place is in the home, however prestigious that might be.

66 Cf. Homer, *Il.* 8.19ff., where Zeus asserts his authority over all the gods. The bloodless annexation of Syria by Pompey in 64 B.C. becomes for Libanius an example of this divine will, to which Antioch had to resign itself. In fact, after the chaos of the last Seleucid kinglets

(130) So then, in return for this complaisance, she enjoyed such fore-thought on the part of our superiors that it seemed that the change of government was merely a change of family, for the crop of blessings was the same as before. It was as if there was no difference between the founders of the city, and those who had come to control it, and as if the Romans possessed something they had originally built, and preserved the kindly relationship towards something of their own creation. They guarded its existing fame, and adding their own customs they retained it in its position as the metropolis of Asia.[67]

(131) So let this narrative suffice for those who think that our city is but lately risen to fame.[68] Now let me demonstrate to those who think that our present fortunes have deteriorated from its pristine grandeur – and may envy not affect my recital. Some cities, like retired veterans, are always singing the praises of their past history, and complaining of their present lot. We however have before our eyes the present, which can compare with the glorious past, and demonstration, rather than recital, is all that is needed.

(132) Now consider whether the city is in complete harmony as it were, in music – and whether like any famous statue, it shows what needs to be done, not half done, but in the fullest perfection.

(133) First, then, consider the council.[69] Upon this, the root as it were,

---

and the interventions of outsiders like Tigranes, the citizens of Antioch were content to accept the relative stability of Roman rule, imposed though that might be. This Libanius recognizes rather ruefully.

67 The honorific title 'metropolis', enjoyed by Antioch from the earliest days under Pompey, Caesar and Augustus, figures in its coinage, cf. Downey (1961), 145–59. It was not merely prestigious, but a due recognition of Antioch's importance as the administrative centre of the East. The title was lost briefly in A.D. 387, as part of the immediate punishment after the Riots of the Statues.

68 Fatouros and Krischer (1992), note *ad loc.*, suggest that these sceptics were likely to have been Christians who claimed primacy for Antioch as a centre for their religion so recently recognized as a legal and favoured cult by the Emperors. But Antioch's claims in the Christian tradition go back to the earliest days, and this view may be exaggerated and misconceived. It is not a topic Libanius would even hint at in a panegyric honouring the Olympia. More likely it is a hypothetical objection to be disposed of with full rhetorical effect in order to introduce the kernel of the speech – the praise of *curia* and commons.

69 The city council (*ordo, curia, boule*) and its members (*curiales, decuriones* as in the Codes, *bouleutae* as in Libanius) are the lifeblood of the community (*Or.* 18.147). A hereditary aristocracy of wealthy local landowners in origin, they were harnessed by the Romans to administer their own community under the supervision of the provincial governor and to

the whole organism of the city is based. Now, our council is the greatest and finest in the world; the councillors can list their fathers, grandfathers, great-grandfathers and ancestors still more remote as belonging to the same order. They have their forebears as teachers of patriotism, and each one of them inherits, along with his property, the idea that he has this property for the common good. **(134)** Thus, by their prosperity, they have inherited their family fortunes, while by their patriotism, they have incurred vast expenses, and by their industry, they have acquired fortunes. They hold their office with no reproach against their wealth: in the expensive duties of state they are most lavish, and in their care and provision they avoid poverty. They take more pleasure in spending money upon the city than others do in making it; so generous are they in their desire to contract these expenses, that sometimes there is a risk that they may be reduced to want, since their expenditure takes so many forms. Sometimes, in time of want, they keep up the supply of food for the populace, and by their donations cause the deficiencies of the harvest to vanish: always they help and refresh the whole city by the enjoyment of the baths or the pleasures of the theatre, and even in their own lifetime they introduce their children to perform services for the state, and in their noble patriotism they end the immunities to which they are legally entitled. Those who have so spent their money are more renowned than those who have never yet acted as *choregus*. **(135)** So everything which in other cities follows upon the acquisition of money, is here linked with its expenditure. We would feel more shame at enriching ourselves by the avoidance of public duties than at reducing

---

perform the services needed, such as those listed in §134, which until recent times they had done with the enthusiasm described by Libanius. In the changing circumstances of the fourth century, however, the central government applied more severe regimentation and compulsion to the performance of such civic services (*munera curialia*, liturgies) and extended them also to governmental services, making the decurions personally responsible for their performance and liable to punishment for failure, as in *Cod. Theod.* Bk 12. It thus became for the poorer members an object to escape such obligations. Libanius does not speak as a disinterested party. His own family were members of this élite, as he constantly reminds his hearers, but in his later years he was only too anxious to get his own son, Cimon, out of the clutches of the *curia*, cf. Petit (1955), 63ff.

The virtues Libanius goes on to mention are personified and depicted in art form in numerous mosaics in Antioch of the fourth and fifth centuries A.D. (cf. Levi (1947), *passim*). Julian in the *Misopogon* criticizes Libanius' depiction of these civic virtues as being too materialistic.

our wealth by their performance. With god to guarantee that they will receive from Fortune twice as much as they spend, they make such lavish expenditure on horse races or gymnastic contests, some in keeping with their wealth, some even exceeding it. **(136)** It is a point of honour for each of them, in the performance of these duties to surpass their predecessors, to preclude their successors from competing with them, to make a finer show in every one they give and to provide novelties, in addition to the usual attractions. **(137)** With us alone, there is as much competition to obtain the privilege of performing these functions as, in other towns, there is to escape it. Many people have often spent considerable sums to attain this end, piling expense upon expense, and by means of their previous expenditure, embarking upon more. They do not spend a small amount to avoid greater loss, but make even more additions to their previous heavy commitments. **(138)** The reason lies in a kind of natural generosity of soul.[70] For this reason, they cannot bear the thought that other cities should have more renown in Antioch than Antioch has among them, and in so far as they can make her supreme, they consider her to be without peer.

(139) Moreover, the council has such wisdom and oratorical ability that you would say that it was some company of sophists in their prime demonstrating their technique. So keen is their intellect, so compact their expressions, so inexhaustible is their flow that many hearers flock to the courts, as though they were regular seats of instruction, to hear the arguments presented before the governors, improvisations which are superior to carefully prepared discourses. **(140)** This ability compels the governors to live up to their name, but not to go beyond it, and play the tyrant. How so? Wherever the council lacks education, though it be ever so wealthy, it is dumb and lies open to outrage by the governors, and must grin and bear it. They who cannot obtain their rights by argument, are obvious targets for wrong-doing, and though they may have the title of councillor, their position is one of slavery. **(141)** Among us, on the other hand, our mastery in oratory maintains

---

70 *Megalopsychia*, generosity of soul, he regards as chief among the virtues of decurions, which is expressed in *philotimia*, competitiveness in ambition. This notion is accepted by the upper classes of his day and later, as is shown by its idealized representation in the Yakto mosaics: cf. Levi (1947), I, 339f., Petit (1955), 142, 382. G. Downey ('Personifications of abstract ideas in the Antioch mosaics', *TAPhA* 69 (1938), 349–63, and id., 'The pagan virtue of Megalopsychia in Byzantine Syria', *TAPhA* 76 (1945), 279–86) discusses personification on Antiochene mosaics and the virtue of *megalopsychia* respectively.

the independence of the council in the fullest sense.[71] It compels those who are set up as administrators of public affairs to live up to the name. If they are men of moderation, it contributes to their search for the highest good, if they are headstrong it restrains their insolence with the compulsion which philosophy supplies, and with its rhetoric, as it were, lulls their temper to rest. The councillors have thus acquired a magic stronger than the governors' power. **(142)** Our council does not make its appearance before the governors cringingly; when they are due to make their decisions they are careful to invite it to appear, so as to be put to the test among them, as men of intelligence, not easily influenced. If there is any infringement of justice they resist resolutely; if justice is upheld, they are loud in their praises. It counts a great deal for a governor's career that the council should be of the opinion that his decisions have been just. **(143)** Yet in other cities the councillors are brought to consider whether they can endure the governor's passion without being overwhelmed. With us, on the other hand, any governor who wins a fair reputation thinks that he gained the crown of virtue, not because he has overcome insubordination, but because he has gained his praises among free and intelligent men. **(144)** So when the council opposes the magistrates, though I would not deny that they have their differences, I would insist that their differences arise from their concern for the common good. The council, divided into three sections,[72] has appointed the best men in each to lead them, while the rank and file follow these commanders who know how to toil for their particular section. **(145)** It is not a case that some may speak and others may not; there is a freedom of speech in which all share. The hearers all rejoice at some fine expression; the young men speak without their elders being annoyed: on the contrary, they give encouragement, advice and confidence, like eagles trying to get their little ones to fly. **(146)** Such prestige has this body acquired that its wishes are put into effect both where they are formulated and by the viceroys,

71 The final justification of the value of the rhetorical education is for Libanius this equation of oratory and independence. His idealized version of the relations between council and governors is over-optimistic, as he is constrained to admit in §144.

72 The *curiales* seem to have been divided into three sections on the basis of wealth, with gradations of duties assigned to each. The most influential were the *protoi* (the *principales* of *Cod. Th.*). Similarly in Tarsus (*Ep.* 1393), where Julian attempted to add a fourth class to counteract the decline in numbers of the *curia*, cf. Petit (1955), 85ff.; A.F. Norman, 'Gradations in later municipal society', *JRS* 48 (1958), 79–82, esp. 83ff.

too.[73] To give is the donor's greatest pleasure, for he knows that he is the benefactor of men of worth and oratorical ability; their worth will cause them to remember the favour, and their oratory will be enough to praise it. **(147)** Yet why need I mention viceroys when the council is respected by the emperors themselves, and sends despatches to them and converses with them before their thrones.[74] In such business the wisdom of the council was revealed to the emperor, and from him the councillors have received the honour of provincial appointments. **(148)** Some, however, have been induced to remain councillors by their affection for their native land,[75] and those who have done so have twin claims to fame – that they were invited to high honour, and yet chose this. Thus, while proving their capability for office, they showed their preference for living for their country as a subject, rather than for leaving it to govern others. **(149)** Thus they made it a pleasure, not a burden, to labour on behalf of their own city. They refused any respite from toil, and were content to continue in its performance, and so they have won reknown either because they refused office, or else because they held office and behaved lawfully.

(150) Of the commons what more need be said than that it fits the council. It would not be right for the council to be the leader of any other commons at all, or for the commons to belong to any other council. Thus the council leads a fine commons, while they, in turn, follow excellent leaders – a fine chorus, as it were, following an even better leader. **(151)** First of all, each one has a wife, children and a household full of furniture. This helps to educate them in carefulness and the pursuit of peace, for those who have none of these things are induced to take part in violent disorders, to grasp the sword, take joy in destruction: they bring misfortune upon every man and run away to some one else, as happens often

73 'Viceroy' (*hyparchos*) for Libanius means 'praetorian prefect'. Fatouros and Krischer ((1992), note 192) here interpret it as his junior, the provincial governor of Syria, but it seems that Libanius distinguishes him – the official of the preceding paragraphs with whom the city council must be in daily contact – from these high-ranking officers, whose only superior is the emperor himself. The prefect in residence at this time was Strategius, a good friend of Libanius who had specific orders to deal gently with the Antiochenes after the excesses of Gallus. Hence the commendation.

74 As ambassadors of the city to the emperors, a prerogative of the *principales*; cf. Petit (1955), 279ff.

75 Cf. Petit (1955), 372. A prime example of such civic devotion was for Libanius his own uncle Phasganius (e.g. *Or.* 62.31). The elder of his uncles, Panolbius, falls into the second category.

enough in Egypt or in Italy, where every word for some people is an excuse for hooliganism and others revel in the misfortunes of their council.[76] **(152)** Among us, however, the commons behave like children towards their parents, and moreover, the council behaves towards them like parents, for it does not allow any dearth to press upon the populace, and in return the populace, the council's wards so to speak, is well disposed towards it. They are grieved at its disappointments, are most pleased at its prosperity, share good and bad fortune alike and think that what it has is theirs also and they would gladly exchange their role of children to preserve their leaders' safety. **(153)** You would get to know the character of the commons, if you examine their grievances, for the charges made against them reveal their worthiness, and the very accusations against them have the quality of praise. When we, city though we are, had to put up with some of the things which were troubling the countryside, it incurred reproach for not having prevented the occurrence, not for having done some dreadful deed. **(154)** Thus it is by nature far removed from wrongdoing, and it is regarded as a corrector of miscreants. Moreover, where is there a commons which can come anywhere near ours in their liberality in making contracts or their reliability in maintaining them? Their tone of voice is not a slovenly drawl; their bearing is dignified; their dress is decent; they shew such deference to their superiors, such affection to their teachers and such complete politeness as can be found in no other commons – or to be truthful, in no other council. They have so risen above their title and in the modest tenor of their life have advanced to nobler state. **(155)** There is, moreover, such an abundance of human kindliness that what other towns omit to perform for their own citizens, here is performed for strangers. When politicians from other places are brought here on charges involving the death penalty, as they are led out to execution the commons has fallen to weeping, surrounding the palace with supplication, and their requests have calmed the seething rage of the governor of the day.[77] **(156)** Thus they would present their requests,

76 Libanius hellenizes the Roman notion of the *patria potestas* of the council over the commons. Elsewhere he speaks of a patron/client relationship. It must be admitted that he has conveniently toned down the bloody riots of the commons during the recent reign of the Caesar Gallus (§153; cf. *Or.* 1.103; Amm. Marc. 14.7.6), concentrating instead on the unruliness of the Alexandrines (cf. *Or.* 26.18; Amm. Marc. 22.6.1). For the steadying influence of the family, cf. *Orr.* 26.8; 56.23.

77 The precise reference is uncertain. Perhaps it refers to the revolt of Eugenius (§159ff.), in which the people of Seleuceia were involved along with Antiochenes. Diocletian, however, was not particularly merciful on this occasion.

because of their inclination to pity, while he would grant them their request since they were fit to receive it. So the cities used to keep their citizens, our city the reputation of having sought and found, and he, fame from overcoming his temper.

(157) It cannot be asserted either that, while virtue is innate in us, yet the city has cast away its courage in danger as well as its training in arms. No! The training has been discontinued by law, but our natural courage has been retained. (158) First, for example, during the Persian invasion,[78] they did not think it proper to save themselves by flight; they stayed clinging to their native city as grimly as Spartans cling to their shield. Secondly, when the usurper at Seleuceia suddenly raised the standard of revolt and fell upon our city, he was brought low by the hands of its inhabitants.[79] The workers in the factories dropped their tools and disarmed soldiers whose life is spent among blood and death.

(159) There would perhaps be no harm done in recounting the story of the revolt, for by this means the valour of the victors will appear more clearly. Eugenius, an officer with a regiment of infantry, was stationed at Seleuceia engaged in deepening the entrance to the harbour. He was aware that there was no military force stationed here, and being held in esteem for his work on the harbour, and gaining confidence at the absence of all who would say him nay, he set himself up as a pretender to the throne. So, without delay, he put on a purple robe which was draped around a statue, and set about the business. (160) They fell upon the farms which they passed on their march, ravaging wherever they went, and late in the afternoon before the alarm could be raised, they had taken the city – as though just the sight of them was enough for that. However, though they were not likely to meet any regiment of soldiers, they met men of daring, more to be dreaded than legionaries. (161) For when they saw this pretender dashing to the palace and snatching the property of their emperor, they were spurred on by the absurdity of the sight and, without waiting for nightfall to concert their plans, they had one thought in their heads – that they would have none

78 For the capture of Antioch by the Persians under Sapor I between A.D. 256–60, cf. discussion by Downey (1961), Excursus 5 (pp. 587ff.).

79 For the revolt of Eugenius, A.D. 303, cf. *Orr.* 19.45f.; 20.15ff. Eusebius, *H.E.* 8.6.8; Downey (1961), 330. The punishment meted out by Diocletian on the decurions of Antioch, which had itself suppressed the revolt, was perverse. Libanius speaks with feeling: his grandfather and great-uncle were executed and the family property confiscated, cf. *Orr.* 1.3; 51.30. *Ep.* 1154.

of him. So with their breasts, not their shields, as their protection, with crowbars instead of spears, thinking everything that came to hand to be good enough as a weapon, they suppressed his bid for the throne that very day. They themselves, with the weapons they had, killed the first of their opponents and used their weapons against the rest. **(162)** Even the women took part in the good work, not just with cheering, shouting and hurling bricks down from the rooftops, like the women of Plataea,[80] but in actual hand to hand fighting experiencing conflict and wounds, and proving true the tale of the Amazons. The result was that Eugenius' men either were slain, or put to flight or captured, and this bid for the throne did not last from one day to the next.

(163) Such is the city, which in pressing dangers preserves in its nature the adventurous spirit of its ancestors. Let us now consider whether it has also maintained the other virtues of the Athenians whom it received as fellow townsmen.[81] **(164)** Now the chief of their praises is that they opened up their land as a place of refuge common to all who were in need, and foreigners flowed in to Athens from all quarters. In this respect however we are, to quote Homer, 'far better men than our fathers were'.[82] There is no city from which we have not welcomed some part. While I would not go so far as to say that we have received the majority of the inhabitants from each of them, it is certainly true that the newcomers we have received here are not much fewer in number than those who have stayed behind. They have moved either in their desire for luxury, or for business reasons, or to demonstrate their learning,[83] or to be rid of their poverty. **(165)** Some are induced to come because they despise their own city for its inferiority, others because of their likes and dislikes of the climate, when, in dislike of the climate at home, they avoid it and develop a liking for ours. Hence the remainder of the inhabitants in any city, upon coming to visit us, associate with their own fellow citizens, although in theory they are in a foreign land. Everyone meets so many who are fellow citizens of his. **(166)** In fact, if one decided to travel through the world, interesting oneself not in seeing the sights of the cities but in getting to know the ways of the inhabitants,

---

80 In the night attack by the Thebans on Plataea which marks the start of the Peloponnesian War, cf. Thuc. 2.4.2f.

81 Cf. §§ 58, 92.

82 Homer, *Il.* 4.405.

83 His predecessors, Ulpianus and Zenobius, were both from Palestine. His assistants also were incomers, cf. *Or.* 31.9ff.

our city would satisfy his curiosity and relieve him of any necessity to go on his travels. If he sat down in our market square here he will scrape acquaintance with every city in the world, so numerous will be the people from all quarters with whom he will come into contact. **(167)** Moreover, those who prefer our city to their own, have never considered it to be a disadvantage not to live in their home town. Those left behind there envy them and curse themselves for not having removed, too – so universal is the participation in the benefits offered here. Foreigners love this land which they have preferred to their own, as if it were their own. Citizens do not claim to be superior to foreigners, but the state welcomes the virtues of the newcomers as, to be sure, it welcomes those of its own sons. In this respect too it is like Athens. **(168)** For just as the Athenians granted a share in their own government to newcomers from Pylos, and employed them in the highest offices, so we especially have honoured foreigners and made the most of them so that even now households of foreign origin are counted amongst the most influential.[84]

(169) This immigration to our city began in the distant past and has never stopped, nor will it ever do so, I think. Naturally therefore our city has experienced an increase in population. The clearest evidence of this is that only Apollo, by whom the oracle says that even the grains of sand were numbered,[85] was able to number its inhabitants. **(170)** It is so great, its area is so vast, and every part is so equally thronged, whether you consider the areas in front, inside or on either side of the gates, whether you make your way to the city centre, go to the side streets, or carry your search all round to the outskirts, everywhere is equally full of teeming humanity and there are as many left behind to look after their homes as there are jostling in the crowd. **(171)** Now when the Athenians, in fear of the Spartan invasion, left the countryside and filled Athens, the throng in the city involved the desertion of their farms.[86] With us, on the other hand, the farms, just as though they were empty already attract many city dwellers, and yet our city still has a flourishing population. All day long in the market square the throng is such that the 'time

84 Pericles in the Funeral Speech (Thuc. 2.39) contrasts the Athenian welcome of foreigners with Spartan expulsions (*xenelasiai*). At Athens, the Neleids, refugees from Pylos, were the ancestors of both Alcmeonids and Peisistratids (Pausan. 2.18.5ff., Herod. 5.65). Libanius takes the same credit for Antioch, cf. §174. A notable example is the family of Argyrius who were accepted and became *principales*, cf. *Or.* 31, note 9.

85 Herod. 1.47.

86 Summer 431 B.C., Thuc. 2.41.

of the filling of the market' is no particular period of the day here, however much it is so elsewhere.[87] This equality between the periods of the day allows none to be singled out for this term; if you use it, you refer to every single minute of the day. (172) As rivers, with current not divided by rocks in midstream, glide on in one continuous flow, so here the throng of pedestrians allows no empty patch to appear in their midst. Thus anyone who first stands and looks at them would hazard the guess that there was a festival being held outside every gate in the city, and that by some custom or another the city was pouring out to visit them, the inhabitants dividing themselves up as they liked. (173) There might be one reason for annoyance with our city, for when one tries to hurry anywhere, it presents the crowd as a barrier to one's progress, slowing it down by the waves of oncomers, like a ship head on to the waves.

(174) Moreover, when one sees the crowds and is unaware of the fertility of the soil, one might have qualms about the food supply necessary for such numbers. On the other hand, upon hearing of its fertility and being unaware of its numbers, one might wonder who consumes all the food. Our population is exactly suited to the land and the fertility of the land to its population. Thus we have never had occasion to violate the divine laws of hospitality through any bias against foreigners, though we have the example of Rome, where times of dearth of the necessities of life are altered to abundance by the expulsion of foreigners.[88] (175) Our land has never obliged us to have recourse to such a remedy; never yet has it got rid of some of its population in order to save the rest.[89] It maintains, I am convinced, its long-established tradition of relieving foreigners of their troubles, not imposing troubles upon them. Even Orestes,[90] after the murder of his mother, when he raged through the rest of the world

---

87 Suidas, *s.v. peri plethousan agoran*, defines this as the fourth to sixth hours, i.e. mid-morning to midday, when political affairs were conducted in the Athenian agora. Libanius, however, is here concerned with business, not politics, since the Antiochene *demos* had no political role.

88 For expulsions of non-citizens from Rome, in the Republic, Livy 39.3; under Augustus, Suet. *Aug.* 42; in the fourth century, Amm. Marc. 14.6.19. Themistius (*Or.* 18.222a) contrasts Constantinople with Rome, in the same way that Libanius contrasts Antioch with Rome.

89 The merest hint of the recent shortages which caused disturbances in Antioch two years before.

90 For Orestes in Syria, Malalas, *Chron.* 142.

hotly pursued by the deities who imposed the punishment of madness on the lad, was restored to his senses once more by our land. As soon as he entered our territory, his madness left him, and the event gave the name to the place. **(176)** However, I have here somehow diverged from my course by the pleasure I have from this tale of Orestes. I must retrace my steps and resume with the examination of our strength. The fact that it is sufficient for the inhabitants is sufficient testimony in itself, but there is yet another which I will proceed to explain.

(177) When the recent Persian war broke out,[91] for which the Persian government had made long-standing preparations, there was urgent need for adequate counter-preparation. For this to be arranged, a place was needed to hold all the host which such a campaign demanded. Our city was the one which in its abundance rose superior to that need, and gathering the forces to her own bosom, in due course, sent forth the whole expedition upon its way. **(178)** Like rivers flowing to the sea, there flowed to our city legionaries, archers, cavalry, horses of war and burden, camels and engineers. The earth was covered with them as they sat and stood; the walls were hidden by the shields festooned upon them; spears and helmets could be seen everywhere; everywhere was the clash of arms, bustling men and whinnying horses. There were so many regiments encamped that their colonels alone would have made no small contingent. So great an army was concentrated that if it had been billeted elsewhere, the drinking-water, too, would have proved insufficient.[92] Yet every one of us here was so glad to have a soldier billeted,[93]

---

91 The Persian War, for which both sides were ready, broke out just before Constantine's death in A.D. 337 and continued under Constantius until well after A.D. 356, the date of composition of this speech. As part of the administrative preparations Constantine instituted a new official, the Count of the East, based in Antioch, whose job it was to co-ordinate the civil administration in support of the military in the Eastern provinces. Antioch, as Libanius describes, became the headquarters base, as it had been for Trajan and Diocletian before him, and the emperor was often personally in residence and in charge, so that she prospered. The Persians, under Sapor II, generally took the offensive with annual invasions of the Roman provinces in Mesopotamia which had been annexed by Diocletian in A.D. 297. These operations are described by Ammianus, a participant in them; their conduct is sharply criticized by Libanius, *Or.* 18.205ff., although they form a major part of his panegyric on the emperors Constantius and Constans (*Or.* 59 of A.D. 349).

92 Unlike Xerxes' army which drank up all the water supply in their passage, 480 B.C., cf. Herod. 7.21.1.

93 Billetting, which included the maintenance of the troops, was normally a source of civilian misery.

and looked after him as if he were a relation visiting us after a long absence. We were so well provided by the land as though in every household the land took the form of a kind of storehouse, of its own self, and so could provide rations to feed them – as much as they could eat. It seemed that no human will or agency made such provision or maintenance, but heaven, in all its divine power, in mysterious ways made these preparations. **(179)** Thus the Persians hold the greatest grudge against us, of all their enemies, because we provided our city as a base which was worthy of our emperor's qualities. Nowhere did we restrain his zeal by neglect of any duty imposed upon us. **(180)** For this reason ours has become the emperor's favourite city. In his absences, he cares for it as if it were his birthplace; he has sworn to return here, too, and he relieves his absences with his despatches. He piles warfare upon warfare without rest; after his labours in the West, he is eager to view the East, and after his labours in the East, he is eager to view our city. So he never proceeded elsewhere, save as the exigencies of war demanded. In very truth he spent here the happiest days of his life, reclining in the arms of his beloved, so to speak.[94]

(181) Then can you admire the physical strength of the city, as in a human body, and yet find the practice of oratory, which can properly be described as the brain of the state, neglected and cast aside? No! This is just what makes her, great though she be, more respected still, and even if she were not so great as she is, would in any case evoke our admiration. **(182)** Though Athens had other claims to fame, in her fleet, her naval victories and her wide empire, yet the finest of them all lay in her pursuit, reverence and acquisition of wisdom. Exactly so with us; though we have nothing which is not admirable, all is of less worth than our love of wisdom. **(183)** In my opinion, heaven which has split the earth in two,[95] has willed that each half shall be equally adorned; and as though to keep the balance in a team in harness, has bidden Hermes to

94 On the evidence of dating in the Theodosian Code in particular, Constantius was resident in Antioch intermittently in A.D. 333, 338–43, 346, 350. Julian (*Or.* 1.40d) reports that Antioch took the honorary title Constantia in consequence of the cordial relations of the emperor and the city. The absence in the West was due to the revolt of Magnentius in A.D. 353.

95 The praises of rhetoric in these sections are heavy with reminiscences of Isocrates (the division of the world into two, Isocr. *Pan.* 179; of Greece, between Sparta and Athens, ibid. 16; the definition of 'Greek' as by culture not race, ibid. 50), and of Plato (Plat. *Menex.* 243c 'strength of the city', *Phaedo* 109a 'balance').

plant the seeds of oratory here,[96] seeds in no way inferior to the oratory of Attica, and to urge mankind to grasp the prize. **(184)** In fact, as previously the Greek world was divided between the two states of Sparta and Athens, so in these days the glories of Greece are divided between Athens and us, if Greeks are to be so named by language rather than by race. **(185)** Indeed, these two torches of rhetoric are held aloft, one illumining Europe, the other Asia, for, first of all, our city has welcomed such fine teachers that if they had not been adjudged worthy of the chairs here, they certainly would have been with regard to those in Athens, since they had such excellence in diction, or in style.[97] **(186)** Secondly, swarms of students have gathered like bees about us.[98] Further, none has left in disgrace; they have gone about their business in the most satisfactory manner, and have then either stayed here or departed. If they stay, they are bound to the city which has given them so much by the ties of affection, because of all they have received. If they go, they take with them their intelligence for the salvation of their own native cities. Again, the renown of those who have returned home has induced others to be initiated in the same rites, and individuals send their sons, brothers, neighbours or friends, – in a word, they all send their fellow citizens. **(187)** And you have become the metropolis of Asia, not more by reason of the superiority of your claim than because here everyone may acquire the most helpful of all accomplishments. Thus, wherever you go, if you find a council well equipped with oratory and speakers of convincing address, you will find that all or most – in any case, no minority – are the products of the colleges here. **(188)** Others, by their forensic skill and by the assistance they provide in legal matters, rise to judge's rank. We provide the provinces with high class pleaders and judges, who direct cities by their judgements, whose sole perquisite

96 Hermes, patron god of eloquence, uses his staff to inspire humans to grasp this prize. The staff is thus important in the conduct of ambassadors.

97 This is not mere self-advertisement on Libanius' part. He was himself invited to a chair in Athens, in A.D. 353, but refused in favour of returning to Antioch (*Or.* 1.81ff.). His rival in Antioch, Acacius, was well enough known to warrant an account next to Libanius in Eunapius' *Lives of the Sophists*, while his predecessor Ulpianus had been renowned for the quality of students he had produced. The intellectual life of Antioch as seen through the writings of Libanius is best presented by Walden (1912).

98 For the students of Libanius, see Petit (1956), a most detailed study. The careers listed are city councillors (§186), pleaders (*advocati*, §188), and provincial governors ('judges', i.e. *iudices*, *dikastai*, §188).

lies in their responsibility for that, and who depart empty-handed but with a crown of glory. You too, in the knowledge of this, have been lavish in building temples of the Muses[99] for students to attend, and as a reward to the goddesses, and you both employ citizens and hold no grudge against foreigners as teachers. **(189)** Your humanity too, has an admixture of acute criticism of oratory, for while the opening of your schools to all indicates your humanity, the praise you bestow only upon the deserving indicates your critical faculty. **(190)** Though you attend upon invitation, you do not gloss over any fault. Any faulty conception, any mistaken figure of speech, any word mispronounced is immediately seized upon. From every side there rises unanimous condemnation of the fault, and the target and object of these censures cannot gaze upon any part of the theatre and try to quell the noisy expressions of their opinion in his ignorance of his audience: wherever you look, you will find a critical examiner there. **(191)** For besides our cultured councillors, there are three classes of orators, of equal number, who gather in the courts.[100] Their ears are no less sharp in judgement than are their tongues in pleading. Thus there is none more fortunate than he who is here judged a skilful speaker, and none more unfortunate than he who has the verdict given against him. In fact, if anyone does not make his entrance here in fear and trembling, he is not so much brave as stupid, since he does not realize the risk he is running. **(192)** So deeply rooted then is the practice of oratory here, and to such like perfection has it grown. Both foreigners who come here for the purpose, and the natives who embrace its study can partake of its waters, so that now it is the current opinion that any dweller in this land has tasted of the art and has shared in the study of rhetoric, – just as if the earth emitted a vapour which induces learning as elsewhere it induces prophecy.[101]

(193) No wonder, then, that, while in other respects she excels others, in the pursuit of wisdom in company with others, she excels even herself, and causes men who come to govern her to be her fervent admirers. For every one of them the beginning, middle and end of his office lies in

99 'Temples of the Muses' are schoolrooms, a favourite notion of his, that seats of learning were hallowed ground. High-sounding though this is, it has basis in fact. Schools were often located in temples, as he is advised to see for himself on his first arrival in Antioch (*Or.* 1.102).

100 The three classes of advocates in the courts are those permanently attendant on any of the three officials based in Antioch – prefect, *comes*, *consularis*.

101 Borrowed from Aristides, *Panath.* 46.

making some addition to the city. Hence those who have been able to make such additions, like men who have made the finest possible offerings to the gods, live the rest of their lives in happiness. They have what they can describe in conversation as their finest achievement, – or to be precise, though they could adduce everything which is glorious for a man, they can pass over the rest in silence and confidently base their claim on this alone, that their work in the most beautiful place on earth will never be forgotten. **(194)** And such confidence is justified. The man who demonstrates his zeal and resolution in a place where men foregather most renders his fame everlasting, – as for instance those painters who have dedicated their works of art to Delphi.[102] Nor is it the case that governors, who can succeed in this by the assistance of the imperial exchequer, have lightly embarked upon such innovation for the city, while those who must spend their own money have revoked. No! Those who have become members of the imperial court have more desire to expend their money here than to make any financial gain.[103] From all the corners of the world they collect fine marble of all descriptions, and this they use upon beautiful buildings which illumine our city like stars. They are leaders in munificence and have many following in their train whose ambitions are too exalted for their capacity. **(195)** So, here, the man who does not build himself a house or buy one already built is thought to have wealth to no purpose, however wealthy he may be; on the other hand, he who does so, though in other respects he may be in some straits, counts himself among the well-to-do. Hence, the extent of the city is never static; just like the human body, it increases from day to day.

(196) However, it is now time to give an account of its size and its site. There is no other city in the world of equal size, I think, which possesses such a fine situation. Starting in the east, it goes in a straight line to the west, with a high pair of colonnades all its length. The colonnades are separated by an uncovered street, paved all the way across.[104] **(197)**

---

102 E.g. Polygnotus (described in detail by Pausan. 10.25.1–10.31.12), in the Lesche of the Cnidians, depicted the fall of Troy and Odysseus in the Underworld.

103 The most eminent of these courtier builders in Antioch up to this time was Datianus (*PLRE* 243(1), *BLZG* 113ff.), *éminence grise* to Constantius. Of the citizen builders, Argyrius and Libanius' uncle Phasganius enlarged the Plethron for the Olympia (*Or.* 10.9ff.), conduct which in A.D. 384 earned his criticism. In fact, in his later years he is as critical of this building mania in Antioch as he is here approving, cf. *Orr.* 2.55; 50.2ff.

104 Detailed study of the topography of Antioch is to be found in Downey (1961), 604ff. Appendices (Topographical Excursus). Particularly interesting is Excursus 18 (pp. 659–64),

Their length, as they extend onwards, is so great that merely to smooth the masonry of such an area would need much labour. If you try to walk from beginning to end, it is a hard job, and you would need the help of a carriage. It is level and continuous all the way, uninterrupted by water courses[105] or steep hills or any other kind of inconvenience. Everything is in harmony, like the perfectly matched colours of a painting. **(198)** From the colonnades, alleys start – some northwards, going over level plain, others southwards,[106] stretching to the mountain spurs, and imperceptibly extending the building-line far enough to stay in harmony with the rest of the city and not to allow it to stand aloof, as it were, by being too much elevated over the rest. **(199)** The city has not overleapt cliffs and precipices, or made intervening areas part of itself, or acquired any little place tucked away in the folds of the mountain. Thus it has not set houses above to loom over houses below, and scare them, like the stone of Sisyphus.[107] It has extended just so far as it could maintain its continuity of progress, and by this means it has also maintained its handsome appearance along with its size. **(200)** The mountain alone stretches the whole way along like a protecting shield held high, and for those who dwell in the outskirts at its foot there are none of the terrors to be associated with mountains, but sources of pleasure – springs, trees, gardens, the breezes and the flowers, the songs of birds and the pleasures of the spring which comes to them sooner than to anyone. **(201)** The colonnades are like rivers in flood, the alleys like streams leading off

---

a discussion of the guided tour of Antioch as given in the mosaic of Yakto. Editors point out that, although Libanius speaks of the long axis of the city as running east-west, it really runs northeast-southwest. Libanius, however, should be allowed some literary licence. His aim is not geographical exactness but the achievement of his conclusion with the description of Daphne, the site of the final day's events in the Olympia, as is only fitting for an Olympic oration such as this.

Libanius does not give precise lengths to the colonnades which were famous in antiquity, but leaves that to the imagination of his audience who knew them well enough. Dio Chrysostom (*Or.* 47.16) exaggerates it with 36 stades, Josephus (*Wars* 21.4) has 20 stades. See Downey, 'Imperial Building Records in Malalas', *BZ* 38 (1938), 306–11.

105 The streams, e.g. the Parmenio or Onopniktes ('Donkey-drowner'), were diverted by culverts or aqueducts under the colonnades, as excavations reveal.

106 Actually, northeast and southwest, cf. note 104 above. The suburbs encroach upon the spurs of Mt Silpius.

107 Homer, *Od.* 11.593. In Libanius' time the suburbs had not yet extended up the slopes of the mountain.

them. Those facing the mountain lead you to the delights of its lower slopes, while those running in the opposite direction lead you to another uncovered street,[108] built up on either side, as canals, which have been constructed for the purpose, connect one river with another. This area also ends in a lovely expanse of gardens on all sides, which in their turn stop on the bank of the river Orontes. **(202)** The colonnades, as I have said, run from east to west, covering such an extent that they would have sufficed for three cities. Right in the centre of the right-hand one are arches facing every direction, connected with a single roof of stone. These are the beginnings of other colonnades which proceed northwards as far as the river, with the mighty temple of the Nymphs nearby which attracts every eye with its gleaming marble, its coloured pillars, its glistening paintings and its wealth of springs. From these colonnades, as from the others, alleys lead off.

(203) Such then is the appearance of the old city. The new city[109] consists of the island made by the river dividing into two. In its upper reaches and for most of its course, the river flows in a single channel, but here it splits, encircles the area and flows by it on either side. One channel can be seen between the two cities, while the other flows on the far side of the new city, and after forming the island, reunites its channel with the other and makes the river as it was before it split. **(204)** The shape of this new city is circular, and it lies on ground completely level and is encircled with an unbroken girdle of wall. From four arched vaults[110] linked to one another in rectangular formation, as though from the navel, four pairs of colonnades extend to each point of the compass – as in the statue of the four-handed Apollo. **(205)** Of these, three of the colonnades reach the circumference of the wall, while the fourth is shorter. Yet the shorter it is, the more beautiful it is, for it, as it were, goes to meet the palace quarter which starts nearby, and serves as the gateway to it. **(206)** The palace itself has absorbed so much of the

108 This is the parallel street to the north of the great colonnade, as shown in the map.

109 The new city is the extension begun by Seleucus II and carried on by Antiochus the Great (cf. Downey (1961), 92), whereby the island formed by the branching of the river was built up and became an integral part of the city, connected to the old by this colonnade. The remainder, situated on the level to the east of the river, was for Libanius the 'old city'. The palace quarter, begun by Gallienus, was built up by Diocletian.

110 The Tetrapylon stood at the main cross-roads of the island at the entrance of the palace. According to Malalas, *Chron.* 328 it was called the Tetrapylon of the Elephants, and here, early in A.D. 363, Julian 'published' his *Misopogon* by putting it on public display.

island that it covers a quarter of its area, for it is close to the centre, which it has taken as its centre too and extends to the further branch of the river. Thus the wall has pillars instead of battlements, and has been made a fitting sight for the emperor, with the river flowing at his feet and the suburbs on every side providing a feast for his eyes.[111] **(207)** Anyone who wishes to give an accurate description of this quarter must make this his whole theme, not a portion of any other. Yet this much I must explain, that of all the palaces in the world which are called palaces from their size or are far famed for their beauty, this palace quarter is in no way inferior to the first and is far superior to the second. Its claims to beauty are unsurpassed, and it wins on all counts in any comparison of its size, for it is divided up into so many rooms, colonnades and halls that even people long acquainted with the place can lose their way when going from one door to another. If this quarter only lay in some miserable little city, as for example many of those in Thrace, where a few hovels compose their cities,[112] – if it lay in one of these, it would without question, in my opinion, give that city which possessed it good reason for pride in any comparison of cities.

(208) But to return to my point; the river, flowing between them, separates the new city from the old, but the gap is spanned by five strong bridges.[113] While the water makes our city two, the bridges refuse to allow it to be two, but link the newer to the older city, like a foal to its dam. **(209)** Now consider! If it be the ideal for a city to extend to great length, the old city was built in this way: if a circular shape is more prepossessing, the new city has this quality; if the very fact that a city has no single form is an indication of its size, here if anywhere is every shape of city. Thus if anyone likes to live in a city which has all four sides of equal dimensions, he should realize that he is happy with little things. **(210)** For as in farming, the small holding is easily worked – like the foreground in a painting – while the arable land of the rich does not allow such treatment, but stretches far and wide into both background and foreground, so with cities the one which has no great size submits to a

111 This gallery of pillars is at the extreme northwest of the island. From here the Emperor Valens conducted his long-range conversation with the Christian monk Aphraates, as recorded in Theodoret, *Historia Ecclesiastica* 4.26.1.

112 I.e. Constantinople, always an object of hostility and contempt for Libanius.

113 Libanius now returns from the island to the old city. Downey ((1961), Map 11; cf. map in this volume) does show five bridges connecting the old city to the island. Two bridges appear on the Yakto mosaic (ibid., 661, 663).

single shape, while a large city extends beyond such confines according to the circumstances. **(211)** While I am on the subject of its size I will not pass over the following fact either, with regard to the length of colonnades which I first mentioned; if those which run from them down to the river, were joined together and put end to end with them, and then, if the colonnades of the new city were in the same way joined to them and increased their former size – and if they were joined so, or even if they were to stay as they are and the distance be observed and calculated, it would be found that the extent of our colonnades is a full day's march.[114] **(212)** As you go along them, you find long stretches of private houses, and everywhere mingled among them public buildings, – temples or baths – sufficiently far apart so as to allow the nearby quarter of the city to make use of them. Every one of them has its front door opening on to the colonnades.[115] **(213)** The point of all this, the conclusion I wish to draw from my lengthy account which has been confined to the colonnades, is this. In my opinion, the most pleasant feature of cities, I would go so far as to say the most beneficial too, lies in social intercourse and association. Indeed, where you have this in plenty, there you have a real city. **(214)** For to have something to say is good; to have something to hear is better; to impart some counsel is best of all, and so is the opportunity of making a fitting contribution to the lives of our friends by sharing their pleasures and their sorrows, and receiving from them the like in return. There are besides thousands of advantages in close association with one another. **(215)** Thus those who have no stretch of colonnade in front of their houses are separated from one another by winter. In theory, they dwell in the same town but in fact they are as far removed from each other as they are from the inhabitants of other towns. They hear news about their next door neighbours just as if they lived miles away. They are confined to their homes like prisoners, by rain, hail, snow and wind; their slaves, now well schooled in reducing

114 The scholiast (*ad loc.*) notes that in Herodotus and Xenophon the *stathmos* equals 24 miles. Editors agree in classing Libanius' statement as rhetorical exaggeration. The *stathmos* (a day's march) was conventionally reckoned as 150 stades, the most common measurement of the stade being 176m. The length of Antioch's main street was about 3km, so that, even if the distance to the island and back is counted, together with all the porticoes on the island itself, we cannot approach the inflated figure here.

115 The Yakto mosaic does show a public bath, but in Daphne. Archaeology has confirmed the statement that the front doors open on to the colonnades, cf. J. Lassus, 'Les Portiques d'Antioche', in *Antioch-on-the-Orontes* V, 33; Martin in Festugière (1959), 48.

discomforts, scarcely make their appearance in the market before they are off again. Thus when the weather clears, they embrace one another in greeting, as though they have come safe home from a long voyage, although they have neglected in their relations with one another many of the duties demanded by the laws of friendship, and they blame not themselves, but all that has kept them apart. **(216)** With us, on the other hand, there is no such biting hail from heaven, no snowfalls, no downpours of rain, which can interrupt the continuity of our intercourse. The year may experience its change of seasons, but there is no alteration in our association; while the rain beats on the roofs, we in the colonnades stroll in comfort and settle ourselves as the chance offers. **(217)** Moreover anyone who lives in the outlying alleys is brought to the main colonnades without a soaking, for lattices project from each wall and protect him from the rain. Hence, while in other towns the inhabitants are split up and their intercourse blunted, among us our friendship grows with our uninterrupted association, and we gain as much as they lose.

(218) Thus the extent of the colonnades has made its contribution not only towards human pleasure, but especially to human wellbeing. Attached to them are the hippodrome, the theatre and the baths. The hippodrome, big enough to satisfy the fastest of horses, has plenty of seats and can give accommodation for seating the mass of the townspeople.[116] The theatre resounds with contests of flute, lyre and voice and the manifold delights of the stage.[117] **(219)** Who would ever succeed in narrating the diverse forms of entertainment in the theatre, the contests of athletes, or of men against beasts, all in the heart of the city[118] and

116 'The fastest of horses', lit. 'the horses of Boreas' cf. Homer, *Il.* 20.219ff. The hippodrome was on the island, near the palace, as shown on the Yakto mosaic and revealed by excavation, cf. W.A. Campbell, *Antioch-on-the-Orontes* I, 34ff.; Martin in Festugière (1959), 49.

117 The Antiochenes were passionately devoted to the theatre, an entertainment of which Libanius and highbrow pagans, no less than Christian moralists, normally disapproved (*Orr.* 41.9; 46.31; Julian, *Misop.* 346a, 357d ff.), although Libanius can produce a rhetorical showpiece in its defence (*Or.* 64), as against the standpoint taken by his model, the orator Aristides of the second century A.D. A theatre had been built under the Seleucids (§125), but this theatre of Dionysus (cf. *Or.* 10.23) was, according to Malalas, *Chron.* 217, built by Caesar, with later rebuilds. There were other theatres, e.g. the theatre of Zeus (cf. *Or.* 10.23), which was most likely the combined Plethrion and Xystos where the preliminaries to the Olympia were held. Cf. Martin in Festugière (1959).

118 Libanius is now in Epiphania, having returned from the island to the centre of the old city where these various temples and baths existed, as is proved by excavation. Note that the

not spoiling the pleasure by the long journey to them? **(220)** And who would not find delight in the baths? Some have their temperature to suit the winter, some suit the summer. Some are sheltered from the gusts of wind, others are, as it were, raised aloft and have no part of earth.[119] **(221)** Of the houses, some under construction are in the magnificent style now in fashion, while those of an earlier day are in a more restrained style, with no element of vulgarity or ostentation.

(222) If I should disclose an idea which has presented itself to me, the zephyrs, I am sure, induced our first founders not to labour incessantly at building. So, while those people who have not a very good climate try every device of building to obtain refreshment, we enjoy our pleasant breezes and, as Homer says,[120] we have the West Wind as a goodly companion and have no need to waste our time, since he allows us to bask in his breezes. **(223)** The story goes that Boreas fought on the side of the Athenians at sea and that he offered them this gift as price for the maiden he had taken; but though he is related by marriage thus, he takes no pains to keep his gift within bounds. With us, on the other hand, Zephyrus is not our benefactor after first wronging us. He is a lover, not of a maiden, but of the whole city, and his love is undying. In winter, he restrains himself, for he knows that if he comes then he will trouble us, so he makes his entry in company with spring, to check the heat. **(224)** He deals with no other city before ours, nor does he pass to any other from ours: he begins here and ends here, like men who, concentrating upon one single object of beauty, do not have their gaze distracted by the appearance of any other body. **(225)** He blows through and about the whole city, and leaves nothing without some part of the aid he brings. He does not blow upon the lofty three-storeyed houses of the rich and pass over the lowly humble dwellings of the poor: as in democracy there is equality under the law, so among us there is equality in sharing the blessings of the zephyr. None has ever thirsted for its

---

displays are *venationes*, not the gladiatorial combats officially banned since Constantine's day.

119 Baths in Antioch for seasonal use, cf. Evagrius, *Historia Ecclesiastica* 6.8. The distinction between covered and open air baths is further developed by the location of some of the latter on terraces on the hillside.

120 Homer, *Od.* 11.7; 12.149. The wind blows along the main street, not across it. For the story of Boreas and Oreithyia and his assistance to the Athenians in 480 B.C., cf. Herod. 7.189.

breezes and charged his neighbours with responsibility for his plight. It just goes everywhere, wafting along and blowing where it may. **(226)** Some people before now have been deprived even of sunlight when a nearby house overshadows them, but there is no let or hindrance for the zephyr to spread its favours broadcast. It lifts the coatskirts and blows around the legs of the pedestrians, its breezes make the sleepers' clothing lift around their bodies, and it makes night a double time of rest when its light airs accompany our sleep.

(227) It is not without reason, then, that there is always building going on in the city: some buildings are up to rooftop height, some half built, or with foundations just laid or else being excavated. Everywhere you can hear the workmen being told to hurry up. The vegetable gardens of yesterday are today built-up areas.[121] Here men know that they can possess in their lifetime all that poets promise the just after their death.

(228) Just consider! The city would be four times as big as it is now had it not suffered three disasters in days gone by.[122] The temple of Apollo Pythius suffered many vicissitudes, and the present temple is the fourth on the site, as a result of the destruction of earlier ones. So with us, our city, inasmuch as it was the work of mortal men was laid low, yet with the blessing of heaven rose again, just like Athena's olive, to which Xerxes set fire when he tried to destroy the Athenian acropolis, but which next day had sprouted an eighteen-inch shoot from the burnt stump. In truth, our city too fell and rose again. **(229)** And now, as you dig the ground to lay foundations, everywhere you find traces of the past, and many people use the material they find instead of what they had intended to use, and bring fresh material to build on top of it. Thus if disaster had not overtaken it, and additions had still occurred, and if

121 Later (in A.D. 386) Libanius is to be bitterly critical of the building mania of the Antiochene magnates, who get labour forced on the peasantry (*angareiai*) for the disposal of the rubble they cause, *Or.* 50 (*passim*), translated in Norman (1971).

122 Antioch is in an earthquake belt. Major earthquakes are noted for 148 B.C., A.D. 37 and A.D. 115. There was evidently a list of quakes in the official records, available both to Libanius and to Malalas who creates confusion by listing that of A.D. 37 as 'second after the Macedonians', with that of A.D. 115 as 'third'. Libanius, whose command of Greek was a good deal better than that of Malalas, makes no mention of Macedonians, and avoids any confusion. He is simply recounting the three major disasters since the foundation of the city. The most ruinous earthquake was to come in A.D. 457.

For his comparison with the rebuildings of the temple of Apollo Pythius at Delphi, cf. Pausan. 6.5.13, Strabo 9.3.9: for the burning of Athena's olive by Xerxes in 480 B.C., Herod. 8.55.

the present activity in renovation had instead been concentrated upon fresh building, many people would have lost good cultivable land.

(230) Now it is not the case either that, while our city is so absolutely unique, the outlying districts are in a condition which would require improvement. They show quite clearly that they belong to this city of ours. First, there are large and populous villages[123] with a larger population than many towns; they employ craftsmen, just as happens in cities; they have a mutual intercourse through their festivals, to attend which each one in turn issues and receives invitations: their relaxations, pleasures and hopes are identical; they allow others to share in their abundance, and make up their deficiencies from them; they buy and sell, and are far more prosperous than merchant venturers, since they make their money not on the surging waves, but with joyous merriment, and there is little which they need from the city because of the system of barter between one another. (231) Consider too the scene before the city gates. You will not think it proper to call them inns,[124] but quarters of a city, and of this city alone. The buildings outside the city are so well matched to the opulence of its interior in their luxurious baths, and equipment, and social life that if you could bring them into one pattern, split up into three as they are, these buildings now before the city gates would suffice to form a city in themselves. (232) Thus, as the outskirts of the palace district partook of the magnificence within even though inferior to the inward parts, and allow us to infer its greater glories from the sight of the lesser ones, in the same way some likeness has passed from the city to those parts beyond the walls. So when you drive out, you will swear that you are seeing what you have left behind, but in miniature, and as you enter the city, you are forewarned by its exterior as to its interior.

(233) Thus every part is on the same lines, but the Western quarter – upon my word, it beats all the rest and beggars description! You should just see it! However pleasant the account you hear of it, you would only hear half the story. (234) As soon as the gates are left behind, one is struck by the variety of gardens on the lefthand side, of places of entertainment, the abundance of fountains, villas hidden among the trees, with rooms overlooking the treetops, – a spot fit for Aphrodite and her

123 For these villages, cf. Petit (1955), 307f., Martin in Festugière (1959), 52.
124 'Caravanserai' at each city gate mark these 'hostelries', each with its own 'souk' (Beroea Gate to the East, Daphne Gate to Laodicea, and Taurian Gate to Seleuceia and the North) – 'mansiones'.

archer son. As one proceeds, on either side of the road can be seen innumerable vineyards, lovely villas, rose gardens, plantations of every kind and streams. One's gaze is attracted first to one side, then to another, and amid such pleasures, one will reach Daphne, the peerless. **(235)** Of Daphne there has never yet been a fitting description, nor will there ever be, unless it occurs to Apollo with the Muses to sing the praises of the place. This road, leading from the city to the suburb I would confidently describe as the tassel of the aegis, with which Homer arms Athena. It is all golden, and ends at the golden Colophon of all things, Daphne.[125] **(236)** At the sight of it, the spectator cannot but leap up with a start, clap his hands and congratulate himself upon the sights and almost take wing in his pleasure. On every side he is delighted and awed by what he sees; while he is still absorbed in one thing his attention is diverted to another, and the radiance which fills his eyes causes the spectator to turn his gaze to view the temple of Apollo or that of Zeus, the Olympic stadium, a perfectly delightful theatre, a thick high mass of cypresses,[126] with shady paths, harmonious bird song, a gentle breeze, and odours sweeter than incense, imposing hotels, vines clinging to the walls of the halls; there are gardens like those of Alcinous, fare of Sicilian profusion, the horn of plenty, sumptuous banquets and the luxury of Sybaris.[127]

125 Homer, *Il.* 2.448. Colophon, proverbially perfection, the finishing touch. Strabo (p. 643) explains that originally the cavalry of Colophon was so good that it overcame all opposition. A variant is that the quality of early Colophonian gold was first class.

For the foundation and cults of Daphne, cf. Downey (1961), 82ff.

126 The Temple of Apollo, with its famous statue by Bryaxis (Downey (1961), 85), was founded by Seleucus Nicator (above §94). It was destroyed by fire on 22 October A.D. 362 (Amm. Marc. 22.13.1ff., Lib. *Or.* 60, Julian, *Misop.* 361b). For that of Zeus, cf. Malalas, *Chron.* 307; the Olympic stadium, which figures on the Yakto mosaic, patronized by both Seleucids and Romans, had most recently been restored by Diocletian (Malalas, *Chron.* 307). The final day's events of the Olympia were held there, the preliminaries in the Plethrion at Antioch (*Or.* 10). For the theatre of Olympian Zeus, by Titus, cf. Downey (1961), 206f. The cypresses, sacred to Apollo (above §99), became in the fourth century imperial property and special permission was required to cut them down (*Cod. Th.* 10.1.2 of A.D. 379) – this to counter bigoted Christian governors who were intent on destroying them (*Or.* 1.255, 262).

127 All these are proverbial descriptions of luxury and profusion: the gardens of Alcinous, Homer, *Od.* 7.112ff.; Sicilian banquets, Plato, *Rep.* 404d, Diogen. 8.7 (*Corp. Par. Gr.* 1.306); the Horn of Amalthea (i.e. the horn of plenty), Zenob. 2.48 (*Corp. Par. Gr.* 1.141); Sybaris, in Magna Graecia, was the epitome of luxurious living before coming to a sudden end with its destruction by its neighbour, Croton, in 510 B.C.; cf. Zenob. 5.87 (*Corp. Par. Gr.* 1.156).

Whatever bath you choose in which to bathe, you may be sure that you have overlooked one yet more pleasant. **(237)** So beneficial is the place to your bodily health, that if you stay there only for a little while and then depart, you go with a better complexion. If you were asked what delighted you most, you would be at loss for an answer, for everything is so well matched. There is no emotion so strong, obstinate and deeply rooted that Daphne could not dispel. As soon as you approach the spot, it drives away your troubles. If the gods really do leave heaven to visit the earth, here I think is the place for them to gather in assembly, for they could stay in no spot more beautiful. **(238)** Such a vision as I have described is not such as to allow its remarkable beauty to lose any part of its wonder because of the fewness of the objects which partake of it. For instance, it is not just a matter of five villas, seven gardens, 300 cypresses or three baths.[128] Though their beauty has no equal anywhere, their total number is greater even than their beauty. **(239)** It has so many of each of these items, that it has remained in the style of a suburb, simply in deference to the city. Yet if it wished to take part in any comparison of cities, it would win on many counts. Even those Romans it has welcomed as visitors, have been won over and induced to refrain from singing the praises of Italy as unsurpassable in these respects.[129]

(240) The chief of the glories of Daphne, indeed of the whole world, are the springs of Daphne. Nowhere has the earth produced such streams either to view or to use. They are palaces of the Nymphs,[130] who have granted them such translucence and purity. **(241)** Indeed, you could assert that the goddesses take no less delight in the spot than does Zeus in Pisa, Poseidon in the Isthmus, Apollo in Delphi or Hephaestus in Lemnus.[131] Moreover, if we are to believe that Nymphs dwell in

128 I.e. the sheer quantity of such perfections makes numerical precision like this merely ridiculous.

129 As noted above (n. 47), Daphne was so famous among the Romans that Antioch was described by Pliny (*N.H.*) as 'Antioch by Daphne'. Although Libanius is generally tepid in his comments about Rome itself, he accepts the received accounts of the natural charms of Italy, although he had visited neither, unlike Constantinople, which he cordially loathed.

130 Hence monumental fountains were called Nymphaea – such as the one near the centre of Antioch.

131 Pisa (Pausan. 6.22.1, Strabo 8.3.31 (p. 356)) was absorbed by the Eleans at an early date, and became synonymous with Olympia, in honour of Zeus; Isthmia, in honour of Poseidon at Corinth; Pythia, of Apollo at Delphi; for Hephaestus in Lemnus, Homer, *Il.* 1.590ff.

water, it would seem that they visit other waters merely on a tour of inspection, but that here, like emperors, they have their capital. Of this too I am convinced, that when the three goddesses began to quarrel about their beauty, it was here that they came to bathe for the judgement, rather than to the place where the story has it.[132] **(242)** No one who has stood and watched the water flowing from the springs and gliding past either wall of the temple[133] could but rejoice at its volume, marvel at its beauty and honour its divinity. He needs must derive some pleasure from the feel of it, more from bathing in it, and most of all from drinking it. It is cold, clear and sweet, redolent of charm and soothing for the body to touch. **(243)** Yet the water does not stay only in the place where it had its source: Daphne, after first producing it, did not allow her gift to stay with herself, to retain the sole enjoyment of it. Though Daphne is its source, the city shares it with her who revealed it, since the water runs from one home to another. Men have not had to tunnel through the hills to construct a channel for the stream from somewhere beyond the boundary of our land. That is a job which involves much toil and risk, since this source of supply depends on someone else's generosity. They have not had to excavate here, to build embankments there, in some places to make a way through mid-air, where cliffs render it necessary, by the use of aqueducts, and to allow the city to share in such amenities which the suburban districts provide. **(244)** Now our chief advantage is that our city has an abundant water supply. There could possibly be disagreement on other matters, but when we mention our water supply, everyone concedes the point. Streams which are lovely are surpassed by ours in number: the majority of streams are surpassed by ours in beauty; – or to be more accurate, ours excel in volume those which exist in abundance, and in loveliness those which are charming. Every public bath takes its fill from the river, and of the private baths some take the same quantity, while others take not much less. **(245)** Any man who can draw water for his bath after other people have done so, draws it with confi-

132 The judgement of Paris – to decide the beauty contest between Aphrodite, Hera and Athena – in myth took place on Mt Ida near Troy. Perhaps Libanius is drawing on a local variant of the myth setting its location in Daphne, but in any case he is giving full rein to his rhetorical invention.

133 The temple of the Nymphs, not that of Apollo, as Downey would have it. On the water supply of Daphne and Antioch, cf. Martin in Festugière (1959), 54ff. The commendations of Libanius and his remarks on canals and aqueducts which follow are confirmed by modern archaeology – illustrated in Downey (1961), Plate 13.

dence. He has no fear that, if he continues the practice in midsummer the place will be called 'dry as a bone' through lack of water. So far from his desire to bathe being thwarted by lack of water, even the man who has not ever much desire to bathe is induced to do so by the water itself. So every quarter of the city has a profusion of private baths which beggar description. Their beauty exceeds that of the public baths exactly as their size is smaller, and there is much competition among people in the neighbourhood that each of them should be the possessor of the most beautiful of them.[134] **(246)** You may deduce from the number of houses, our wealth of fountains. There are fountains as many as – no, more than the number of houses, and the majority of the workshops boasts one.[135] **(247)** So we have no free fights around our public fountains, as to who will draw water before his neighbour, which is a nuisance to many a wealthy town. There they push and jostle around the fountain, and there is weeping and wailing when bowls are broken and at the injuries received around the springs. We, however, all have our fountains inside our houses, and the public ones are for show. **(248)** Besides, with regard to the purity of the water, you could make a fair test, if you were to fill a swimming pool and then check the water from entering. You would think it to be empty, for the floor of the bath stands out so clearly under the water. So I am not sure whether the sight would serve to inflame your thirst rather than to quench it, for it entices you to drink and gives such pleasure before even you begin to do so.

(249) With regard to the friendly rivalries which you exercise with each other, no final judgement is possible since here there is such general equality. You are so obviously superior to other people, yet towards each other you are all on the same plane. **(250)** So those who dwell in the Eastern quarter can claim that the greater part of the grain is imported through their district, and they can also cite their possession

---

134 There were eighteen *phylae* ('tribes, wards') in Antioch (*Or.* 19.62), each under an *epimeletes* (supervisor). They had no political function, but did retain some religious functions (e.g. the boxing festival of *Or.* 5.43ff.), and had responsibility for some public amenities, such as baths (as here) and street lighting (*Or.* 33.35ff.). The maintenance of the public baths was an imposed duty on the lower classes, and so done perfunctorily. That of the ward baths was voluntary and its performance an object of competition. The actual heating of the baths was a liturgy imposed on decurions. Cf. Downey (1961), 115, Liebeschuetz (1972), 123.

135 Such abundant water supply was, in the ancient world, luxury indeed. Contrast Pliny's account (*Ep.* 10.37) of the expensive fiasco of building an aqueduct at Nicomedia.

of Alexander's fountain.[136] Those again, who live in the Western districts cite their plantations, their general elegance and the pleasant proximity of Daphne. Those who live on the hillsides can boast of their fresh air, their repose and their view of the whole city, while the inhabitants of the new city point to their wall, the island and palace, and their neatly planned lay-out, while those who dwell in a central position, boast of the fact. Who could express a preference on hearing this, when faced with the list of equally valid claims? **(251)** May we, by the grace of heaven, never lose this sense of rivalry, which is instilled in us by the desire of each to outdo the rest! For what can be more abundant or satisfying than the profusion of goods on sale? These are so widely distributed over the whole city that no one part of the city can be called the market area, and purchasers need not go to one special place; it is suited to every man's convenience, for he has but to stretch out his hand, either before his own front door or anywhere in the town, and he can get whatever he wants.[137] **(252)** It is impossible to find a street so mean and obscure that it sends its inhabitants elsewhere to procure any of the necessities of life. Both the centre and the outskirts of the city are equally flourishing, and just as every part teems with human beings, so it teems with goods on sale. **(253)** Though you have often enough before now passed by many which you do not need, no one has ever yet looked for anything and found it wanting. Exquisite delicacies vie with necessities, for in our city they cater for both purses, in providing enough for the poor while still satisfying the desires of the wealthy. For their entertainment it produces a store of luxuries, while for the more slender purse there is more moderate fare, and not too little of this nor too much of the other. Indeed, it is our proudest boast that our city carefully provides for the poor in various ways; it ensures for them not merely a bare existence, but a pleasant existence.[138] **(254)** You can appreciate the vast trade of our market in this way. Any other city we know of with a reputation for wealth has only one row of stalls, that in front of the houses. Nobody plies his trade in the area inside the columns. With us, however, this

136 The eastern suburb by the Beroean Gate: Alexander's fountain is that named Olympias, cf. §73 above.

137 Martin (in Festugière (1959), 56) points out the significance of Libanius' comments for an appreciation of the difference between Hellenistic town-planning, where the markets are grouped, and the Roman, where each street had its own sales pitch.

138 In his enthusiasm, Libanius has blithely ignored the shortages experienced two years before under Gallus, which would recur, with more severity, six years later under Julian.

space also is part of the market, so that practically every house has a workshop facing it, wooden stalls and roofs of brushwood. There is not an inch without its craft, but if anyone gets hold of a square yard or two on the edge, it straightaway becomes a tailor's shop or something like that, and they hang on to their stall like grim death – an Odysseus hanging on to his fig tree.[139] **(255)** The display of goods is remarkable enough, but an even greater source for wonder lies in their unbroken line. Thus shoppers in the Eastern quarter have no need to have recourse to the vendors in the Western district. In rather the same way as you come upon waters which are everywhere alike, whenever you need them, so you can enjoy the various shopping centres, between which there is nothing to choose. Not even nightfall dispels the activity but here you can see something which excels all the proud boasts of the Ethiopians. **(256)** They provide what they call the table of the Sun,[140] laden with meat, at sunrise. It is the duty of the authorities to place the meat on it during the night, but they make up a strange story that this is the produce which the earth of itself provides. Now here you cannot tell at what time our wares are prepared: you can look upon this profusion, it makes no difference whether it be day or night, for at both times everything is there in the same abundance. **(257)** Hence, when night overtakes travellers on the last few miles of their journey here, they cheerfully continue upon their way for they know that they will be welcome there after dark, and they will be able to bathe, wine and dine more sumptuously than guests at victory celebrations – just as if they had sent their cooks on ahead to prepare the feast. **(258)** Everything is to hand; there is no need to go scurrying round for fish to buy: all you need do is to lend an ear to the fish-sellers crying their wares. Indeed, landsmen though we are, we have a greater supply of fish than many who live on the coast. Though we live at a distance from the sea, the fishermen catch the fish of the sea for us, and every day heaps of fish of every variety come into the town.[141] **(259)** Another advantage here, too, is that not

139 Again Libanius exaggerates. Such stalls, or booths, were known in other cities (cf. Martin in Festugière (1959), 57), but those in Antioch were notable enough to appear on the Yakto mosaic. His mock-heroic comparison with Homer, *Od.* 12.432 is the more pointed since fig-tree wood is notoriously brittle.

140 Cf. Herod. 3.18, and W.W. How and J. Wells, *A Commentary on Herodotus*, 2 vols., Oxford 1912, note *ad loc.*

141 Downey ((1961), 23, note 47) notes the large numbers of mosaics found in Antioch, many on the floors of baths, which show fish of many varieties, 39 on one floor. This is re-

even the poor are excluded from such a diet. Fortune has provided each man with his due: to the rich she has given the harvest of the sea, to the rest that of the lake, and to both alike, the river which for the rich feeds the kind which come upstream into it from the sea, and for the rest, feeds many others of all varieties.

(260) The river and the lake are a source of profit to the city not merely in that they provide fare for our tables, but also because all the produce of the soil comes into the city's possession through the ease by which it is transported, for the import of corn is not reduced to the meagre amount brought in by pack animals. The countryside is divided up between them; the river flows through the areas which derive no assistance from the lake; similarly, the lake extends over those areas where there is no aid from the river. By lake and river craft they empty the countryside of its produce and transport it to town. (261) The first stages of transportation are separate, but then, instead of both being used, the river acts as host for the convoy of lake-borne goods as well as of its own, and brings them into the centre of the city, setting down the freight at everyone's doorstep for women and children to clear the cargo. In Thesprotis exactly the opposite of this occurs; there the river flows into the lake, while here it receives the outfall from the lake.[142] (262) Most important of all, its course below the city is navigable. It is not impassable because of rocks, as much even of the Nile is;[143] hence it is of great advantage to us and deserves the praise which Pindar bestowed upon the river Hipparis in Camarina, that it 'swiftly weldeth together a soaring forest of steadfast dwellings' by providing carriage for timber from all quarters.[144]

(263) Since I have mentioned the outfall of the river into the sea, I am brought to an account of the harbour. This, in my opinion, is not one of

---

plicated throughout the Roman world, e.g. at Pompeii (in the National Archaeological Museum in Naples), and even in the mosaics from villas in Roman Britain. The Mediterranean pattern books of mosaicists travelled widely. Fish was indeed a staple diet. In Antioch the cheaper fish, produce of the Lake of Antioch a little upstream, consisted mainly of eels and catfish.

142 A comparison of the Orontes and the Lake of Antioch with Thucydides' description of the Acherousian Lake in northwestern Greece (1.46.3f.). The Orontes does not flow into the lake, lying northeast of the city, but receives overflow from it.

143 Another comparison with Herod. 2.29.3, the Nile cataract at Wadi Halfa.

144 Pindar, Ol. 5.14ff. – a fitting citation in an Olympia oration. The Orontes was navigable as far as Antioch, where Seleucus marked out its earliest commercial area by its banks. For timber floated down from the mountains, cf. §19 above.

those which our provident rulers have merely improved by alterations. In Seleuceia there was excavated from the solid rock for our city's sake a harbour, at such expense that all the treasure Croesus got from Pactolus[145] could not cover it. **(264)** And so ships put in from every port with the produce of the whole world, Libya, Europe, Asia, the islands and highlands. The choicest products of every land are brought here, for a quick sale encourages the merchants to come here, and so we reap the fruits of the whole world. Indeed, more sea-going vessels stow their sails in our harbour than in any other.

(265) Hence it is no wonder that we, who dwell in such a land as this and possess such trade as this, who have the lake as our ally and the river's course as our helpmate, have made our city very like a holiday centre. **(266)** For is there anywhere else in the world where a holiday is celebrated with such a profusion of things as we have here on every day of the week? Who, on his first view of the city, does not think that he has arrived for the holy month? Who is so dejected in spirit that it does not cheer him up? Where is there such a stream of delight elsewhere? What source of pleasure do we lack here? Have we not a genial climate, delightful baths, a wonderful market, a winter presaging long spells of sunshine,[146] spring agleam with flowers, summer bright with the colours of the fruit trees, and with its colours making an Arcadia of our city? Is it not more pleasant to stroll through the midst of the merchandise than through the midst of the gardens, and is not conversation in the Market Square preferable to staying at home? Is not the throng which flows through the city a pleasant sight? Is it not proved among us here that Homer praised Sleep beyond his deserts? **(267)** For here, at least, Sleep is no 'lord of mankind'[147] nor does he draw them to him against their will, nor yet force them to rest. On the contrary, we alone of mankind

145 By Diocletian (§159 above, cf. Downey (1961), 330), and Constantius (ibid., 361, note 198). Libanius dismisses the notion of the harbour construction as inspired by military needs, concentrating instead upon the economic advantages to the city, which were real enough, although of secondary importance to the administration. His comparison of the cost of harbour construction at Seleuceia with the legendary wealth of Croesus (for which cf. Herod. 5.101.2) is a rhetorical demonstration of the importance of the harbour to the Roman authorities, and implicitly gives the lie to his claim about their intentions. On Seleuceia, cf. *s. v.* Honigmann in *RE* II A, 1190ff.

146 Reiske's supplementation of an alleged lacuna is here translated.

147 Homer, *Il.* 14.233. The street lighting of Antioch was famous in antiquity, in contrast with conditions in Rome; cf. Amm. Marc. 14.1.9. The shopkeepers had to supply the oil for it. The service was regulated by the governor and administered by the *epimeletae* (cf. *Orr.*

have shaken ourselves free of the tyranny he exercises over our eyes, and other lights succeed the sun's light. These far surpass the Egyptian Feast of Lights and night here differs from day only by the kind of illumination. It is just the same in the workshops, where some busily ply their trade while others give themselves up to joyous merriment and song. Night belongs to Hephaestus and Aphrodite[148] alike, as some work in the smithies while others dance. In other towns, however, it is sleepy old Endymion who is more honoured.

(268) There is no class of man which does not derive advantage from the city. Here financiers may easily obtain a fortune,[149] professors of philosophy a reputation, the lover his desire. Though it is a good place for serious pursuits, it is a proper place to have a good time. There are horseraces, where the rivalries do not involve riot, the delights of the stage, and a gladness of heart which matches our serious reflections.[150] The pride of Elis has been transferred here, and those who instructed us in the ways of the Olympic festivals we have surpassed in our honour to Zeus.[151] (269) Why, an emperor once

---

16.41; 22.6; 33.35ff.; Martin in Festugière (1959), 60). For the Egyptian Feast of Lights, cf. Herod. 2.62.

148 Smithying (the province of Hephaestus) whether in precious or base metals was one of the major industries of Antioch – especially so in times of war against Persia, when it became more tightly controlled by the government; e.g. *Ep.* 197, where a retired decurion is saddled with the job of supervision of the smithies by the Count of the East in A.D. 360. There were also arms factories there.

All-night entertainment (the province of Aphrodite) provides the light relief of song and dance. Endymion is the proverbial sleepyhead; beloved of Selene, Zeus granted him his choice – either frail mortality or everlasting sleep in which he remained forever youthful, cf. Apollod. 1.56.

149 Banking was very important. Antioch's import and export trade, and the centralization of so many imperial offices there, dealing with financial no less than political administration, ensured that it was the centre for both direct and indirect tax collection of the Orient.

150 See Petit (1955), ch.3, ('Les Jeux et les Spectacles'). Libanius is ambivalent towards the Games. He certainly does not regard them as among the more laudable forms of entertainment, for they cater for the tastes of the vulgar, but he condescends to tolerate them if they have a 'good' object in view – i.e. one sanctioned by religious or social tradition. So even the chariot races can be regarded as acceptable, but he carefully notes that there are none of the circus factions and their riots, which were a feature of life in Constantinople. The popular mimes and pantomime shows remain for him beyond the pale.

151 Malalas, *Chron.* 248.5ff. says that Antioch successfully petitioned Claudius to be allowed to 'purchase' from the Eleans the right to hold Olympic Games. This was granted, but the full-scale games were reorganized by Commodus, as described by Malalas, *Chron.*

opened the festival, and postponed his own expedition so as to go in procession to the Olympia.[152] Another was seen acting as president of the games with a garland of bay leaves on his head.[153] Both of them honoured and were honoured by their actions. If the festival brings some renown to the Eleans, though in general they do not perform it as well as might be expected, what must we think of our own, since, discounting all other blessings, we are supreme in the glories of the Olympia?

(270) What city then brooks comparison with ours? She is more prosperous than the oldest states, while to the rest she is superior either in size or origin or fertility of the land. Moreover, if she be inferior to any in respect of her walls, she yet surpasses that town in her supply of water, the mild winters, the wit of her inhabitants, the pursuit of philosophy; and in the most noble feature of all, in Greek education and oratory, she rises superior to a city still greater.[154] (271) In general, you will find some towns small, others unlovely because of their bulk. Here the goddess mother of Love has poured her charm over our bulk; if you leave our city to go elsewhere, you will remember it, while if you come here from elsewhere, you will forget those towns you knew before. Thus we should pardon those who have neglected parents and homeland

---

283.1ff. The officials in charge bore titles harking back to those at Olympia, the *alytarch* or *agonothete*, representative of Zeus, the *grammatistes*, of Apollo, and the *amphithales*, of Hermes, patron deities of Antioch, and also various officials, the *Hellanodikae*. The venue was, for the preliminaries, the Plethrion (Plethron in *Or.* 10), in the city, the final day's events in the stadium at Daphne. There was, however, no hippodrome in Daphne – the horse-racing events taking place exclusively in the hippodrome on the island.

152 This emperor is Diocletian; so Malalas, *Chron.* 300f., who confuses the issue by adding that after the games, meaning presumably those of A.D. 304, he and Maximian abdicated. This cannot be: commentators are agreed that Diocletian's alytarchate was in A.D. 300.

153 By Malalas, *Chron.* 311f. the 'other emperor' is named as Maximianus (M. Aurelius Valerius Maximianus Augustus), who, he notes, was preparing for a campaign in Armenia. But Maximianus Augustus never operated in the East. However, Diocletian's junior colleague (C. Galerius Valerius Maximianus Caesar) was active against Persia and did engage in a campaign in Armenia in A.D. 296 – so named by Sextus Rufus, *Epit.* 25, Eutrop. 9.25. Libanius' interest was not the identification of the rulers – the event was familiar to his audience and himself, having happened within living memory. His object was to emphasize the prestige gained by them and the games by so officiating. Malalas, writing 150 years later and in an exclusively Christian context was, not without reason, confused.

154 The two cities are, respectively, Constantinople and Rome.

through the charms of our city. They have seen no other like it, and know that they never will.

(272) Now, gentlemen, to the city which bore me I have paid my debt, to the best of my ability, but not half so well as I could wish. Of the future, I may confidently assert that, though men may perhaps make better speeches than her citizen has done, none will in his speech, do full justice to the glories of our state.

ORATION 31:
TO THE ANTIOCHENES FOR THE TEACHERS

INTRODUCTION

This Oration is addressed to the city council of Antioch as a plea for special financial assistance to be afforded to the four assistant lecturers who, together with Libanius himself, form his school. Libanius is firmly settled as the sophist of the city in succession to Zenobius, but has found his educational system to be out of favour with the imperial administration, with the consequence that the social position and the standard of living of his assistants have slumped disastrously, thereby opening up the possibility that their scholastic efficiency might become impaired.

The four assistants, described here as 'rhetors', not 'sophists' (i.e. as assistant teachers of rhetoric, and not the head-teacher), as members of Libanius' teaching staff, receive an official salary (*syntaxis*), and are evidently official appointments, as befitted the staff of the 'sophist of the city', whose schoolroom was attached to the City Hall. A severe pruning of their emoluments, in line with that suffered by Libanius himself, seems to have occurred. Collectively, they have been allocated the single salary, without emoluments, which had been assigned to the sophist Zenobius, and experience frustration and delay at the hands of the officials, both provincial and municipal, in securing payment. Official obstruction provides a model for parental reluctance in the payment of fees, so that these teachers, for whom Libanius is head, colleague and mouthpiece, are examples of the new poor.

It is clear that there are other schools and other teachers in Antioch, probably privately run, but since his is the municipal school, Libanius addresses his plea to the municipality. In view of his reticence concerning the whole teaching profession in the town, it may be conjectured that his establishment has been singled out for unfavourable treatment by hostile officials and councillors at this time, and that these assistants are also being penalized in the disfavour shown to their superior.

From the Letters certain assistants of Libanius at this time may be identified with the four listed in this speech. Herodianus, a Phoenician, and owner of a small estate in that province, appears to be an appointment of Libanius' own (*Epp.* 454; 307; 640). Gaudentius, already a teacher settled in Antioch on Libanius' arrival, had connections with Arabia (*Epp.* 329; 543; *Or.* 38 *passim*). Uranius (*Epp.* 357; 454) also appears to have been long established in Antioch. There is no indication of his place of origin. A fourth teacher seems to be Cleobulus (for whom cf. Wolf (1952), 71ff.). His assistants at a later day include Calliopius (dead in A.D. 390; *Ep.* 1064), Eusebius (*Epp.* 904; 908) and Thalassius (*Or.* 42).

The source of revenue from which Libanius requests his councillors to provide support for his assistants is the municipally owned estates. It is evident that, despite the confiscations of municipal lands and temple property by Constantine and Constantius, so often deplored by Libanius (e.g. *Orr.* 30.3; 37f.), the city still retained possession of certain lands in its own right. These cannot be identified with any allocated by Julian, whether by his general act of restoration of municipal properties (*Epistulae, Leges, Fragmenta* 47) or by his specific grant of 3,000 *kleroi* to the city of Antioch (cf. Julian, *Misop.* 370d). Libanius explicitly states that these estates have come to the city by inheritance, thereby providing an instance of the application of the enactment of A.D. 319 (*Cod. Th.* 5.2.1), that the *curia* should inherit the estates of those decurions who die without issue. Another means by which the *curia* could acquire land was in certain cases of confiscation, *Cod. Th.* 12.1.6. Normally, the possession of such estates was allocated to the *principales*, the rents provided by their peasant tenants being reserved to defray the expenditure which this highest class of decurion was called upon to make for the performance of the liturgies and their other civic obligations. The residue of these lands, generally consisting of smaller farms, could be allocated by the *curia* at its discretion in return for meritorious service, such as that of Libanius' predecessor as municipal teacher, Zenobius. It is clear that Libanius himself receives no such special emolument; but he here requests for his four assistants, conjointly in their present financial stress, the allocation of the revenues of such an estate, so that the quality of education in Antioch should not be impaired and the reputation of the *curia* as the patron of the arts be diminished. These decurions whom he lists in §47 are all of the class of *principales*.

The date and circumstances of the oration have been much debated. Foerster (III, 119) originally dated it to about A.D. 355, just after Libanius' appointment as sophist in succession to Zenobius, and hesitantly identified the sophist in Caesarea (§42) with Acacius (for whom, cf. Eunapius *VS* 497; *BLZG* 39ff.). In this, he is followed by Petit ((1955),

261), Festugière (1959), 101, Martin ((1988), 264), and Fatouros and Krischer ((1992), 61–2). Later (XI, 632) Foerster accepted the suggestion of Sievers ((1868), 199), placing it near to A.D. 390, with Priscio (cf. *BLZG*) as the sophist of §42. Walden ((1912), 267) and Wolf (1952), 94ff. more convincingly place the speech in A.D. 360/1.

Sievers' suggestion of A.D. 390 is ruled out by considerations of prosopography. Of the decurions listed in §47, Eubulus, after the intrigues described in the *Autobiography* (*Or.* 1.156ff.), never appears in Libanius' narrative except in retrospect (cf. *Orr.* 35.10; 52.31); Arsenius dies in A.D. 364, and Obodianus, son of Argyrius the elder and father of Argyrius the younger, may be presumed dead by the time that Libanius writes the letters of commendation for the younger Argyrius in A.D. 390. The dating to A.D. 355 is equally inappropriate. The sophist of Caesarea, rival to Libanius in his early days in Antioch, is, as Eunapius certainly shows, none but Acacius. He, though distressingly active in Antioch as late as A.D. 358, had clearly removed by A.D. 361 (*Epp.* 274; 289; *Or.* 1.120). In any case, in A.D. 355 Libanius would never have appealed to an anonymous cousin but to his uncle and patron, Phasganius, who had been instrumental in securing his removal to Antioch. Phasganius, however, died in A.D. 359 (*Or.* 1.117; *Ep.* 96). The dating to A.D. 361 is quite certainly correct. In addition to internal hints for a later date (see notes 2, 14), at that time Eubulus, according to Libanius, gets his own way in everything (*Ep.* 289.3), this 'dunce Elpidius', praetorian prefect since A.D. 360, impugns Libanius' standing and cuts his salary (*Ep.* 740), and the death of Phasganius has removed Libanius' most influential support in the *curia* and equally Eubulus' need to have Acacius to hand as propagandist against a rival pressure group. Libanius, depressed by private griefs, racked by chronic ailments, and sadly out of favour, was able to hold his own professionally only with great difficulty. Naively he confesses the efficacy of presenting his case before a mass audience. It is the one way he can put pressure on Eubulus. From such frustrations he was to be rescued within a few months by the advent of Julian, whereby he and his profession were once more valued at their true worth.

The oration is notable as being the first overt admission in his extant works of Libanius' recognition that all was not well in the circumstances of his profession. It is a far cry from the heady excitement which marks his settlement in Antioch (*Or.* 1.86ff.), or from the idealized picture of Antioch as a centre of purest Hellenic culture, so characteristic of the *Antiochikos* five years before. Harsh reality has now obtruded itself. He may well be unchallenged now as leader of his profession, but the circumstances in which he practised it had changed, and the situation was full of uncertainty. From A.D. 358 onwards his personal worries had increased with the deaths of some of his closest friends, his mother and of his uncle Phasganius, who had been his chief supporter in the local *curia*. Grief and ill-health induced in him a deep depression verging on nervous breakdown (*Or.* 1.117f.). He was also a marked man: he had made no secret of his devotion to the old religion, and though he might support and befriend Christians as individuals, in his published work he had ignored this new-fangled religion entirely, and this at a time when religious attitudes in Antioch, a notable centre for Christianity, were becoming more polarized, and news of Julian's movements in the West became more ominous. He was, from A.D. 360, no longer in official favour, and he saw his official salary cut (*Epp.* 28; 740), and this feeling of increased vulnerability had its counterpart in his relations with the local community, and is evidently not unconnected with the remissness of the councillors towards his subordinates. Indeed, his loss of confidence may be measured, even after the bloodless change of régime late in A.D. 361, by his cautious advice to a young kinsman (*Ep.* 679) to wait upon events, and by his own reluctance to communicate with Julian, still unpopular in Antioch, until the famous meeting in summer A.D. 362.

The tone of the oration, as befits the occasion and the audience, is one of sweet reasonableness. There is none of the acerbity or descent to personalities which mark the later rebuttals of criticism of the reign of Theodosius. Any criticism of the educational policies of the current administration remains generalized and muted, and it is no accident that his initial appeal in §47 is to Eubulus, who was now and will remain the most influential member of the Council, and that this appeal is founded upon his appreciation of the importance of *philotimia* for a local grandee.

Available editions are those of Foerster and, with more difficulty, of Reiske. The speech is the basis for Wolf's study (1952), and for Petit (1956). Discussion appears in Schemmel (1907), repr. Fatouros and Krischer (1983), in Festugière (1959), and in Walden (1912), a most useful book for the study of Libanius. It should be noted, however, that references in Walden and Schemmel, of necessity, are to Reiske's edition for the Orations and to J.C. Wolf's Amsterdam edition of 1738 for the Letters, a concordance to which may be found at the end of Vol. XI of Foerster's Teubner edition.

TO THE ANTIOCHENES FOR THE TEACHERS[1]

(1) Men of Antioch, you would all agree that I am not one of those persons who have gone about stirring up trouble for the city, and that up to this day you have never incurred any expenditure, whether great or small, upon the teachers as a result of any words of mine.[2] My attitude in this has been dictated not by any thought that I might fail in my request, however much it might involve, but because I felt it incumbent upon me to show a restraint proportionate to the enthusiasm I knew you would show in your decree. But I can now maintain silence no longer, however much I might wish to do so, and therefore I have come to tell you of facts which it would be improper for me to leave untold, and on which it would be right for you to accept advice, for the consequence will be that, although you appear to be granting a concession, you will gain a name for extreme generosity with no loss to yourselves.

(2) Now, if I had quantities of money enough[3] both to satisfy my own needs and to provide for my assistants, I would have addressed to myself the considerations I now put before you, and I would gladly have relieved my colleagues in their distress for two reasons – for the performance of a most creditable action and so as not to publicize people's lack of means, the blame for which, no matter how circumspect I might be, it would be hard for the city to escape. **(3)** However, the extent of my property removes me equally from the need to take and from the power to give, so that the alternative, fellow citizens, is for the cure to proceed from you. In this way you may do away with the reproofs of your accusers too, if indeed there be any such, for by your present assistance you will demonstrate that you would long ago have acted so if you had known the facts and the reproach may perhaps be transferred from you, because of your unawareness, to those who failed to inform you.

(4) Perhaps I shall bring tears into the eyes of these people whose cause I have espoused, for when I explain their situation and reveal their grievous impoverishment, they are bound to be despondent under the gaze of the rest, but it is better for them to endure the tale of their

---

1 *Or.* 31, ed. Foerster (III, 119–46); *Or.* 29, ed. Reiske (II, 204–22).

2 This passage indicates that this speech was not composed almost immediately after his accession to the municipal chair in A.D. 355, as some modern commentators assume. Cf. Introduction.

3 On Libanius' financial standing, cf. Petit (1955), Appendix III, pp. 407–11. On the social status and salaries of teachers in general, see now Kaster (1988) esp. 115ff.

poverty in order to be relieved of the evils it produces, and you, even if any of my remarks makes unpleasant hearing, must bear it so that your future time may be spent amid acclamation.[4] **(5)** For, had I chosen the topic out of a desire to disparage them or to accuse you, I would be malicious: but since my approach is made to ensure that an end be put to their lack of means and to your neglect of a matter which least of all deserves to be neglected, I might reasonably be regarded as the benefactor both of those whom I advise and of those on whose behalf I have come forward. Thus you should pay particular attention to my argument, unless you want to segregate yourselves from them in attitude no less than in station.

(6) What then is my plea? And let none of you, if he has no children at all, or if the many fine sons he had are dead, or if he is the father of daughters only, or if he has sons who do not yet require a rhetor's care or who have ceased to need it – let none of you for these reasons I have mentioned consider himself relieved of concern about the present issue, under the impression that he will suffer no harm if the better course does not prevail, for you are now assembled to take counsel on behalf of the city, in whose administration you all share alike, even if your situations are different as regards parenthood.

(7) The sole matter you should consider is this – whether it is more advantageous for our great, fine city of Antioch[5] to maintain its teachers of eloquence in their present plight or to alter the situation. You must concern yourselves with everything that makes a city famous and prosperous, and especially with what has advanced our city to its present station. And this – unless I am talking utter nonsense – is rhetoric and the ability to overcome the irrational impulses of governors by dint of rational argument.[6] If peoples who win power from arms and victory in battle ignore any decline in the manufacture of arms, they would injure themselves as regards what they have won and they would encompass their own destruction: similarly, those who have made the greatest

---

4 Public assistance thus has two purposes for the donors, that they should incur no financial loss, and yet gain a good name for their generosity.

5 Antioch is distinguished from the several other cities of that name by the epithet 'the great', which by this time had become a stock term: cf. *Or.* 21.2; Amm. Marc. 22.9.14; Auson. *Ord. Urb. Nobil.* 4–5.

6 Libanius optimistically always pits the power of persuasion against his well-founded suspicion of the administration for its excesses, cf. *Or.* 1.2.

contribution to the art of eloquence would be held to blame if they did not maintain the profession of rhetoric.

(8) So I will postpone discussion of other aspects of the unfortunate situation in our schools, but it is right that some assistance should now be sought for those persons entitled 'rhetors', my four assistants who direct students towards knowledge of the classics:[7] and that account and consideration must be taken of them, I shall briefly demonstrate.

(9) If they were to be asked, 'Tell me, are you natives of Antioch, and were your parents from here? Or have you come here owing to force and fear, in alarm at the influence of your enemies or punishment you expected?' they would not admit any of these reasons. 'What then was it that induced you to choose someone else's city instead of your own?' Their reply would be, 'We shunned the disturbances that prevail in other professions, and we longed for the peace and quiet of teaching. If we stayed at home, we all thought that we would spend our lives in pettifogging matters, not much different from people who sit in idleness, and we were induced to come here by much great expectation, for there were many examples to guarantee it, since you welcomed any pauper who possessed nothing but intellectual ability.[8] These people you promptly displayed, some as owners of broad and fertile acres, others of silver and gold and all else that usually is a mark of wealth.[9] It was in expectation of this,' they will declare, 'that we made our way here, intending to deposit our eloquence in a congenial locality and ourselves to obtain a share of the prosperity which our predecessors enjoyed.'
(10) Does it then redound to our credit, citizens of Antioch, that in experience this reputation should be proved unfounded, and that you should be thought of, in their anticipation, as better than you have shown yourselves to be, and that, despite their joy at their first arrival, they live a life of unrelieved misery? They told the fine story to the relatives they left behind, that they were off to seek a fortune so that they could provide for them too, but now, so far from sending them any contributions, they would be only too glad to accept anything that they offer. **(11)** And please don't delude yourselves with hair-splitting termi-

---

7 For these assistants, cf. Wolf (1952), 60ff.

8 For the immigration of intellectuals into Antioch, cf. *Or.* 11.185f.

9 A good example of this is the elder Argyrius, whose entry into the *curia* of Antioch was secured by Libanius' own grandfather, and who became president of the Olympia in A.D. 332 (*Orr.* 10.9ff; 49.18; 63.4).

nology – that they are teachers not rhetors, or that they are not in occupation of a chair, or that they do not enjoy the other perquisites of their station – but learn the truth from one with intimate knowledge of their situation. Some of them have no little place of their own but live in rented rooms, like cobblers. Anyone who has bought a house, has not yet paid off the loan, so that the house purchaser is worse off than those who are not. As for slaves one has three, another two, another not even that many, and, because they are not in service with more for company, these misbehave and are insolent to their masters since some have not often had slaves and others have them under conditions degrading to themselves. Then one thanks his lucky stars that he has only one child, another regards his large family as a disaster, another must take good care not to fall in the same trap, and the one who avoids marriage altogether is held to be a sensible man. **(12)** In times past people of the same standing in the teaching profession as these used to go to the silversmith's[10] and give their orders for their wares, and they often used to converse with the craftsmen while they were working on the job, pointing out faulty work or suggesting something better, commending them for speed or urging them on if they were slow. But for these people here – and don't let anyone give me the lie – the greater part of their conversation is with bakers, and not bakers who have borrowed their corn[11] and from whom they are wanting payment for it, but those to whom they themselves are in debt for corn, whom they are always promising to pay and always asking for a further advance. They are in a quandary, forced to run away from and yet run after the same people, for they are in debt and so run away from them, but in need, and so run after them: ashamed at not paying their debts, they are yet urged on by an empty belly, and stare them straight in the eye. Then, when their debts have reached mammoth proportions and there is no sign of anything with which to pay them, they take their wife's ear-rings or bangles from their persons, cursing the profession of letters, and hand them over to the bakers, and so take their leave. And they have no thought for what they can give the wife to make up for it, but for what there is left at home that they can resort to next. **(13)** So when lesson-

10 Antioch was noted for metalworking in general, cf. *Or.* 11.267, Athenaeus, *Deipnosoph.* 5.193d; but silversmiths formed an important element in the smithies, *Or.* 28.20.

11 The baker takes the customer's corn and is paid only for the baking of it. Thus he owed the customer for the corn he had provided.

time is ended,[12] they do not, as they might do, hurry home from their labours straightaway to rest, but they dilly and dally, for if they go home they will have a clearer appreciation of their troubles. Then they sit down together, and tell the tale of their woes to one another, and when one recounts his own desperate plight, he hears tell of others worse off still.

(14) And I, in such a situation, hang my head in shame for two reasons, first as a citizen of yours, secondly as head of the school,[13] and though on both counts I might have lent them a helping hand, in times past[14] I have confined myself to deploring what was happening, but I have now at last decided that this is a sign of weakness and indecision, and that some means of remedying the trouble must finally be devised for them which, while not inconveniencing the council, may yet satisfy the rhetors. (15) Many suggestions have been made, the best and most practicable of which in my opinion is the one I will now put forward, first requesting you to listen to my arguments without disturbance. For at this time I would not dream of asking you to contribute money, or corn or wine from your own resources, for I am well aware of the expenditure you undertake every day on behalf of the community. Then how should you act so as to save these people for the city?

(16) You members of the council farm practically all the city estates,[15] and this, while ensuring that the income is forthcoming entire for the city, does not leave the workers without profit either. Some of these estates can be big ones, others quite small, and the first are allocated to the councillors according to the properly and justly established convention, and the rest to other individuals who hold a position outside that of civic service, and to them you have voluntarily assigned it, while retaining the power to deprive them of it. (17) Well, the larger estates must belong to you, for you spend your money and contribute to the community, and are subjected to great expenditure, partly of annual regularity, partly

12 I.e. at the end of formal lesson-time.

13 Sievers ((1868), 41) followed by Foerster (note *ad. loc.*) interpreted the phrase κορυφαῖος τοῦ χοροῦ as appertaining to Libanius' official position as a 'sophist of the city' (Jo. Chrys. *Hom. de S. Babyla* 18, Migne, *PG* 50.560). Wolf (1952), 63 more correctly views it as a simple metaphor, describing his position in his own school.

14 Another indication that this oration is to be dated well after his removal to Antioch in A.D. 354; cf. Introduction.

15 On the question of the city estates, cf. Liebeschuetz (1972), 149ff. For a different view, cf. Petit (1955), 96ff.

recently instituted. But from these smaller estates grant the rhetors a respite and raise their morale, and regard them as more deserving than those who perform no civic services, for if you were to say that they were such contributors, you would not perhaps be wide of the mark.[16] Alternatively, if this seems preferable, give up some part of what you hold, but in any case give them a share in the estates, for however slight the assistance they will have from it, half a loaf is better than no bread. **(18)** If they obtain such aid, fellow citizens, their gain will be nutritional, that of their students educational. The countryside, when blessed with rain, returns crops of high quality and quantity, and droughts are of their nature hostile to the crops: similarly with teachers, concern for their daily needs holds their tongue fast, while a good supply of the wherewithal calls forth their eloquence in streams. So won't you get more than you give, and by means of a pittance of corn cause the meadow of learning to bloom? **(19)** 'But look here!' I may be asked. 'Don't they get their salary every year?' In the first place, it is not every year: sometimes they get it, sometimes they don't; sometimes it comes in part, sometimes late. And I leave unsaid all the trouble we have to go to for it, before the governors, their staff, the city treasurer[17]and any swaggering jackanapes, before whom we must grovel with words and postures unbefitting gentlemen, fawning upon our inferiors. A decent, self-respecting man, such as a teacher should be, finds this harder to bear than absolute starvation. **(20)** But I let this be. But as for the amount of the salary, which some people will tell me is adequate, I would be ashamed to mention it. It is so huge, so worthy of our city's name! But just step out and tell the answer to this question first. Had Zenobius[18] a salary or not? Of course he had. Oh? And didn't he farm the best and finest wine-producing estate of the city, that lies on the right as you go towards Daphne, by the actual riverside?[19] Nobody set

16 Teaching is thus, metaphorically, a kind of liturgy.

17 Cf. Liebeschuetz (1972), 152. *Apodektai* are mentioned in *Orr.* 28.16; 57.51. Their primary duty was to receive and distribute taxes in kind. The *syntaxis* (salary) was evidently paid in money: these officials were thus responsible for the receipt of payment in kind and its transfer into cash by *adaeratio*.

18 Libanius' teacher and predecessor as municipal sophist in Antioch, cf. *Or.* 1.100ff; *BLZG* 315(i).

19 Daphne, the famous suburb of Antioch, site of the legendary metamorphosis of the nymph and of the temple of Apollo. Antioch is often defined, e.g. by Pliny, as 'by Daphne'. Cf. *Or.* 11.234ff., and *Or.* 11, n. 47.

up the protest, 'Good heavens, this chap is milking the city with two sources of income,' but they stuck to their opinion that anything they were likely to give was less than he deserved, however many times they gave it.

(21) 'Ah, yes! But he was more capable than these fellows.' My opinion exactly, but for all that his extra proficiency in rhetoric is no good reason for neglecting them, nor yet should the living be penalized for the excellence of the dead. If you believe that the present lot are no good for our students, then tell them to pack their bags, and start looking for someone better; but if you agree that they are good teachers, don't treat them as experts and yet disdain them as incompetent, or else those who experience this treatment will suppose that you are more concerned about the estates I am speaking of than you are about your sons. For if you won't allow them any part of the estates because of their alleged incompetence, and regard the proposition as scandalous, and yet entrust your children to them for their education, as though you are not taking much of a risk, then obviously you concede that your children now take second place to your property, since you take it upon yourselves to subject the rhetors to scrutiny over the matter of a proposed grant while neglecting to conduct any examination of them in considering your sons' education.[20]

(22) In short, on the question of their maintenance, the consideration must be whether the grant is proportionate to or falls below their needs; if it appears sufficient, pay no attention to any proposal for an increase, but if it be found far too little, accept the suggestion of some addition, for even Zenobius acquired the tenure of the place in order to be kept in the state befitting a gentleman. It certainly was not the reward for his teaching. If it were, you had precious little regard for his learning, which, I positively declare, deserved a crown, a public address, a bronze statue and all the money in the world. **(23)** But if in any case your payments to these must be reduced and it is something unconstitutional for them to receive maintenance on the same scale as he did, then so be it: they will suffer a reduction. Yet they are four and they have been allocated the salary he received as a single individual, so that, even if they be allowed possession of the estates, since the salary scale remains unaltered, their circumstances still cannot be equated with his.

(24) So, that I am making no novel proposal in my suggestion about

---

20 The assessment of teachers' competence is resumed in *Or.* 43.

the estates is proved by the man who held them and farmed them previous to these people, but I believe that, even if I devised some aid for the teachers that had never been granted before, it would still be no good reason for me not to come away without persuading you. It is not the novelty of the proposal but disgrace that men of good counsel must guard against. For it is absurd that, while obviously inferior aspects of current practice are jettisoned and the facts of the matter prevail over precedent, yet, in matters by no means clear cut, the fact that the argument is unconventional should be decisive.

(25) For all that, some of the tradesmen sitting at their workshop doors gossip about the teachers' high incomes. They tot up the numbers of students and, using their fingers, reckon up a vast amount of money. And now I suppose that I will be presented with the question of where it all is that is paid by the pupils. It is hard to give an answer to this question, not for lack of a proper explanation, for I have one, but because the truest will appear the least convincing. Those who made a fortune out of school-teaching in earlier times have given currency to the idea of the profession as a prime means of making money. Well, this ought to have been the situation all along, but it does not happen nowadays. Times have changed, and for reasons which those of you who have followed my career will realize, but which I will give for the benefit of those who remain in ignorance.

(26) All arts that are favoured by the emperors lead their students to influence[21] and simultaneously bring fortune to their teachers: the services are held to be great, and the rewards are great. However, when any profession, even though intrinsically good, is despised by the ruling emperor, it loses its prestige; and if the prestige vanishes, the rewards vanish along with it, or rather, if they be not entirely lost, from being great they become small. (27) So, do you believe that rhetoric is highly influential and of paramount importance at court, that capable orators obtain all the official posts and are summoned into conclave on issues of government and are persons of some standing? Or is it the reverse, that rhetoric and rhetors are rejected, rebuffed and insulted and, like the Megarians,[22] are regarded as mere ciphers and of no account? No one is so out of touch with recent developments or so maliciously delighted as to venture to assert that our profession has not plumbed the depths of

21 Cf. *Or.* 18.158ff.; *Or.* 62.8ff., 51, with reference to the preferment of *hypographeis*.
22 Proverbially ill-fated, cf. *Or.* 14.28; Theocr. 14.49; Suidas, *s.v.* ὑμεῖς, ὦ Μεγαρεῖς.

degradation. **(28)** For in cases where people, who have undergone the laborious training for the acquisition of learning, either go the whole hog and direct their sons to shorthand-writing,[23] regardless of intellectual ability, or else have regard for both alike, for rhetoric as good and shorthand-writing as prestigious, what greater proof yet do you need of the insults to which education is subjected? Come, tell me this – is it possible that, while the practice is regarded as useless, the teachers of it should have many to admire them? Who has ever seen priests held in honour while their temples are being demolished?[24] or a ship-builder making a fortune far inland?

(29) For this reason alone, gentlemen, these people have suffered the loss of their income. However, there is another one yet, of far greater impact, which has not allowed that income to be forthcoming as before. Many of the families of long established renown, who were characterized by learning and generosity, have been reduced to beggary by the present circumstance, and this, while not preventing them from receiving an education in rhetoric, has rendered them incapable of providing the financial reward for it. Certainly, no one is unaware of people of famous family who have sold their property, and of others who, descended from mere nobodies, have bought it.[25] **(30)** The teacher shares in the misfortunes that attend every such family. When they possessed wealth, he would enjoy it; and similarly, now that they are poor, he must teach them free.[26] So, if you claim to observe the merits of the teachers in the numbers of their pupils, you will find them great indeed, but if you take the number of pupils as indication of the teachers' incomes, your judgement is faulty. **(31)** What need is there for guessing about this, when you can proceed to an actual investigation and learn the simple facts of the matter as they stand? Anybody who thinks that students' fees are large may enter the classroom, sit himself down by the teacher's chair, call out each pupil and ask him what fee he gives. With precious few exceptions, I am sure, they would all run off to whatever hiding-place they could find, once they realized the purpose for which they were being called, for they haven't the heart to tell a lie and they are ashamed at their non-payment. And there are some whose payment is such that

---

23 Cf. *Orr.* 1.154; 2.44ff.; 62.10ff.; Wolf (1952), 53ff.
24 A sour comment, by way of aside, on Constantius' religious policy.
25 A topic resumed at length in *Or.* 62.
26 For Libanius' attitude to fees cf. *Orr.* 3.6–9; 4.17; 34.3; 36.9; 62.19.

they would want to make themselves scarce, more even than those who don't pay a penny. **(32)** Still, this is not a matter that demands exhaustive treatment. It is better to leave out of account some of the things that could be said than to hurt the feelings of people who would gladly pay but have no chance to do so. This much I would venture to assert, that, since the income from fees is small, I expect some provision to be made by the community, and upon an estimate of the rhetors' incomes, those who hazard conjectures from afar should not command more belief than I who am their intimate. **(33)** In fact, I would like to enquire whether anyone ever expected to see these teachers of shorthand making a fortune from their trade or doing better than cobblers or carpenters. No one, of course. Yet for all that, they are making a fortune, dining and wining and putting on airs. What need to wonder, then, that my teachers' status has declined, as theirs has been undeservedly raised?

(34) 'And why,' I will be asked, 'do you distress yourself and speak on their behalf, yet don't advocate the cause of the rest of the teachers?'[27] Simply because I am more fully aware of their condition, since they are my intimates and colleagues, my fellow-workers and fellow-lecturers, instructors of the same class, and though the circumstances of the rest may perhaps not be very satisfactory either, they have certainly not approached me with a request to make overtures to you on their behalf. It might perhaps create ill-feeling to refer to poverty before a larger assembly against the wishes of those who are so affected. **(35)** Moreover, my inability to cite precedents on their behalf induced in me a reluctance to refer to them. At any rate, the estate held by Zenobius supports the case of my assistants, but there was no instance to be seen of anyone else receiving assistance from such a tenure to support the rest. So I was afraid that those who have determined to oppose my suggestion should seize upon the weakness of their case to try to demolish my justified claim for my assistants. So if I find you generous towards my initial plea, I will be encouraged with regard to the next step, and every particular in education that requires amelioration – and there is much that is

27 Although he is sophist of the city, and thus the recognized mouthpiece for the profession, Libanius is pleading for help for the teachers in his own, officially recognized, school, not for the numerous private teachers in Antioch, one of whose number he had himself been immediately after his return in A.D. 354.

wrong! – will receive care and attention; for the enthusiasm of the audience will produce proposals in plenty.

(36) 'And what need is there,' comes the objection, 'for a set speech, and a meeting of the council, and the waste of a day when you could just approach the councillors individually, have a few brief words with them and achieve the same result?' That is the sort of thing a fellow will say who directs his witticisms at all and sundry, and thinks he is amusing his companions, whereas in fact he causes more displeasure than any amusement he thinks to give. (37) First, then, the fellow who demands that advice should not be tendered in this way should realize that he is the Muses' foe, for if set speeches are like a painful wound to him and if he thinks that the days spent on declamations are a waste for the community,[28] then he is obviously far removed from the rituals that belong to the Muses. Secondly, he does not recognize that this method of advice is at this time a twin adornment for the city, when the person capable of delivering it is a citizen of yours and you are seen to delight in the orations he has composed.[29] (38) Besides this, he should realize that any subject, however well justified, would not have the same effect if it were carelessly delivered as it would if it were narrated with meticulous care; while an indiscriminate treatment is no different from silence, as far as persuasiveness is concerned, a speaker who deals with his subject carefully and as it deserves, makes the fullest contribution. (39) Moreover, I anticipated that the very numbers of those who will be assembled and the fact that a crowd of all manner of persons will attend the recital would help to encourage you no less than the actual speaker, for generosity, if unobserved, deters prospective donors, and if there is none to know of it, one prefers not to give what one would have spent had there been many witnesses of it.[30] When you reflect that, if you reject any advice you listen to before a packed audience, you will have thousands to complain about you, whereas, if you give way and accept it, you will have as many to commend it, fearful of the first and desirous of the other, you decide upon the course which will show you in the better light. (40) How many are they now, do you think, from Phoenicia, Palestine, Egypt, Cyprus,

28 Cf. *Or.* 34.15, 26.

29 Cf. the introductory apology to *Or.* 11. For an example of the enthusiastic reception of his declamations in Antioch, cf. *Or.* 1.89.

30 *Philotimia* is thus a method of advancing personal prestige. Any altruistic motive, on this argument, is secondary.

Arabia, Cilicia, Cappadocia, wherever you can mention, who are listening and attending to what I have to say and what your attitude to it will be? Then allow them to take home with them a good report of you and to say that the city of Antioch's attitude and decision is worthy of the Muse, its tutelary deity,[31] that it regards all expenditure on education as a burden lightly borne, and that it is not niggardly with land, whether waste or cultivated, or with anything else at all whereby it thinks it may maintain here the practice of education. **(41)** But, by Helios, our noble who breeds horses,[32] collects athletes from every nook and corner of the earth, buys up herds of beasts and tracks out men to fight against them – and all these items are of the sort that shatter the fortunes of those who perform such services – is he going to be miserly, niggardly and parsimonious on a matter where the future of education is at stake and the means of rescuing it is an acre or two of land? Surely not! Let such activities proceed as now, and let this be added to them. **(42)** I trust never to see teachers abandoning us for another city, not in flight from earthquake or any other disastrous act of god, but from lack of sustenance and the disappearance of that consideration you once held for education. It is intolerable and unpardonable for the people of Antioch to have less regard for learning than those of Caesarea, who by lavish promises induced one of your teachers to pick a lesser city in preference to the greater; and now he possesses what they promised.[33] **(43)** Shall we not even imitate them in these practices where we ought to be their teachers? No, in the name of Apollo leader of the Muses who observes all from close at hand. We should not think of him as losing the person of the nymph he was pursuing and so falling in love with the place[34] –

31 Calliope. Cf. *Or.* 1.102, 'I addressed Calliope thus: "Most glorious of the Muses, our city's guide . . ." .'

32 The invocation to Helios, the principal horse-breeder among the gods, naturally introduces this description of the Antiochene *principalis*, for whom the chariot races, athletic contests and beast fights were the most important and expensive liturgies to be undertaken. The chariot races were a major part of all holiday spectacles, especially those of the New Year, cf. *Or.* 1.230, *Ep.* 811, *Ekphrasis Kalandon* 8 (Martin (1988), 201). The beast shows seem to be peculiar to the Syriarchate, a position held recently by Libanius' cousin, and demanded great effort and expense, cf. *Epp.* 586–8, 598–9. The athletic contests were part of the Olympic games in Antioch, cf. *Or.* 10 *passim*, *Epp.* 1179–83.

33 Acacius (*PLRE* 6(6), *BLZG* 39(ii)), Libanius' rival in Antioch in A.D. 353–5, now retired to his own city, Caesarea, cf. Petit (1979), note on *Or.* 1.90 (I, 228f.), Wolf (1952), 93f.

34 For Daphne, cf. §20 above. According to legend, Apollo's pursuit of Daphne occurred here (*Or.* 11.94), and the actual laurel into which she was transformed was shown there

children's stories, this[35] – but, more likely, of the original inhabitants as admirers of music, and so preferred to all others by the god. **(44)** Let us emulate our ancestors then, gentlemen, and imitate them, and keep Apollo among us by our zeal for education, and let us regard these people, on whose behalf I have come before you, as his servants and friends no less precious to him than swans,[36] for you know the post they hold and the present title they enjoy, though they could have been, if they wished, leaders of the whole school, such is their ability.

(45) And if we disregard their professional capacities, every other qualification they possess would secure for them a good will that is thoroughly well deserved. One of them has spent more than thirty years in continual labour without protest, and has lived the rest of his life with no hard words from him or about him. Another, though intimately connected with the noblest families, has been the soul of discretion, never breathing a word of what went on among them and never damaging an old friendship by seeking a fresh one. The third is a man of spirit, never guilty of any wrong, maintaining his post to perfection, and hazarding his own security for those who entrust him with their confidence. And as for the youngest, nothing more need be said than that, before even he left the company of boys, he was the leader of boys and gave no opening to the tongue of slander.[37]

(46) So, since they are such gifted speakers and of such good character, won't you take care of them and grant them, at my wish, what no one at all would have objected to me personally receiving, if I so wished? Look here! If when I came here, especially when I saw that my removal was not without hazard, I had told you all that I had ever got in other places, and said, 'Instead of this, then, grant me some of the city's estates, as is usual', I hardly think that there would have been anyone so

---

(Eustathius, *Comm. in Dionys. Perieg.* 916 = Müller, *Geogr. Gr. Min.* 4.378). For a mosaic from Daphne reproducing the story, cf. Levi (1947), I, 211ff. The Temple of Apollo (to be destroyed by fire in October A.D. 362) was located there, *Or.* 11. 236, *Or.* 60. Apollo, as Musagetes, is patron of learning, including rhetoric.

35 For Libanius' scepticism about such legends, cf. *Or.* 11.162, 241; *Or.* 64.16.

36 The swan (the *canorus ales* of Horace, *Od.* 2.20.15, from the story of its dying song, a story which can refer to the whooper swan only) is sacred to Apollo not only because of its song but also because of its powers of divination (e.g. Aristoph. *Birds* 869ff., Cic. *Tusc.* 1.30.73). Libanius here endows his assistants with these same qualities of bardic minstrelsy.

37 For these assistants, Uranius, Gaudentius, Herodianus, Cleobulus by name, see Introduction and Wolf (1952), 63ff.

insensitive, so arrogant and cantankerous as to get up and make an exhibition of himself, and try to stop it. So think of me today as the recipient, and even if you make the grant to them, say that you have made it to me, and I personally will acknowledge to everyone that I have received this mark of esteem. This decision will heighten your prestige and win you universal fame, and even if displeasure is aroused by my present remarks, pleasure will be the consequence of your action.

(47) Eubulus,[38] the occasion summons you to the fore. Son and sire of Argyrius, emulate the elder of these. As for my cousin, he should regard the proposal as his own. Let the family tradition of philosophy inspire Hilarius, and the reason for his title inspire Letoius. You, Arsenius, even now nurtured in the halls of the Muses, would support me even without being called to do so. The future president of the Olympia must concern himself so that he may find orators for the occasion.[39] What need is there to address you severally by name? All you members of the council have as a compelling reason to assist education your own educational gifts.

(48) I know how to sing the praises of those who reach a right decision and how to write appropriately about those who oppose it, so choose the means whereby you may both confer advantage upon the city and delight the gods of learning.[40]

---

38 A list of *principales* of Antioch follows. Note that Phasganius does not appear among them. Eubulus is recognized as their head. For Eubulus, cf. Petit (1979), note on *Or.* 1.90, cited above in note 33. The notice in *PLRE* 287(2) is wrong. All references to him as a sophist and to his domestic life belong to Acacius (6). Eubulus was the chief of the clique among the *principales*, employing Acacius as their mouthpiece, who opposed Phasganius and his mouthpiece, Libanius. Obodianus, son of Argyrius the elder and father of Argyrius the younger, Libanius' pupil, is urged to imitate the elder of these, who is now advanced in age. This passage has been misinterpreted to make Eubulus the elder brother of Obodianus (as by Seeck), cf. *BLZG* 222. Hilarius (*BLZG* 178(vii)), *PLRE* 435(8)), son of a philosopher and pupil of Libanius, was envoy to Theodosius after the riots of A.D. 387. Arsenius, the younger, pupil of Libanius, *Epp.* 540, 1260, died A.D. 364 (*PLRE* 111(3)). Letoius (*BZLG* 197(i)) is described as ὁ καλός, *Ep.* 146. The name of Libanius' cousin is not known.

39 For rhetorical competitions as part of the Olympia, *Ep.* 1183.

40 Apollo, Hermes and the Muses.

PART II

IN THE REIGN OF THEODOSIUS

ORATIONS 62, 43, 36, 34, 42, 58, 3

ORATION 62: AGAINST THE CRITICS OF HIS EDUCATIONAL SYSTEM

INTRODUCTION

This oration is undertaken to rebut criticisms currently levelled against Libanius concerning the ineffectiveness of his educational programme. He is accused of an inability to produce from his ex-pupils any examples of a successful career in the higher professions or in the ranks of curial or imperial administration. This is a matter on which he had touched in the concluding section of the original *Autobiography* of A.D. 374 but, whereas there it had appeared as a mere generalization, here the criticisms are specific and personal, made by a particular unnamed individual, and in consequence the tone of his rebuttal is more personal and bellicose. It was evidently delivered before a real, not a fictitious, audience – probably before one of the gatherings of local literati which provided the audience for his more personal and professional apologias, such as *Oration* 2 or the original *Autobiography*, and under none of the controlled secrecy which must have characterized his more violent vituperations such as the *Pro Thalassio*. The views he expressed were intended to reach a wider audience, albeit not on the scale envisaged for his formal display orations.

The dating and circumstances of the oration have not been fixed with any certainty. It was composed after the suppression of the revolt of Procopius in A.D. 366, when Andronicus was executed, but at what interval of time remains unclear. Sievers' dating of it to that year ((1868), 149, note 51), a view accepted by both Seeck ((1897–1921), 106) and Festugière ((1959), 94) remains highly improbable, even granted that other persons mentioned here are best attested in the period A.D. 355–65 (e.g. Celsus §61, Dulcitius §11, Themistius §55), and that Libanius had not yet lost touch with his curial friends in Ancyra, as he was later to confess that he had done (compare §38 with *Ep.* 921 of A.D. 390). Indeed, the speech does not belong to the last years of his life: besides an impressive list of *argumenta ex silentio* (e.g. the lack of reference to his honorary status, held from late A.D. 383, to his services in both famine and riot in the 380s, to the institution of the Latin rhetor in A.D. 388), his assistant Calliopius, here mentioned (§35f.), is dead in A.D. 392.

Internal evidence suggests a date c. A.D. 382 (as stated by Petit (1979), 264 (note on *Or.* 1.214)). His professed reluctance to engage in another bout of self-praise in answer to criticisms made against him (§3) seems to hark back to *Oration* 2, delivered in such circumstances in A.D. 381. The account of the fate of Andronicus has the same nostalgic tone as that in *Or.* 1.171, written c. A.D. 382 (cf. Petit (1979), 12), and Libanius' claim to have produced successful scholars in these lean years (*Or.* 1.213) is here expanded in the account of the geographical distribution of his pupils (§27ff.). The death of Eusebius (*Or.* 1.188) may perhaps occasion the comment of §29, although admittedly such morbidity is never far from Libanius' writings. Nor are the conditions as here described inconsistent with his other comments (e.g. those of *Orr.* 24 and 2) which belong to the first years of Theodosius. Indeed, after the decade or more of enforced silence under the repressive régime of Valens, a more combative tone marks these speeches. He is no longer content to maintain a purely passive role, and at the advent of a new reign he once more presents himself as a protagonist of the old values of educational, religious and social purity, such as had been embodied in Julian's shortlived programme of reform, and which remained his ideal. Against the encroachment of the new meritocracy with its crude notions of success he is once more prepared to take issue, and personally to defend himself against criticisms of his conduct in his profession and in society, in a very different way from his more abstract examination of his Fortune in A.D. 374. This change of front bore fruit. He was able to overcome opposition and his prestige was once more increased during the early years of Theodosius; public opinion was not yet so hostile towards him as it was to become after A.D. 388. He enjoyed the ear of the great, personal advancement, and was able to override criticisms. Disillusion had not yet set in.

The criticisms which he here attempts to evade are only partially refuted. His opponent admits that Libanius is a good enough orator, but asserts that he is a poor teacher: his pupils know nothing and he can show no successes among his ex-students. In reply to this, he half concedes the case; he points out (§6ff.) that the times are out of joint: first, the régime of Constantius had seen the abandonment of the literary education along with that of the old religion: illiterate secretaries ruled the roost. Then (§19ff.), he had never pressed for his fees, and anything cheaply got is cheaply held. Third (§21ff.), the growing competition of law has reduced the number of his students, and lastly, there are the growing problems of student indiscipline and parental indifference (24ff.). These general points are here merely asserted, without argumentation. They are to be hobby-horses which he will ride in later, more choleric orations.

More positive refutation follows (§27–62). In the types of career where parents expect their sons to shine and to become successful in the eyes of the world – those of curial administration, advocacy, provincial government in particular – he proves the accusation false simply by citing specific examples of success in each category, claiming to have ex-students of proven ability in almost every province of the East. He seems to fail to notice that, by doing so, he has gone far to undermine the credibility of his initial argument of the encouragement of illiteracy by the administration. To this point he reverts (§63ff.) in his conclusion, a vituperative depiction of his chief critic as an ignorant upstart, one who had undeservedly attained the rank of *honoratus* and used the wealth so obtained to become an enemy of the social order, a usurer who, far from supporting, delights in oppressing respectable curial families, but whose cardinal crime was not to have composed but to have purchased the speeches which had gained him advancement.

Clearly, such flawed arguments, based as they are on his personal prejudices, failed to allay criticism, and he encountered increasing opposition hereafter, as his attitude hardened and the discontent became more manifest among pupils, parents, and fellow teachers, as revealed in *Orations* 36, 34, 3 and 58. Moreover, he is ready to cross swords with yet another class of the disaffected, the *honorati*. It is notable that here for the first time he falls foul of one of their number, who are later to be subjected to the same criticisms (e.g. *Or.* 36.5).

Available editions are those of Foerster, and, with more difficulty, of Reiske. Walden (1912) is again a most useful aid, and various passages are discussed by Petit (1955) (see *Index locorum*) and (1957), as well as in the commentary on *Oration* 2 in Martin (1988).

On the purpose of rhetorical training, see now Brown (1992) 35–70; Kaster (1988).

AGAINST THE CRITICS OF HIS EDUCATIONAL SYSTEM[1]

(1) For a long time certain worthless dunces, who yet arrogate much for themselves, have employed many slanders against me and my students, against them alleging that they have learned nothing, against me, that I don't know how to teach. (2) While ever they did so in secret and obscurity, afraid that I would find out, I kept silent, thinking that I had punishment enough from them in that they were afraid when they misused me so. But since they have become so insolent as a result of their ill-gotten wealth that now they even abuse me openly in the presence of many people in the City-Hall Square, I shall attempt to stand up for myself and to show both them personally and those whom they have deceived, whether or not I have any skill in eloquence. (3) And though I resent these people for their ignorance of their own deficiencies and their readiness to criticize the abilities of the rest, the chief cause for resentment, I declare, is that once again[2] they set me upon eulogizing myself and impose upon me the necessity of doing something it is my habit to avoid doing, that is, of giving some account of the advantages I have conferred on others. (4) If it were possible for me to dispose of the accusations while avoiding such an account, it would be wrong for me to proceed in the course of self-praise; but since in the favourable recital about myself their assertions are shown to be utterly false, you will, of course, pardon the manner of my refutation, if I cannot do otherwise. Indeed it would be absurd for the speaker to be more afraid of the truth of the commendations than of the slanders which people have broadcast about me for some time now.

(5) What is it that they say both when they sit around and when they stroll about? That I am good at composing orations, better than most people, but nowhere near so good a teacher. Then they go straight on and ask, 'Why! What pupil of his has become a leading light in the courts? Or in the position of city councillor? Or in the teachers' chair? Or in that of the governors?' And before their listeners can reply, they give themselves the treat of replying, 'None.' (6) That there are some of my late pupils who have gained fame as a result of their rhetorical abilities, I will demonstrate very shortly. But let us now assume the truth of their statement that there are none. Well? Must the incapacity of others immediately involve

---

1 *Or.* 62 Foerster (IV, 342–83); *Or.* 65 Reiske (III, 434–61).
2 'Once again' seems to refer to a comparatively recent composition of *Or.* 2 (To those who called him tiresome), and may thus be taken as indication of dating to c. A.D. 382.

disparagement of me? If I personally am ignorant of anything that befits the would-be teacher, or if, out of envy, I keep my art concealed and to myself, or if my teaching is affected by incompetence and if I provide my students with insufficient training, or if, when I provide it in proper measure, they refuse to accept it and I have not reproved the lazy-bones, then let people abuse me, accuse me, blame me, or rather prosecute me, contest the case, and have me punished, since I have deceived many cities and in particular have injured them by means of my students. If, however, there is some eloquence in me, and I impart all that I know, and if I employ all the means that are now employed, and against the idlers I utilize the cane, or words more painful than the strap, how much more just and generous it would be to seek the cause of the matter somewhere else, rather than to level unfounded criticisms against one who is inno-cent? But since you refuse to see the reason for all this, although it lies in plain view, now pay attention while I demonstrate it.

(7) In any matter, circumstances alter cases. If they are favourable, everything goes quickly and well: but should they exert any opposing influence, then in any venture, it is labour in vain. For what good do sailors get from contrary winds, or the tillers of the soil from bad weather? Circumstances assist generals, doctors and envoys, – in a word, every trade and profession. It was a circumstance without prece-dent, says Thucydides,[3] that set the Lacedaemonians on the invasion of Attica; and I have entered upon a highly unfavourable set of circum-stances, under the impulsion of a necessity which I need not mention in the circumstances.

(8) 'What, then, are these unfavourable circumstances that you speak of?' I shall be asked. Constantius and his régime. He inherited this spark of evil from his father, and fanned it into a mighty flame.[4] For though Constantine had stripped the gods of their wealth,[5] Constantius demol-ished the temples too, erased every sacred law, and entrusted himself to those we know well enough,[6] extending his disparagement from religion to oratory. And with good reason, for religion and oratory are, I am sure, interconnected and inter-related.[7] (9) As for the philosophers and

---

3 Thuc. 3.13.
4 For Constantine's responsibility for starting the Persian War, cf. *Or.* 49.2.
5 For his religious policy and the confiscation of temple property, cf. *Or.* 30.6.
6 For the religious policy of Constantius, ibid.; cf. *Cod. Th.* 16.10.2ff.
7 This passage is discussed by Petit (1955), 191ff., Festugière (1959), 229ff.

the sophists, and all those devoted to the rites of Hermes and the Muses, he never invited one of them to the palace, never set eyes on them, or commended them or had anything to say to them, and never listened to their addresses. Instead he welcomed, kept around him, and made counsellors and teachers of a collection of hooligans, confounded eunuchs.[8] He abdicated the functions of emperor to them, leaving himself the title; he had the trappings, they the power. (10) And they harassed the rhetorical education by every means, humbling those who partook of it, and telling one another to see that no educated man should slip in unnoticed and become his friend; they began to introduce the pale-faces, those enemies of the gods, denizens of grave-yards,[9] whose proud boast it is to belittle Helios and Zeus and his fellow-rulers; and they hoisted to senatorial rank secretaries, who weren't one bit better than their own slaves either in intellect or manual dexterity,[10] but in some cases were even worse, in one particular or even in both. (11) And the transformation was very prompt. The cook's son, or the laundry-man's,[11] the street-arab, the creature who thought he was in clover if he wasn't actually starving, was all of a sudden a fine man on a fine horse, nose in the air, with a mass of attendants, a great household, wide estates, toadies, parties, gold. And if, by any chance, an orator obtained any office by their gift, he got it as the reward for toadying; and if he had any self-respect, it would have been better for him to be yet further humbled rather than to be elevated by their agency. But the contemptible, tipsy eunuchs became so insolent and unconscionable that they promoted the secretaries to the prefects' chairs and settled them on it. And our glorious Constantius rejoiced, as if he had gloriously discovered the sole means of preserving his realm.

(12) So when the students in the schoolrooms see this, don't you think they have often said to themselves, 'What profit is there for me from these countless labours, whereby I must go through many poets, many orators and all kinds of literature, if the result of my exhausting efforts is that I hang around in dishonour, and somebody else becomes successful?'[12]

8 In particular, Eusebius, chamberlain of Constantius throughout his reign, *PLRE* 302(11).

9 For Christian martyr cults (that of St Babylas being proper to Antioch), cf. Julian, *Misop.* 357c, 361a. For monkish pallor, *Or.* 30.8.

10 Shorthand writers, for whom *Orr.* 2.46; 18.158; 31.28; 42.25. Festugière (1959), 410ff.

11 Dulcitius, cf. *BLZG* 125(iii), *PLRE* 274(5). For him and others, cf. *Or.* 42.23f.

12 For the same complaint, e.g. *Or.* 1.154, 213f., 234; *Or.* 43.3f.

(13) And why speak of the students? From such reflections as these their fathers, men who have laboured in rhetoric, began to bring up their sons in a combination of rhetoric and its alternative, respecting the glory of eloquence but seeing the power that lies in the other system. They personally were penalized in comparison with the other system, because of their rhetorical training, and they caused despondency among the rest, for it was thought that eloquence was not an adequate training for success. (14) You may see more clearly the distemper of the times, if you observe the number of official agents who come from Athens. For after their scholars' gowns, their attendance at the Lyceum, their declamations and their introductions to them, and, indeed, after their study of Aristotle come the breeches and belt of those who serve the emperor's despatches which must be borne from the palace over the length and breadth of the world.[13]

(15) This affliction, then, that has affected even Athens, has affected my pupils, but more so, and it has harmed them the more, because it is not the same thing, nor anything like it, to be a teacher in Egypt, Palestine and Athens as it is where I am. For where is it the same to hear of the success of the secretaries and to see them in person? To listen to the accounts of prestigious entrances and exits, whether at dawn or in the afternoon, and themselves to be able to give such accounts?[14] Thus in the first instance absentees are involved and less harm done; in the latter case, in three cities alike, in Constantinople, Nicomedia and Antioch,[15] what has been particularly hostile to me and blunted the inspiration of my students is that there are no rewards for their efforts to induce them to sustain the tedium, and to quote Plato,[16] though we would know what he meant even without him saying it, 'Whatever is respected at the time becomes the fashion; what is not is ignored.' (16) Well, if the profession of rhetoric was one of those respected by Constantius, the teachers have made ill use of an excellent opportunity. But if none of the intellectuals was a friend of his, nor yet the speakers, but if shorthand writers who quickly took down the words of someone else have obtained the

13 The breeches and belt are, like the *zone* (*Or.* 2.57), part of the uniform of the *stratiotes* (i.e. civil servant, *officialis* or *agens in rebus*, cf. *RE* XVII, 2047 *s.v. Officium*).

14 A possible reference to Valens' stay in Antioch in the 370s, as viewed by an eyewitness. However, the problem of influence improperly obtained by such audiences as *eisodoi* was a matter of criticism for the rest of Libanius' life, cf. *Orr.* 51 and 52.

15 For his early career as a teacher in these cities with their imperial connections, cf. *Or.* 1.1–100.

16 Plato, *Resp.* 8.551a; cf. *Or.* 18.156.

greatest success, what surprise is it that a certain numbness with regard to studies has affected our students?

(17) This then was the trouble and this the cloud that was dispersed by the emperor Julian, who took in his hands both weapons and books, and loaded his trains of camels with these as their burdens, not with wine, unguents and soft bedding, such as followed his predecessor in large quantities.[17] And work was for the students more pleasant than idleness, as for the Achaeans war was more pleasant than sailing away, once they had received the inspiration from Athena.[18] **(18)** But this amendment was made brief by the unhallowed steel in Persia, which murdered Julian and caused our students to take another toss. Had not an evil spirit a grudge against the cities, the fortunes of mankind would have improved in every way, and would have reached their zenith, as far as oratory was concerned.[19]

(19) So when the one throughout his long reign had waged war against oratory, and the other, who revered rhetoric, no sooner made his appearance than he vanished, a certain reluctance affected my students. If this has reached such proportions, I too accept responsibility for some of the harm, for the very attitude that gave me a name for kindliness induced idleness in my pupils. This is due to the fact that each pupil who attends me pays me his fee or not as he chooses, for non-payment appeared a nice thing even to those who could pay. The inclinations of the rich were in line with the inability of the poor, or – to be more precise – of the rich, some paid, others did not. **(20)** The non-contributors became even more numerous, and were idler for this very reason, – the opportunity to get something free does not compel eager acceptance: if you don't pay for a thing, you aren't worried if you don't get it – and, as I say, when the majority were in evil case, the payment of the fee vanished with them. And it was more the case that the impoverished were drawn to idleness by the others than that these others were improved by them, for inactivity is easier, I believe, and more pleasant than toil, and the consequence was that even for them the profit to be obtained by paying was minimal.[20]

17 Cf. *Or.* 18.216, 232.

18 Homer, *Il.* 2.453.

19 Libanius insists that Julian did not die in battle but was assassinated, cf. *Or.* 24 (on the *murder* of Julian), an oration slightly earlier than this. For the post-Julianic reaction, cf. *Orr.* 17.23ff.; 18.283ff.

20 For Libanius' attitude to fees, cf. *Orr.* 31.30; 3.9f.; 43.7. Themistius also made a point of not exacting fees (Them. *Or.* 23.289a).

(21) There was yet a third factor that has ruined the profession. Grant that this impediment is honourable; commend it, if you like, but it still has been the greatest hindrance to the prestige of the literary education. Always before this, you could see youngsters from the factories whose concern was for their daily bread, going off to Phoenicia to gain a knowledge of law, while those of well-to-do houses, with illustrious family, property, and fathers who had performed civic services, stayed at school here. And it was thought that to learn law was a mark of lower status, while not to need it indicated a higher standing, but now there is a mass stampede towards it, and lads who know how to speak and are able to move an audience race to Berytus with the idea of getting some advantage.[21] (22) But what they haven't noticed is that, instead of getting some advantage, they are getting an exchange. For it isn't the case that with the advent of the alternative, the original is preserved for those who had it: the alternative arrives, perhaps, but inevitably the original departs. The intellect is incapable of acquiring something fresh and, simultaneously, of retaining the other; whoever concentrates on the one, relinquishes the other, so that it would have been better if they spent all their time in the study of law rather than wasting it for the most part in vain. (23) So as to whether they behave so with the idea that their pursuit of law is the pursuit of a more useful acquisition, I believe that it is no matter for inquiry, for at present there is no question of the law being granted a formal confrontation with rhetoric, but it is enough for me to demonstrate that the eloquence instilled by earlier studies must inevitably be ruined by the effects of the later, and these must prevail, while the former vanishes, in some cases completely, in others, to no inconsiderable degree.

(24) Besides the considerations I have mentioned, there is now yet another, which I will leave on one side, in case anyone should think I am envious. Instead, I will proceed to the crux of this disastrous business. You see, parents no longer threaten their children or bar them from the table or the baths if they are negligent, nor yet do they punish them so,

21 The law school of Berytus in Phoenicia was second only to that of Rome, cf. *Orr.* 48.22ff.; 49.27f. On the competition between rhetoric and law, cf. Festugière (1959), 411f., Liebeschuetz (1972), 243ff. Soon after his return to Antioch Libanius had made strong efforts to induce a teacher of law to settle there, with a view to co-operation (e.g. *Epp.* 433, 478 of A.D. 355/6). His attitude to the subject hardened in the next generation, his basic criticism being the opportunities for curial evasion offered by a period of study abroad, even though he himself was a good example of this.

or threaten that they will expel them, disinherit them, leave their inheritance to someone else. They can't approve but they dare not blame. They have changed position with them, so that the sons wear angry looks and the parents cower before them. **(25)** Students get this licence, and sleep, snore, drink, and get drunk, and hold high revelry, and make it plain to the teachers that, unless they put up with any and everything, they will go off to somebody else, and their fathers won't stop them. And the wretched parents, as Andromache did, connive at their sons' desires.[22] Some have already commended their sons when they were bent upon illicit intercourse,[23] and admired them when they fill the school room with fighting and disorder,[24] and declare that that conduct, which ought to make them choke with anger, will make him cock of the roost when he becomes a man.

(26) My critics ought to observe this and take it into consideration, and to find in it the cause for my students not attaining perfection in oratory; they certainly should not pass over the real causes, and invent fictitious ones, and, leaving the truth aside, parade a string of falsehoods, making a double departure from what is right both in what they say and what they don't say.

(27) Such considerations, then, and others besides, have robbed me of the growth of eloquence that ought to have increased in my students; but still after all these reverses, as Demosthenes somewhere remarks,[25] I will not bluster or exaggerate at all, and say that I have filled the three continents and all the islands as far as the Pillars of Heracles with orators. I will confine my remarks to what I can prove, that I have children – for it is right so to call those who have enjoyed attendance with me[26] – some in Thrace and the capital, others in Bithynia, or Hellespontus, Caria, and Ionia, and you could find some in Paphlagonia, if you cared to, and in Cappadocia – not many there, for not many have come to me from there, but still you would find some. **(28)** In the cities of Galatia, however, you would see many, and no less a number in Armenia. Again, the Cilicians outnumber them, and these too are far

22 Eurip. *Andromache* 223.
23 Pederasty, cf. Festugière (1959), 195ff.
24 Cf. *Or.* 3.6.
25 Demosth. *de Cor.* 3.
26 The teacher standing *in loco parentis* to his students is a commonplace of the classical education, and Libanius believes in it most sincerely, cf. Festugière (1959), 95n. Cf. n. 57, below.

outnumbered by the Syrians. And if you go to the Euphrates, and cross the river and go to the cities beyond, you will come across some of my pupils, and perhaps not bad ones, either. Both Phoenicia and Palestine are under some obligation to me, together with Arabia, Isauria, Pisidia and Phrygia.[27] **(29)** In saying this, I do not imply that everyone from every region has taken home from me a pre-eminence in eloquence, but that each area has gained some orators. And I will not mention the dead, for if I were to assert that these have been my greatest glory, I don't think that I shall hurt the feelings of the living.[28] Some of them are my fellow-citizens: two, from Galatia, were the namesakes of mine. Just recently there was a Cappadocian, and a Cilician not long ago, and a Phoenician besides. If they, and they alone, had reached old age, they would be enough to crown me with the garland of fame.

(30) 'Who of these took up a teaching career? Not one,'[29] it is retorted. No, for they didn't want to, though they would have been very capable, if they so wished. So prove it, if they don't have the capacity. If they have it and preferred to undertake another career, refusal would not indicate incapacity. We avoid many things we could do if we chose, in some cases when no consideration induces us to act, in others even when none prevents us. **(31)** How many physically strong persons have not enrolled themselves among the athletes? Thousands. And how many potential governors have preferred to be governed by others rather than govern cities themselves? Leaving the rest aside, my younger uncle who was in no way inferior to his elder brother in this particular quality, and in some respects even surpassed him, rejected many governmental positions, preferring the position of city councillor to the status of governor.[30] I could mention many councillors to you who continue to do the same although they could long ago have progressed on a career

---

27 The list of provinces in §28 (like that of *Or.* 31.40) marks approximately the recruiting area for Libanius' pupils after his removal to Antioch in A.D. 354. There is some overlap with the area of his earlier teaching career in Nicomedia and Constantinople (outlined in §27), owing to the number of students who accompanied him from Constantinople. This is the case with Galatia in particular, students from which (e.g. Hyperechius) finished their course with him in Antioch after beginning it in Constantinople. It had dropped out of the reckoning by A.D. 390, however.

28 Cf. *Or.* 1.151ff.

29 For the same criticisms of Libanius' teaching abilities, cf. *Orr.* 1.151; 2.50; 35.25; 62.53 and comments in Petit (1956).

30 Phasganius (*BLZG* 234) and Panolbius (*PLRE* 665(1)).

of office and could disdain some of those who have become so puffed up after a period of office.

(32) What cause for surprise, then, if, just as others have deemed it more advantageous to be governed although they know how to govern, some of those who are capable of teaching decide not to take this course? If I must also state the reasons on their behalf, my statement would be nothing complicated but something that is obvious even to a child: they see the profession despised, dragged down deep, and without reputation, influence, or income, but, instead of this, involving a grievous servitude, with many as their masters,[31] – fathers, mothers, attendants, the students themselves, whose reactions are most absurd, since they think that the teacher of rhetoric has need of someone to receive it and that the harm involved in the lack of reception falls upon the teacher, not upon the non-recipient. On seeing all this, like navigators avoiding reefs, they avoid a profession that has gone wrong.

(33) And who will look on me and hanker after the profession? I am held to be lucky, but my life is more miserable than that of prisoners, for I am ordered about and needs must both dislike and court the same people, the first in consequence of my past experiences, the second so as not to experience more and worse in future. For this is the nature of present-day parents: they seek the undoing of those to whom they send their sons as pupils, and if they cannot manage that, they give vent to their temper by abusing them.

(34) Well, would the matter of my declamations induce any sensible man to believe that teaching is not a disaster? If you don't issue an invitation, you make an enemy; if you do, you are a nuisance. There is no forgiving even the slightest mistake; if you succeed, envy is rife; and in either case you are abused. Moreover, anyone who doesn't demand his fee would never get it; and if he does, then war is declared by the payer of it. So when they see troubles and inconveniences of this sort, and more besides, to be part of the job, are you surprised that sensible men shrink from it?

(35) However, if I must in any case reveal myself as a teacher's teacher, just cast a glance at Calliopius here.[32] He is quite satisfied with the position of understudy, when he could, if he wished, be the star. Let

31 Cf. *Or.* 25.46ff.
32 Calliopius, pupil and assistant teacher of Libanius, died in A.D. 392. *PLRE* 175(4), *BLZG* 102(iv).

me refrain from demonstrating this: for qualities, at present concealed, will become apparent, given the chance. Many people, comparable with him, have embarked on a legal career when they saw him grieving at the troubles in which he had involved himself and which he endured. **(36)** And should any carping critic argue that this ability is present in him alone, while ever he agrees that teaching ability exists in a single person, he concedes that I have the ability to produce people capable of teaching. For from the same training many people could have had this ability, just as from the same hands many acres could have received the seed.

(37) 'Who are the councillors that you can show?' is the next question. Many. 'Then how is it that they don't outshine the rest?' says my inquisitor. In Ancyra, the capital and greatest city in Galatia, the sons of Agesilaus certainly do so. In reputation they surpass their esteemed father Agesilaus, and they are not inferior to their uncle.[33] Nobody else is fit to look at them, even; this is something they have won not so much from the vastness of their expenditure upon their city as from their ability to speak effectively upon matters under discussion at the moment. It is said too that in Cappadocia a person with a similar literary training is pre-eminent, and in Cilicia,[34] we practically see them directing their community by education.

(38) What is more, even here you could be shown young men who perform civic duties better than many of their elders, and orators far better than them without curial rank, while people who are far inferior to them, hold that position and express themselves upon civic matters. **(39)** And how has this come about? There are two things necessary for a decurion these days, eloquence and money, and money is the more important, for unless he performs the most important duties with greatest expenditure, even were he Nestor, or Pericles or Demosthenes, he would be absolutely bound to stay silent of his own free will and, should he not wish to do so, then he would do so against his will, especially since he could not even proffer any hope of services because of his present poverty. Anyone who cannot himself demonstrate men of sense to be talking nonsense, can, provided that he is renowned for his services, put a gag on would-be speakers because they have not laid out money.

---

33 Strategius and Albanius, sons of Agesilaus, nephews of Achillius, *principales* of Ancyra and connected by marriage with Hyperechius (for whom *PLRE* 449). They were all staunch supporters of Libanius, cf. *BLZG* 50, 284(ii), 47(ii).

34 E.g. Apolinarius and Gemellus (*PLRE* 83(2), 388(2); *BLZG* 80(iv), 162).

(40) Some who are not very clever happen to be well off, while capable orators have no money, and the result is that these don't handle civic affairs, while the others handle them less efficiently. And if some god had combined the virtues of the two of them and had given to the first group the fortunes of the wealthy or to the second the ability of the others, then, though they could not have competed with Phasganius, in my opinion, for his gifts were divine and surpassed human nature, they would still have made many of the so-called orators of the present sing small.[35]

(41) A further question of theirs is as follows: 'How is it that those taking up the position of legal advocates don't have very many people having recourse to their services?' Because, my dear good fellows, they have learned while with me, along with rhetoric, a sense of decency. For this reason they don't hire publicity men, they don't grab litigants, or flatter hawkers, or send humble letters to neighbouring communities: they aren't slaves to the underlings of the governors, don't make agreements with the criers for the pickings that they will get, nor yet purchase audiences from the magistrates' clerks. The strong points of present-day oratory are shouting, lying, breaking oaths, creating riots and disturbance, giving promises and bribes. **(42)** Pupils of mine neither can nor will do anything like this, and by heaven, I trust they never can or will; I hope they will retain their present position, assisting those in need and providing themselves as sufficient protection, without seeking or hunting out those who don't approach them.[36]

(43) Moreover the pressure of business upon the governors regarding the levy of taxation and their allocation of a brief part of the day to court actions, while taking up the greater part of it on throttling and hacking the debtors,[37] has expelled long, fine discourses and has revealed the

35 Libanius, especially from A.D. 388 onwards, begins to criticize the *principales* of the council of Antioch, a class to which his own family belongs, for what he alleges to be their oppression both of rhetoric and their lesser fellows in the council; see *Orr.* 48 and 49 especially. He reproves his curial ex-students for their silence in its debates, in *Or.* 35, where they excuse themselves with arguments similar to those presented here. Legislation of the Theodosian age on the treatment of the city councils did in fact rapidly produce a distinction in treatment, not least as regards physical punishment, between the *principales* and the rest, cf. *Cod. Th.* 12.1.75ff. For Phasganius, cf. §31 above, note 30.

36 For the career as advocate in Libanius, cf. Petit (1955), 78ff., 363f. It was an attractive career, and could, at its best, lead to curial immunity and office.

37 Cf. *Or.* 45.23f. (of A.D. 386). The rigour which attended the collection of taxes in the Theodosian age was a constant grievance, cf. Liebeschuetz (1972), 161ff.

true function of the orator to be a nuisance; if anyone makes a full statement and brings forward some matter of considered opinion, he is
thought to be a fool and a time-waster, and this has hoisted to power
this crowd of ignoramuses, who are no better than street-corner-boys,
who inform us of the matters for which they come into court by a nod of
the head rather than by well-intoned delivery. **(44)** If the profession had
retained its old rules and the judge had demanded a well-composed
address and sent back to the schoolroom anyone who was incapable of
producing one, you would have seen all my pupils besieged by those
who requested their assistance and unable to protect the masses of those
who appealed to them. As matters stand an inability to speak is an
advantage, and 'rhetorical ability' dirty words. In consequence the
tortoise has outstripped the horse in reputation, not as in Aesop's
fable[38] because they exerted their efforts while the horses were slack, but
beating them simply by their deficiency in speed. **(45)** So don't, if you
please, judge your first-class orator by the amount of his rewards, but by
the skill he really has, and if you do so, you will find that these people
who gain little profit are better than those who have made a success of
things. And if you require me to cast a glance at the money that comes
their way, I in turn require you to look at their souls so totally lacking in
culture. The people whom we used to regard as a joke with the teachers
are now held to be specialists in law. Every single day they leave court
with hands full of gold.

(46) But my pupils, even if they were deficient in the power of
eloquence, at any rate sought to get it, and they paid a fee before getting
one. They became members of my class and shared a more honourable
title; but one fellow, named Heliodorus,[39] a hawker of fish-pickle who
plied his trade by sea, in the course of his trade once came to Corinth.
The friend with whom he was lodging was involved in a law-suit and
happened to fall ill, so Heliodorus took his place and entered court,
listened to the pleaders, and conceived the hope, upon hearing them,
that he too could become a successful pleader if he paid attention to
law-suits. So he divided his interests between the sale of fish-pickle and

---

38 Aesop, *Fab*. 420. Libanius refers to it elsewhere, *Or*. 1.114, *Ep*. 72.

39 *BLZG* 166(v), *PLRE* 411(2). Libanius is our only informant for this remarkable
success story. It presumably came to his attention during his days as student in Athens
(i.e. before A.D. 340), since Heliodorus began his career as advocate in the court of the proconsul of Achaea at Corinth, where cases from Athens were heard.

listening to law-suits, and in a short time, Heliodorus suddenly made his appearance as an orator. **(47)** Influence came as a result of his impudence at first, in no small measure; it became greater thereafter, and, as time went on, reached its peak. He never managed to get rid of jokes about fish-pickle, but he got the better of the jokers, bought himself a house, slaves and land. Before any court action the prime concern for the litigants who would take part in it was to get Heliodorus for their shield and defence. Such a name does a man get from sticking at nothing. He went the rounds of every type of court and he finished up in the palace making the speeches that a man of his kind must make, and as a result of these too he attained pre-eminence. **(48)** And his reward was many estates in Macedonia, more in Aetolia and Acarnania, gold, silver, vast numbers of slaves, herds of horses and cattle; moreover, of the property of which, by his advocacy, he had made one woman the mistress, he took one half as his reward. He even became a governor, for it was held that he had been through the mill of oratory! **(49)** So, my dear man, it is no cause for surprise that ignorance in law-suits is a means of attaining wealth. Although I could mention many similar instances, I have confined my account to him alone, since not many people know of them, and my story might not be believed, whereas about him I can call many witnesses from all over the place.

(50) However, people tot up the numbers of pupils of other teachers who have held office – ten in one case, more in another, twenty in a third instance, and they ask, 'How many different provinces have you administered for us through your pupils?' – just as if one criterion of the art of rhetoric is the attainment of office. I agree that those who are going to be good governors need rhetoric, yet to obtain provincial governorships is no proof of its attainment. It is possible both to obtain office without being an orator and not to obtain it if you are. This is the gift of Fortune,[40] not an innate characteristic of the art. **(51)** This has always been the case, and especially in the reign of Constantius who appointed his prefects from the class of notaries.[41] They sat on their chairs of office and issued their orders, while the orators stood and trembled. **(52)** And though it is important in some forms of service to win praise and not to

---

40 Fortune, the most potent and personal of Libanius' deities, is the inspiration and the title of his *Autobiography* (*Or.* 1, *The Autobiography* or *Concerning his own Fortune*). J. Misson, *Recherches sur le paganisme de Libanios*, Louvain 1914, studies it in depth.

41 E.g. the list of such notables in *Or.* 42.23f. Cf. Liebeschuetz (1972), 245f.

be thought behind-hand, yet if we attribute to the teachers what the gods have in their power to grant or not, the Rhodian becomes more important than Ulpianus.[42]

(53) Moreover, it is quite ridiculous to compare young and old, and to expect those only just out of school, the majority of them dead anyway, to have obtained honours which men in their later years have scarcely acquired. Wait until they reach their prime, wait for their old age. Perhaps the course of time, when I am no longer alive, will produce some such result. But if the situation demands the man, they too will be given office without solicitation or flattery. As things are, some of them spend their time hanging around the doors of the magnates.

(54) In actual fact, some of my pupils have already revealed their qualities in office, – one from Paphlagonia,[43] who by his labours so cared for his subjects that, after his departure, they still weep for him, – and a Galatian[44] who even now governs Cappadocia so competently that they praise his actions and want nothing more. (55) And before them there was the Heracleote[45] who was governor of Lycia before reaching the age of twenty-five. He found the province ruined by the speculations of his predecessors, and had no good word for them. He restored his provincials to prosperity, judging his salary from the emperor to be enough for himself; the fortune he won was that he left behind him his ex-subjects wealthy. And while he so improved their fortunes, above and beyond his cares of office he performed a sophist's job by honouring the festivals of every city with an oration, so that teachers in Lycia gained more advantage from hearing than delivering orations.

42 The allusion is unclear. The Rhodian is unknown: an Ulpianus was a teacher in Antioch c. A.D. 330, *PLRE* 973(1); another is a jurist and provincial governor A.D. 361–4 (ibid.(5)). *PLRE* toys with the idea that the reference is to the famous jurist, Domitius Ulpianus, of Severan times, which seems unlikely since he wrote in Latin, which Libanius did not know.

43 Probably Alexander, governor of Bithynia in A.D. 361; *BLZG* 52(ii), *PLRE* 40(4).

44 Petit ((1979), 264, note on *Or.* 1.214) dating the present speech to A.D. 382/3, identified this unknown Galatian with Africanus (*PLRE* 27(4)) who received Gregory Nazianzen's Letter 224 at that time. Since Olympius (*PLRE* 646(10)) is known to have been governor of Cappadocia Secunda then, Africanus' province was that of Cappadocia Prima.

45 Themistius (*BLZG* 307(iii), *PLRE* 894(2)). Libanius' pupil in A.D. 357, and governor of Lycia at a very early age, in A.D. 361. *Epitropeuein* is not here used in the technical sense of procurator but as a general term for governor (so *Or.* 1.36).

(56) I could not mention the name of the noble Andronicus[46] without weeping, and if I failed to mention him in the number of my students, I would do him serious wrong, for he was no less an adornment to me than they say Achilles was to Chiron.[47] He was governor of Phoenicia, that province so free with its bribes, but he was a protector of each man's property, even more meticulous than the owners. The provincials brought their usual offerings, calling them presents, and disguising their bribe under the title of the New Year feast,[48] and he very nearly arrested the slaves and had them imprisoned; and he let them off with this much punishment and ordered them to distinguish a future governor from a hireling. **(57)** He was the only governor to have to employ the minimum of executions against those he governed. So forcibly did he demonstrate his hatred of injustice that the fear he inspired allowed no one to venture upon any action deserving of death. Past holders of high office[49] were in the habit of issuing orders to the governor of Phoenicia, some by letter, others by personally rushing into court with clamour and disturbance and angry looks, and forcing the governor to regard their own whims as higher than the law. He, however, did away with all such tyranny as this, not with clamour and insult, so that they would have reason to complain, but by revealing that he respected no person more than he did justice. And they were schooled, on approaching him when the court was not in session, to request only those things which it was not unjust to obtain. Hence he gained the reputation for administrative ability. And no one was such an enemy of Andronicus as to rob him of this. **(58)** So he ought to have stayed at home and enjoyed the beauties of Tyre, and that ill-starred summons should never have come his way. But it did, and when the revolt occurred in Thrace the pretender to the throne[50] immediately

---

46 Andronicus (*BLZG* 71(i), *PLRE* 64(3)), governor of Phoenicia in A.D. 361 (where R.A. Pack (*Studies in Libanius and Antiochene Society under Theodosius*, Diss. Michigan 1935, 119) identifies him with the just and clement governor of *Or.* 45.30). His uncle in high places, identified by *BLZG* and *PLRE* with Nebridius, is proved by H.F. Bouchery (*Themistius in Libanius' Brieven*, Antwerp 1936, 87ff.) to have been Strategius Musonianus.

47 Chiron as teacher of Achilles, cf. *Or.* 59.30; *Progymn.* (Foerster VIII, 405ff.)

48 Cf. *Or.* 9.8ff., and *Ekphrasis Kalandon* 3 (Foerster VIII, 405ff.; a French translation, Martin (1988), 202). The giving of New Year gifts (Lat. *strena*) was standard courtesy by friends, or by clients to patrons.

49 The *honorati*, for whose position and power of influence over the provincial governor, cf. Liebeschuetz (1972), 186ff.

50 For the revolt of Procopius in A.D. 365/6 cf. Amm. Marc. 26.5ff. The execution of Andronicus in consequence of this attempted usurpation is mentioned in *Or.* 1.171 (a

appointed him a governor, though there were many available, for he thought the genius of Andronicus to be a strong bulwark. Andronicus, unwillingly but with the glint of steel all around him, accepted the post and was of the greatest use to the one who trusted him, for he was no traitor, nor was he unaware that they would be fighting against a far superior enemy strength and that he was participating in a dangerous enterprise. Despite all this, he preferred not to be a villain, though he felt that he was backing a loser, to enduring the reproach of Thessaly,[51] and becoming rich thereby. **(59)** And as governor of Bithynia he was both loyal and energetic, and better still when he was despatched to administer the whole of Thrace. And when the enemy gained the upper hand, though he had it in his power to decamp, when he had harbours in sight and vessels ready and many who advised him to take this course, he refused to lurk in caves or hide himself in the forest and live in a guise that was foreign to his nature.[52] While regarding compulsion as sufficient excuse for his acceptance of the offices, he considered the fact that treachery was an ignoble business as reason enough for not being a traitor, and delivered himself up to the conquerors and was robbed of a longer span of life, departing this life in the perfection of the glory he had won. The confiscator of the property[53] of the deceased, viewing the paucity of his possessions, admired the character of him who had received the death stroke.

(60) Does not Andronicus' staunchness of character alone and the administration which it produced deserve to be contrasted with you and your hordes of governors? Should a man be more justly judged fortunate in his sons when he has one good one than when he has many who are bad?

(61) Though Andronicus has departed, and made you happy by his death, yet Celsus is still alive.[54] He is not a bit like you, but he too is the

---

passage also written early in Theodosius' reign), where Valens is acquitted of blame, the responsibility being fixed upon the treacherous one-time friend of Andronicus, Hierius, introduced to him by Libanius himself.

51 Notoriously and proverbially treacherous, cf. Eurip. *Phoen.* 1407, Demosth. *c. Aristocr.* 112.

52 As Procopius himself did, Amm. Marc. 26.5ff.

53 The emperor Valens.

54 Cf. *Orr.* 15.51; 18.30; Amm. Marc. 22.9.13. *BLZG* 104(i), *PLRE* 193(3). He was a student under Libanius in Nicomedia. This invitation to teach in Athens (cf. *Or.* 2.14),

product of my efforts. He was capable of governing properly his fellow citizens, his kinsfolk and friends without transgressing the law by any favour towards them and, what is the most uncommon thing of all, by maintaining his friendships and justice also. If you came to him and asked him, 'Tell me, whose pupil are you, then? From whom do you get your rhetorical ability?', you would be told that it was from me and from his studies with me. For he, in the heart of Athens did not hesitate to declare this, nor will he conceal it now. He went there under a false impression, but when experience proved his impression to be false,[55] and the student body was present in the Lyceum, he declared that he was in the proverbial situation, and had simply swapped horse for donkey.[56] This remark stung the Athenian state and forced it to pass a decree inviting me there, since it resented it if there was any eloquence elsewhere superior to what they had in Athens. **(62)** Well, don't just consider the fact that Celsus went to Athens. Examine the ability he possessed on arriving there. You will find him truly a son of mine,[57] and like his earlier teachers, not the later ones, and this would be indication that he regarded his later training as poor, and the earlier as better.

(63) So will you still level objection and abuse against my declamations, you ignoramus in everything except praise for yourself and slander against others? For you have filled everywhere with comments like these; 'I am the only one with money, with a capacity for speaking, with administrative ability. It's an insult for me to live in this world.' **(64)** You have got money, true, but wrongly! Your wealth comes from your brutality in usury, whereby you have been the ruin of many a

---

which occurred in A.D. 352/3, is described at length in *Or.* 1.81f., where the initiative is attributed to Strategius, proconsul of Achaea. Sievers ((1868), 61 note) reasonably suggested that Celsus made the first unofficial approach, with Strategius giving his official confirmation. Libanius always took great pride in this prestigious invitation, and in his refusal of it.

55 Disillusion with the stereotyped quality of teaching in Athens was not uncommon at this time, cf. Lib. *Or.* 1.17ff.; Themist. *Or.* 27.336d f.; Eunap. *V.S.* 491 (of the prefect Anatolius); Synesius *Ep.* 135.

56 Proverbial; cf. Zenobius 2.33, Diogen. 1.96 (*Corp. Par. Gr.*).

57 A commonplace view, but sincerely held, that pupils are the sons of their teachers, cf. *Ep.* 1051 (of Calliopius (*PLRE* 175(4)), 'assuredly a child of mine, not by blood but reared by my labours'). Similarly, of Eusebius (*PLRE* 305(24)), *Ep.* 960.2, 'my child Eusebius. Arrhabius (Cimon) is my child too, and more so than Eusebius, for he is connected by eloquence also, whereas there is no blood connection with Eusebius.' Cf. n. 26, above.

family, without compassion for widows, without pity for orphans, unbending before floods of tears, bawling and bellowing, 'Sell your estates, sell your slaves, sell your family tombs, and, if you can, sell yourself, too.' Those were the remarks he made when he sat and took his piece of gold from women and naked children. Then they would go away to beg for their living, while he, having obtained in this way the sum they gave him, would depart joyfully, calling himself happy as a result of gains that are more disgraceful than utter beggary. **(65)** For usury such as this he relinquished the position of governor which he had got by his importunities,[58] and for five months was assessor to a prefect, and he didn't leave that job until he had sacked over thirty households, acting the part of brigand instead of reasonable creditor. A brigand spares nobody, a decent creditor has it in him even to make some allowances. But he smiling upon his debtors and presenting a kindly face is, in the collection of his dues, more savage than the Cyclops, practically tearing the flesh from the starving.[59] **(66)** This is our Croesus; instead of the Pactolus,[60] he personally turns his inhumanity into profit; waking or sleeping he counts up his interest, hated by everyone, happy at the troubles of the rest and aggrieved at their success, demanding preferential treatment and quarrelling with those who treat him well, as if he had been ill done by, afraid that, if he condescends to accept a favour, he will inevitably be bound to repay it. Of course you would make a fortune if you rob your friends and regard their ill-fortunes as a chance for you to thieve.

(67) 'But,' some will say 'he has delivered speeches.' Yes, of course. Somebody else's. That is how he got married, deceiving the bride's father, a man who loved eloquence. I know the person who sired[61] the

58 He had thus obtained the privileged position of *honoratus*, and used it to oppress the decurions.

59 Homer, *Od.* 9.287ff.

60 The proverbial river of gold of the Lydians, Herod. 5.101, Strabo *Geogr.* 13.4.

61 For the metaphor 'sire of speeches' cf. *Or.* 18.14. The vividness of Libanius' diction indicates his disgust at what he alleges as professional misconduct. It may be noted that such examples as this of literary pretensions providing a passport to office give the lie to his repeated claims that the importance of the literary education has collapsed. Thus, Themistius' recommendations are his philosophy; Icarius also attains office as a reward for his poetic talents (*Or.* 1.225), and even Eustathius (*PLRE* 311(6)) gains attention by his rhetorical ability. That the situation is not as bad as Libanius would have it is indicated by his repeated, and very natural, commendations of his protégés as models of culture and eloquence. Cf. the discussion in Petit (1955), 359–70.

seven speeches that you hawk around, and how he composed them, you bought them, and insist on being thought their composer, though you are a mere actor, with no qualification for that except the diction. **(68)** For you, as a student, to buy speeches like anything else on the market, is a disgrace – ye gods of eloquence, of course it is – but you might in other circumstances be pardoned for it, but for you, an inmate of the palace who for a long time served the emperor with your tongue upon his dispatches, to have bought speeches surely merits the deepest dishonour. **(69)** Or do you think that the identity of the writer of the treatise[62] about the armour which makes invulnerable the cavalryman who fights under its protection has passed unnoticed? He was not able to keep quiet on the subject: he got his price for his composition but he also got the credit for it by talking about it to his confidants. They took a leaf out of his book, and chatted about it to others, and you often used to tell the tale to people who knew the whole story, believing them completely ignorant of it, when you might have heard it from their telling, if they only dared. **(70)** Alas, for my untimely generosity. Recently one of those who have been ruined by his rapacity in usury begged for a little moderation. He received none and made his mind up to gather together as many as he could of both citizens and outsiders, and in the great theatre to proclaim the secret aloud, but I stopped him. **(71)** And now he enjoys the freedom of his position through me, for had I not then restrained the man, he would be living the rest of his life with veiled head, cowering before his slaves; yet though I saved his position for him, this young fellow takes this line against me and mine, and he asserts that no orators have originated from me, while he is the cleverest of men. But his stupidity, or rather his sheer craziness, is such that he claims to be no whit inferior to Zeus; and he wants the god to relinquish his rule over the world to him. **(72)** Despite this arrogance and the ridicule he inspires, he has not learned his lesson and stopped, but he is always looking for something more absurd than before, and doesn't realize that he is making a laughing-stock of himself. It is a great blessing for him that he has no children, for he would have been revealed as

---

62 Such tractates, mostly in précis form, were common enough in the later empire. Specialist and utilitarian, they form part of the tradition, of which Vegetius is the best known today, which culminates with the *Tacticae Constitutiones* of the Byzantine Emperor Leo VI, c. A.D. 900. One example can be found in the work of Modestus, *Libellus de Vocabulis Rei Militaris* in the Didot edition of Ammianus and others pp. 643–51 (Paris 1851).

loathing even his children. As it is, this no small wickedness escapes remark because of Fortune, who in her concern for mankind makes this accursed[63] fellow childless and rescues the cities from some base seed.

(73) You see that it does no good to enter a contest lightly, don't you? At any rate, although you could have a reputation higher than you deserve, by provoking a man to oppose you, you have the one you do deserve.

---

63 *Aliterios* is a term of abuse generally used by Libanius to indicate Christians, in the plural. This adds spice to his venom.

ORATION 43: ON THE AGREEMENTS

INTRODUCTION

This oration was delivered to members of the teaching profession in Antioch to deal with a recurrent problem of student indiscipline which had once again reached alarming proportions, namely the withdrawal of students from the teacher with whom they had registered and their transfer to another.

Internal evidence of dating shows that Libanius was now well on in years (§18), and that he had no challenger for his position as sophist of the city (§2), a situation which does not apply after A.D. 388 (cf. *Or.* 1.255f.), but which had been triumphantly vindicated in A.D. 382 (ibid. 186f.). It was certainly delivered in the earlier part of a school session when this unwanted mobility among the students had become critical. External evidence which provides more precise indications of date (although Wolf (1952), 48 would deny this) is (i) *Or.* 36.13, of A.D. 386, and (ii) *Or.* 1.241f., a narration of events which can be firmly dated to the winter of A.D. 385/6, and which runs:

> (*Or.* 1.241) The emperor put a fitting end to that winter ... when, refraining from inflicting the death penalty (for a charge of oneiromancy), he imposed a sentence of exile on a couple of people and corrected the rest with a few floggings. However, a disturbance of different origin affected me, when not all the students in school kept the rules of discipline. The majority did behave properly, but a certain section misconducted themselves and made a point of being a nuisance, showing that, if they took it into their heads, they would go to even greater lengths. (242) Naturally I felt aggrieved, but I decided to remain silent until they recognized their misconduct and returned to their former station. Yet their attitude gave no grounds for confidence, and so some compulsion was applied, so that they could not leave even if they wanted to. What this was precisely, I have decided not to say.

Students, before admission to their course of higher education in rhetoric when they assumed the academic gown, faced two hurdles. First, they must take an oath, a form of contract between master and pupil, and so the equivalent of the modern registration or matriculation; secondly, they must normally undergo at the hands of their fellow students a ritual initiation of the ceremonial bath and banquet. Such rituals were time-honoured and universal, and are described by such varied authors as Eunapius (*V.S.* 485ff.), Gregory Nazianzen (*Or.* 43.15 (Migne, *PG* 36, 514)), and Olympiodorus (*FHG* IV fr. 28), and supplemented by Libanius' own lively account of his misadventures upon arriving as a student in Athens (*Or.* 1.16ff.). Desertion after such rituals of admission thus became a serious matter, and Libanius here records that any such transfers were most unusual in his own student days and invariably accompanied by social stigma – a matter of concern, if not to the student, certainly to the average parent. Loyalty had thus been ensured by custom and by peer pressure, both in pupil and parent. By the 380s, however, in a changing society and with the prestige of the Greek rhetorical education declining and its monopoly broken, such desertions had increased alarmingly, the reason here alleged being economic, the intention of both parent and pupil being to bilk the teacher of his fee.

The present speech presents Libanius' solution to one part of the problem, as he suggests to his junior colleagues measures to be taken corporately to scotch the business in the long term. He first suggests that they should voluntarily accept a self-denying ordinance by which they might bring the disaffected to heel by influencing the parents. They should agree among themselves to refuse to admit to their courses any registered student who took it upon himself to do the rounds of all the teachers in town. Then, any parent dissatisfied with the progress of his son could have him examined, to determine whether or not there had been any negligence on the part of the teacher. Should the case be made out, the father could bring a formal complaint against the teacher before a board selected from teachers and others, and only then, with negligence proved, should the student's transfer take place – but in due form. Thus the problem of the mobile student is to be tackled indirectly through the parent, but Libanius accepts that the criticisms currently levelled against the teachers were in part justified, and his proposals represent an encroachment on the independence of the private teacher. In a profession where personal vanity loomed as large as it did among the teachers, any such voluntary agreement became very difficult to implement, and certainly, from the tone of *Oration* 36, it was to create some resentment against him.

The *Autobiography* supplements this general solution with a résumé of the measures employed against the dissidents in his own school. Clearly he did not assail these malcontents with the oratory of reproof, as he was later to do in *Oration* 3, but he proceeded by a more devious route. First, he remained silent. In other words, he refused them instruction in declamation (§242), which brought down upon them yet more indirect pressure from both their peers and parents, and cowed them temporarily. He then resorted to an ultimate sanction which finally brought them to order but the nature of which he quite deliberately refuses to mention. What this was can only be a matter of conjecture, but it was certainly effective. It was no form of legal action, nor was it any back-stairs influence applied on his behalf by officialdom, for he was personally unpopular with the *comes* and *consularis* then in office. The suggestion of Petit ((1979), note *ad loc.*) that his solution involved conduct not normally permissible, and the further canvassing of the possibility of his resort to the practice of magic, though unproven, is tempting. His narrative of the events of A.D. 385/6 reeks of the atmosphere of magic, whether feared, alleged, or demonstrated, and he believes in it implicitly. It may also be noted that he is equally reticent about imputing responsibility for the spell of the chameleon to any individual (*Or.* 1.248, 250).

However that may be, the sanction was convincing; the recalcitrants at last came to order. The proposal for a general self-denying ordinance among the teachers seems, to judge by *Or.* 36.13, to have been put into practice for a while at least, but by the time of composition of *Oration* 3 academic discipline seems to have deteriorated once more and student restiveness was now as bad as ever. In the meantime, the institution of a chair of Latin in Antioch in A.D. 388 made the position of Libanius himself more vulnerable (cf. *Or.* 3.24; *Or.* 38 *passim*), and there was open dissatisfaction from parents, pupils and pedagogues concerning both the method and the contents of the rhetorical education then current (cf. *Or.* 34).

The problem of such desertions was not new, nor was it a merely local phenomenon. As he states in this speech (§1), he had encountered it himself in A.D. 355 just after his return to Antioch and before he had time to become firmly settled in his sophistic chair (cf. *Ep.* 405.8). The responsibility then he ascribed to pedagogues, who were hawking their charges around the teachers with a view to their own aggrandizement and to the detriment of discipline in the schools. He records that a

speech he made then to his fellow citizens, i.e. to the parents, produced
some resentment against the culprits, but since his views had met with
some opposition, he had let the matter drop. Now, forty years later, the
causes are different and the responsibility lies with the parents, who,
under increasing economic pressure, are themselves only too eager to
cheat the teacher of his fee. The practice is confirmed by Augustine in
Italy (*Confess.* 5.12), and in the East by Synesius (*Dio* 15) and Himerius
(*Or.* 34), who also confirm his statement that the object was to rob the
teacher of his fee. These economic pressures remained a dismal feature
of academic life.

Available editions are those of Reiske (obtainable with some difficulty) and of Foerster. For a translation into French, with notes, see
Festugière (1959), 455–66. There are useful discussions by Schemmel
(1907), repr. in Fatouros and Krischer (1983); by Walden (1912) and by
Wolf (1952).

ON THE AGREEMENTS[1]

(1) The best opportunity for the remarks I am now about to make has
passed, my friends. When I first began my career as a teacher here I
should have presented you with this advice in a written discourse, but
when, after a short verbal exposition, I failed to convince you, I refrained
from pursuing the matter further and from composing and producing my
suggestions. So, reproaching myself for not having done so long ago, I
have come to perform what I then failed to do.[2] I would like you to
show your appreciation of my argument by following its suggestions,
especially when the advantage accrues both to me and to those who will
commend the idea, for you provide me with increased renown[3] and yourselves with deliverance from serious trouble.

(2) Now, had I not continued to maintain an impartial regard for

---

1 *Or.* 43; Foerster (III, 334–48), Reiske (II, 420–34).

2 Cf. *Ep.* 405.8 (of A.D. 355): 'seeing that the pedagogues were ruling the roost from the
sale of their students, and that discipline in the schools had been ruined, I counselled my
fellow citizens not to ignore this, but to take issue with it and to stop it; and no little anger
was directed against the culprits. My rival threatened to speak in their support.'

3 I.e. as head of the whole teaching profession in Antioch whether public or private, and
of which he is, as 'sophist of the city' (as he is described by John Chrysostom, *Hom. de S.
Babyla* 18 (Migne, *PG* 50, 560)), the acknowledged leader and spokesman. This he had not
yet become in A.D. 355 when he had made his original proposal.

each and every one of you up to this day, had I supported one section and opposed another, I might now be reasonably suspected of not seeking the common good, but of approaching the problem out of deference for certain individuals. But since it is obvious that, on the many occasions when parents have given me the responsibility of choosing a teacher, I have never shown any preference for one over another,[4] I may be believed with good reason today to have set about amending a state of affairs, which I regard as unsatisfactory, out of my concern for all alike. This situation has done me no harm since I have no rival as professor, but it has for long enough now harmed the position of the rest of you and, if not stopped, it will not cease to cause harm, so it should now be brought to an end.

(3) In an ideal situation, if our educational system enjoyed good fortune, and all were plain sailing[5] for us, as it was for our predecessors who were in charge of the classes of pupils and who were fortunate in having a large number of students eager to learn, it would for all that be a natural precaution to see that no circumstances should ever arise to damage this position. As things are now, as you see, our profession is in rough water and blasts are directed at it from all quarters, and whatever your desires in the matter, it is not possible now to harbour malice and of your own free will to inflict hardship above and beyond that which is inevitable.

(4) You are well aware that the present critical situation has endowed other forms of teaching with the pre-eminence that was formerly ours and has transferred their inferior status to our studies: it has made the less admired studies more acceptable, and the more admired, less – or rather, it has succeeded in making those be regarded as the dispenser of all blessings and ours as mere nonsense and trouble and a cause of impoverishment.[6]

(5) In consequence we see the frequent embarkation of our students, and the boats that set a single course – towards Rome[7] – and the cheering of the lads they carry in high hopes of what awaits them, office, power, marriage, a life at court and hob-nobbing with the Emperor. As a matter of fact, such a journey has been of use to precious few of them;

---

4 A good example of professorial patronage.
5 Cf. Soph. *Ajax* 1083, a proverbial expression.
6 The studies of Latin and law, cf. Festugière (1959), 92f., Liebeschuetz (1972), 243ff.
7 Cf. *Orr.* 1.214, 234, 244; 40.5ff.; 62.12f.

for the majority, besides offering them nothing, it has robbed them of some of the sense they had left. Yet for all that, they are still attracted to it and are expectant. In anticipation, they grasp hold of something that they have not yet got, and the business is judged upon a lower standard: there is no examination of it in the light of anything higher. Such is heaven's decree upon both systems of education. So, sorrow is what we take home from our class-rooms and we can do nothing but deplore the iniquity of the times.

(6) But this is an unfortunate accident and we are not to be blamed for what I have described above. However, with regard to the defections which have adversely affected the teaching profession, whom can you blame but yourselves? Are you going to tell me that they don't upset you much? Don't you go home, cut to the quick, if yesterday's pupil today turns up as somebody else's? Isn't your lunch displeasing? Your afternoon distressful?[8] Your dinner distasteful? The best part of the night passed in sleeplessness? The next day you loathe your chair, hate the place where you teach and suspect those who still remain, while the absconding student, bold as brass, with deliberate insolence, comes face to face with his former teacher, forgets everything he has done, expels from his glance the respect he owes him, and puffs himself up with arrogance towards him, eager to annoy him with his every action and attitude. If you should mention a fee, he sets up a howl and protests that he has spent even his time to no purpose, that he has learned nothing, heard nothing, has been slow to leave him, and that he should have done that long ago, and that it is not done to pay fees for learning nothing.[9] (7) His father makes the same remarks to other parents too, and though father and son are both liars, they still have the cheek to tell the tale, so that they should not be regarded as defaulting over the fee. And the teacher seethes with anger at the thought of all the work he has put in and at his unawareness that he was building for the soul of an ingrate. So, if he mentions his fee, these are the straits in which he finds himself, and if, alarmed at them, he keeps quiet, he is irked because he cannot even open his mouth, and in consequence he probably takes his seat, eating his heart out. Either he does not turn to his book and the nurture to be derived therefrom, or, if he does, he does so in vain,[10] since he

---

8 Formal teaching ends at midday.
9 For similar criticisms of Libanius' teaching by his pupils, cf. *Orr.* 34.5; 3.19ff.
10 Upon his attitude to fees, cf. *Or.* 31.30n.; *Or.* 3.6n.

cannot concentrate his attention properly to benefit from it. And as a result he becomes less efficient. So, besides the loss of his fee, it comes about that his ability is impaired, too.

(8) This business of defection is no doubt of long standing,[11] but it has never reached present-day proportions. I know of two or three who behaved so in my school-days and gained no good name for their defection. Their friends and acquaintances grew scarcer in consequence, for any who demonstrated his disloyalty towards his own teacher proclaimed to one and all that he did not know the meaning of friendship. So it was something rare then, but it is commonplace now, and defections almost match the days of the week. You can find the same people going the rounds until they turn up with the teacher they first left. And then a second cycle starts, and a third. With every teacher you can often see both things happening at once – one student leaving to go off to another teacher, another entering after rejecting someone else. And those, who stay all along, do not stay without provoking the suspicion that they are likely to do the same, so that even from the better students there arises some discomfort.

(9) How then can each teacher rely on keeping the pupils he has? By suppressing these defections by an agreement and making it impossible for them to chase from A to B and then from B to A, as children do when playing at rounders. Let every student realize that this craze for defection is finished, and let fathers, mothers and attendants realize it too. All these now are the bosses of the occupants of the teachers' chairs,[12] but if my recommendations are put into effect, they will recognize their position and that of the teachers, and, instead of requiring the teachers to defer to them, they will follow these leaders, as the order of justice demands. The strap and the cane will come into play. As things are now, some schools do not even have any, and in others their use has been renounced, for their user knows full well that, if he makes the punishment fit the crime, he makes the boy somebody else's pupil. This is the consequence of corporal punishment;[13] but failure to cultivate the

11 Cf. note 2 above, and Introduction to the oration.

12 Cf. *Or.* 25.47 (On slavery), where in a moralizing declamation to demonstrate that all the world is a slave, he points out the influence that the pupil's family exercises over the teacher.

13 E.g. *Ep.* 555.4, of A.D. 357, where his rival 'sees a student of mine who had deserved a beating and as a result of it had taken umbrage, and he makes him believe that he is going to take over a good part of my class'.

boy's attendant, by sitting him down in the class-room,[14] paying him
cash, dining him and the like, has the same effect too. Put up with this,
and you can keep the lad; if you don't, then you hear that he has left.
(10) So, by this agreement not only will you be able to gain your independence, but the students also will be improved, if, owing to the compulsion
applied, they cannot idle away their time, for they will have to stay and
either be ready to work or be made to, and the fear of defection will not
inhibit corporal punishment. As things are, the pupils are idle and the
teachers do not reprimand them: they doze, and the teachers do not
wake up their ideas; they misbehave, and the teachers hold their peace,
for though they know that they are not doing their job properly, they
discover that reproof is not without risk for themselves.

(11) But it is outrageous, the parents will say, for their decisions about
their children not to be put into effect, and for someone not to allow them
to entrust them to whom they like. Quite so; and the teachers will say that
it is outrageous for someone not to allow them to decide which of the
students they should be associated with and which not. You have a son,
and you want him to have his share of the art of public speaking. There
are many teachers holding professorial chairs who have shown their
mettle over a long period and who have given proof of their ability in
their successful training of people already. Weigh the pros and cons, pick
the one you think best, entrust your lad to him, and let him stay. **(12)** But
to take the lad first to one, then to another,[15] implies no admiration for
the latter but disrespect for the first, and this second teacher, when he
takes stock of the matter, will tell you in a few studied words that he
could not possibly accommodate you for such a purpose, nor could he
associate himself with you in insulting his colleague. And if you hale him
into court and accuse him, he will have no lack of arguments: there will
be plenty, and good ones too, and they will show such wanton intrusions

---

14 For the influence of pedagogues cf. *Orr.* 34 and 58. Libanius can describe them as
sacrosanct (*Ep.* 1475). They often recommend a teacher to the parent (*Or.* 58.36). Here, to
curry favour with the pedagogue, the teacher allows him to sit and wait inside the classroom.
Normally they sat outside (*Or.* 34.5).

15 Responsibility for these latter-day defections is here clearly placed upon the parents,
whereas for those of an earlier day it had been attributed to the pedagogues. Too much
should not be read into this difference, however. The character of his audience on each occasion should be considered. In A.D. 355 it consisted of the parents themselves, and he could
hardly apportion blame to them however much it might have been deserved. Now, addressing the teachers, there was no need for him to prevaricate. They knew by bitter experience.

to be wrong and that once a person has made his mind up, he should abide by his decision. **(13)** It is as plain as a pike-staff that parents introduce the second teacher out of no regard for greater efficiency, for it was open to them, at the very start, to enquire of people who were knowledgeable in such matters, and then, if any found himself deceived and hoodwinked, he ought to have taken the next step without delay. As it is, the years roll by and the seasons[16] bring the question of the fee to the fore, and then, and only then, do the veils of mist clear and they distinguish the good and the bad. They claim to have been diverted from the right course from the start, not because they think they have found something better, but so as to put a good face on their chicanery and be thought devotees of what is best. And the proof is that many have returned to the very same teachers that they left because of their incapacity, claiming that they are superior. Yet how can the same person be both superior and inferior? It is impossible. But the year that has been spent with the second teacher, and the return of the season and the time for paying the fee – that, I feel, is what makes them change their mind.

(14) 'Ah,' it will be said, 'people will get the idea that, because of our self-confidence as a result of the agreement, we shall be more lax in the conduct of our classes in future, since transfers will be impossible.' Such a view as this will be held by people who know nothing about us. Besides, it is indication enough of our devotion to duty that we do our job even on the days when we might be on holiday – those, for instance, when the governors summon the public to the theatre or the hippodrome, out of respect for such occasions as conferring some blessing upon the emperors.[17] Then the heralds raise their cry both when the governors arrive at the spectacles above-mentioned, and again at their departure, while we listen and know what is going on, and still busy ourselves upon the duties which we need not perform unless we wanted. If all the schools were silent and on holiday, this would be no reason for leaving. **(15)** And besides, our wish for an increase in student numbers should encourage us in our task, for everyone wants good said about him because of the advantage he will gain from his model pupils, for successful students mark the path even for those who have not yet

16 The beginning of the school session and the time for the payment of fees come with the autumn.

17 On public holidays, and especially the occasions when *vota* are officially offered, e.g., for imperial birthdays, anniversaries and triumphs.

begun their schooling.[18] **(16)** Moreover, it is only right that parents, either present or absent, should test their sons, personally, if they are capable of such judgement, or else by employing persons who are so capable: and if, in the students, any negligence on the part of the teachers is observed, let it be possible for the parent to express dissent, disapproval and complaint and to institute proceedings, and let him, if he so desires, have as many judges as he likes convened, composed both of teachers and lay-men, and let him produce the lad in court and bring a charge against the negligent teacher. And if he is content, in a case of proven negligence, merely to liven up the teacher's ideas, then let him leave with a name for kindliness and generosity: and if the decision should prevail, by vote of the tribunal, to transfer the boy, then let him do so and let the agreement remain in force. And let a rider be added to this effect, my friends, 'should any teacher be found guilty of excessive negligence towards any of his pupils, he should not think that he suffers injustice if it is thought necessary to assist the student'.

(17) This, I believe, will satisfy the parents. But some of you perhaps, hopeful of gaining pupils by means of defections, are irked at my recommendation about the agreement. Such a one must consider, not just what he will gain, but also the fact that he himself may lose pupils in the same way. It is human nature to be not so much pleased at what one gains as sorry at what one loses. So which is the better, then – to experience neither such pleasure nor such pain, or to live in both such hopes and fears, spending night and day distressed in soul, in desire of the one and fear and trembling of the other? **(18)** In fact, our school-rooms now ring with the curses of the teachers who, victims of their pupils' wrongdoings, call down imprecations upon them as they relate how they have been rewarded for all their efforts; but once the cause of the trouble has been removed not one of the gods will ever hear any such lament. So if such a fellow finds his hopes dashed, let him learn self-restraint by balancing the discomforts against them; and if he wants to get his own back for the wrongs he has suffered, let him first reflect on what he has himself done, and then, if he thinks that there is need of something further to ensure justice being done, let him reflect that it is an Hellenic quality[19] to let such matters pass, and be patient. Let him not pay less

18 A truism already developed at length in *Or.* 62.
19 I.e. a civilizing quality derived from his Hellenic education, cf. Festugière (1959), 219ff.

heed to the peacemaker than to the firebrands, to the professor[20] than to the touts, and to the senior than to the junior.

(19) For long enough now have you experienced warfare and strife. Now try concord and friendship. If your situation changes, you may perhaps put a stop to what goes on now, when one teacher complains that he should have been a farmer, another a sailor, another a member of some other profession or of the governor's staff.[21] Everyone makes a song of his present poverty, and claims that his income would be greater from any one of these. These are your laments when you come to see me in the City Hall[22] after class has been dismissed, and though you don't abuse each other face to face, once lunch is over, you spend the rest of the day at it, some seated among the advocates, others among the military, and some you can see entering private houses and venting their spite upon their colleagues.[23] There may perhaps be other reasons for this spite, but the most important is these defections.

(20) Well, if I could produce a complete cure, I would do so, but since no means of correcting the greater part of the trouble has yet presented itself, I am putting a halt to what I might well be able to stop. Good Lord! look at yourselves, and see not what you are, but what you will be, once the principal source of irritation is removed. You will look more kindly on each other; and you may have better words to say of one another. You will speak in independent tone to those before whom you now cringe. You will stop envying the good fortune of those in other walks of life, and you will be able to send packing those who claim to be devoted to learning but yet induce students to be idle, for they would no longer have the means of injuring you when you are annoyed at their misconduct.

(21) So let us make this day the start of better things, and let us proceed to an agreement. If we find it to be as I have suggested, let us keep to it; if not, let the advice presented by the facts carry the day.

---

20 Libanius himself.

21 Cf. the teachers' arguments in *Or.* 31.9.

22 Where his school was located.

23 After the ending of school at midday, the teacher's time could be spent as he liked, in social or professional activities, or in the cultivation of persons of influence, a quasi-professional activity in which Libanius himself had participated with great success in the 350s, cf. *Or.* 1.108. Here the dispensers of influence are the military, the serving members of the governor's staff (there was no standing garrison in Antioch until after the Riots), the advocates who attend his court, the private houses being those of the *honorati* or *principales* – the Pooh-Bahs of the city council.

ORATION 36: ON THE MAGICAL PRACTICES

INTRODUCTION

Having brought the episode of the agreements (cf. *Or.* 43) to its cryptic conclusion, the narrative of the *Autobiography* continues:

(*Or.* **1.243**) My old migraine ... attacked me again after sixteen years of respite. Commencing straight after the festival of New Year [i.e. of A.D. 386] ... it became worse, and it was feared that I would collapse when seated in front of my class or even as I lay abed. Every day was painful; every night I was thankful for sleep, and when day dawned it brought my affliction back with it. I began to pray heaven for death in preference to any other blessing, and I was convinced that the malady would affect my reason. **(244)** At the time of writing this has not yet occurred, but I can have no confidence as regards the future. Yet the fact that it has not yet occurred is the gift of the gods, who through a soothsayer forbade me to open a vein for bleeding, though I was very eager to do so ... **(245)** While I was in this state I had the following dream. I thought I saw people sacrifice two boys and put the dead body of one of them in the temple of Zeus behind the door, and upon my protesting at this sacrilege against Zeus, they told me that this was how matters would stand until evening, but that when evening came, he would be buried. This seemed to portend spells, incantations and the hostility of sorcerers. **(246)** And so it turned out in fact, when those fears beset me and I wished for nothing save to die. This was the sole topic of conversation with each fresh visitor and of my prayers to heaven. I loathed any mention of bath or of dinner. I avoided my classical books and the writing and composition of discourses, and my eloquence was undone, even though my students loudly demanded it. Whenever I ventured upon it, I was carried off course like a boat in a contrary wind, so that while they kept expecting some discourse, I would fall silent. My doctors bade me seek the remedy somewhere else, for there was no such remedy in their art. **(247)** They and others besides also attributed to the same cause the double visitation of gout, winter and summer alike, saying that I would be dead before morning ... **(248)** So some of my friends kept urging me and each other, too, to prosecute certain individuals who were regarded as practitioners of such arts, but I did not share their attitude and I restrained them, telling them that they should offer up prayers rather than prosecute anyone for such goings-on. **(249)** However, a chameleon turned up from somewhere or another in the classroom. It was an old specimen and had been dead for several months, and we saw it there with its head tucked in between its hind-legs, one of its forelegs missing, and the other covering its mouth, as though to silence it. **(250)** Nevertheless, not even after such a revelation did I name anyone as responsible for its appearance, but it seemed that the guilty parties were overcome with panic and relaxed their pressure, and so I was able to move about again. Anyway, it was a stroke of good fortune that what had been buried deep should lie above ground, exposed for all to see.

This incident of the chameleon, the subject of the present oration, is therefore the culminating point of a protracted period of stress, both physical and psychological, which Libanius had suffered in A.D. 386. His physical ailments, the recurrence of his combined gout and migraine, exhibit the regular symptoms which he faithfully records, neuralgia, arthritis, vertigo and above all a depression which laid him open to private and personal fears. The year 385 had not been without its alarms and excursions caused by allegations of magic in which he had risked being involved, and his nervous state was a concomitant of the new visitation of gout, so that, in an age when such superstitious beliefs prevailed, it was natural to translate these physical symptoms into the consequences of magic practices, spells directed against himself. It is, in fact, these threats of magic, magnified by fear of the unknown, that cause him much more alarm than the actual discovery of the spell, in the form of the chameleon. This actually had the result of diminishing his alarm, for, by the interpretation of the sympathetic magic it embodies, he could come to a conclusion about his symptoms, which had previously been unknown. He could see from the evidence of the missing forefoot, why he was afflicted with gout, and from the position of the other foot, why he was unable to declaim, and the psychological pressure was thereby relaxed.

The experience affected him profoundly. His depression he refers to in *Or.* 36.15 in terms almost identical with those of the *Autobiography*, and to his illness and its bitter cures in *Or.* 34.17, almost a year later. His present accounts have a note of hysteria, verging on persecution mania, but with the discovery of the chameleon, the spell is broken, and there is no more mention of magic. Yet even so, he refuses to point the finger at the persons responsible although in this oration he hints strongly that he could do so, if he were so minded. The reason for such restraint is once again a matter of conjecture. It may well be that he thought he would be stirring up a hornet's nest if he resorted to law, and in any case he always felt uncomfortable in a court of law (e.g. *Or.* 1.277). One thing is certain: Libanius and his friends and, it may be assumed, the other parties, were in deadly earnest in their assessment of the efficacy of the spell cast upon him. The suggestion of Festugière ((1959), 113) that the incident of the chameleon was merely a practical joke runs counter to the whole tone of Libanius' account and to the climate of opinion of the age.

Available editions are those of Reiske (with some difficulty) and of Foerster. A French translation, with notes, appears in Festugière (1959), 453–8; discussion by Campbell Bonner in 'Witchcraft in the Lecture Room of Libanius', *TAPhA* 63 (1932), 34–44. Further references are in A.A. Barb, 'The Survival of the Magic Arts', in A. Momigliano (ed.), *The Conflict between Paganism and Christianity*, Oxford 1963, 100–25, and 230.

Further information on magic can be found in P. Brown, 'Sorcery, Demons and the Rise of Christianity: From Late Antiquity into the Middle Ages', in *Religion and Society in the Age of Saint Augustine*, New York and London 1972, 119–46, esp. 127–8 on Libanius; Ch.A. Faraone and D. Obbink (eds.), *Magika Hiera: Ancient Greek Magic and Religion*, New York and Oxford 1991; J. Gager, *Curse Tablets and Binding Spells from the Ancient World*, New York and Oxford 1992 (ch. 3); F. Graf, *Magic in the Ancient World*, Cambridge, Mass., 1997.

ON THE MAGICAL PRACTICES[1]

(1) My greatest affliction is the devices that have been contrived and the acts perpetrated against my soul and my body by certain sorcerers,[2] but I have no small cause for mortification in the fact that, upon the revelation of the plot, when practically the whole city had heard tell of the crime, numbers of my so-called friends, upon meeting me, either did not condescend to utter or listen to a word about the matter, or, if they did, found it so unpleasant that they were no different from the others. **(2)** Yet even if I had tried to stop them talking of it when they wanted, the right thing was for them to disobey me in this much at least and to take every action proper to such a situation. But these fellows go their own road and show themselves for what they are: you, my students, would deserve due praise for your anger at what has happened and your annoyance at not knowing the person responsible. You, I believe, would not even have waited for trial and judgement, but would all have resorted to blows instead of an indictment. **(3)** But though I am unable to shake off the chains that bind me,[3] and lament therefore, and though I would sooner be dead than living, I am afraid that people at some future time – for no one today, I feel, is unaware of my condition – upon hearing of sorcerers, spells and chameleons, will conceive this as the revenge of persons who believe themselves injured by me and whose behaviour, though illegal, is a natural reaction, in the resentment they feel against me. I must therefore speak of myself and of my attitude to every class of person in the city, for by so doing I shall be seen to be suffering not the punishment, but the experience of wrong-doing.

(4) So, among which class should I seek the person responsible for this? Among the ordinary folk, the commons, and those who make a living by their hands? But my attitude towards them is such that for them I have become better than a father or a son or a brother, by reason of my daily courtesies and the frequent provision of assistance that has freed them of great perils.[4] In the case of this heavy

---

1 *Or*. 36, ed. Foerster (III, 225–35); *Or*. 35, ed. Reiske (II, 307–15).

2 See the narrative of his tribulations in *Or*. 1.241–50 (cited in the introduction to this speech).

3 The spells of sorcerers.

4 For his attitude towards the urban working class, cf. *Orr*. 2.61; 58.4. He had spoken vigorously against oppression of the bakers in time of famine under Philagrius in A.D. 382 (*Or*. 1.206–10), and under Icarius in A.D. 384–5 (ibid. 226–9; *Or*. 27.9), and in A.D. 385 he

taxation,[5] all that could be effected by indignant outcry, I have done: flog-gings of the weaker by the stronger have been prevented,[6] as has the insen-sitivity of employers towards the employees in their service. So if any such crime has been committed by any of these against my person, I have been foully wronged. **(5)** And I have been wronged, too, if any member of the council has resorted to it. For who, of them all, is unaware of my words and actions on behalf of our council here during all this time before the governors of the province and of the greater circumscription, before the prefectural powers, before the very masters of the world?[7] Who is unac-quainted with this constant warfare on the council's behalf which I have waged against the ex-holders of office?[8] These regard its good fortune as their own particular misfortune, its misfortune as their good fortune, and they form themselves into an army, assault and grapple, and indulge in words and acts of abuse. Yet despite obtaining the greater part of what belongs to the council – and it is not the time or place to relate how – they are irked at not having got the lot. **(6)** They have left nothing untried in their desire to detach me from the council and to make me a member of their own clique, promising that I would be their president, their leader and all such like. And I shall not let pass in silence their frequent solicita-tion. Why! They used to say that they would even do obeisance to me! For all that, this did not induce me to desert my post, but out of deference for my own forebears I thought that I should stay as I was, maintaining towards the ex-magistrates their legitimate claims and not robbing them of the respect that was their due, yet deeming it my duty to remain loyal to the council so that its members also would be unable to level any such

---

had protested against forced labour imposed upon the peasantry (*Or.* 50). He could there-fore with some justification claim to be their patron.

5 Above and beyond the normal tribute, the taxation that bore heaviest on the trades-people was the *chrysargyron* or *lustralis collatio* (for which see Petit (1955), 145ff.). These were critical times for the imperial treasury, since in A.D. 387 imperial anniversaries had to be financed and meanwhile the revolt of Maximus was raging in the West. Provincial gov-ernors, like Tisamenus, governor of Syria in A.D. 385/6, were under severe pressure. He was most strict in squeezing the last brass farthing out of the wretched commons.

6 As by Candidus, *epistates* (supervisor) of the bakers under Icarius, *Or.* 27.9ff.

7 The *consularis* of Syria, the Count of the East, the Praetorian Prefect (of the East), and the Emperor, respectively.

8 The *honorati*, ex-officials and *ipso facto* members of the senatorial order, whom Libanius always represents as oppressors of the decurions (cf. Petit (1955), 370ff.). As sena-torials, they form an ever-growing class of landowners immune from the liturgies and taxa-tion to which the decurions were subject. Furthermore, they had the ear of serving officials.

accusation against me.[9] **(7)** Nor do I believe that any of the advocates[10] either could make one such complaint against me that would justify his resorting to this revenge: for I will be seen always to have spoken favourably of them to the governors, and I have taken up arms whenever anyone abused them. I have never spoken a word to accuse any of them of not maintaining the law, and I have never advised those in need of advocacy to avoid A or seek the protection of B, asserting that A was no good or that B was all powerful. If one of them greeted me before I him, I used to think that I was misconducting myself towards him: in their illnesses I would either visit them personally or send to enquire about the state of their health.[11]

(8) Well! But was it any of you students who committed this act of impiety? Now there are some whose behaviour towards me has not seldom been one of impudence when they wish to prefer what is essentially second-rate.[12] Yet I have never sought nor imposed punishment for this, though I could easily have done so had I wished, but I let them make fools of themselves and bore with their folly, without reproof for their non-attendance or rebuffs when they did decide to attend – and whether you want to call this simplicity, stupidity or generosity I will not cavil. For all that I did not neglect them in their illnesses or involvement in trouble at the hands of those persons who delight in abusing youngsters and who find in the title of 'soldier'[13] ample opportunity for outrage. In such cases, I have watched over them, protected them, defended them and rescued them from heavy-handedness. **(9)** Moreover, as regards fees,[14] who on earth has not marvelled at my practice, except for the teachers who have been penalized by my habit, since the students

9 Upon receipt of his honorary prefecture in A.D. 383 (cf. P. Petit, 'Sur la Date du *Pro Templis*', *Byzantion* 21 (1952), 291–4, a view contested by Martin (1988), 250–2), Libanius automatically became an *honoratus*. They naturally wanted him as their mouthpiece, but he refused, partly because of his pride as a member of a curial family in Antioch and partly from distrust of their motives.

10 Syndics = advocates, cf. *Or*. 3.19; Petit (1955), 78ff.

11 One of the social courtesies which he was punctilious in performing, cf. *Orr*. 1.105; 2.21f.

12 Reiske saw this as an expression of the rebelliousness of youth, as opposed to his old age, but it is more likely to be their support of the new-fangled studies as opposed to his Greek education; cf. *Or*. 3.24.

13 The staff of the various officials stationed in town. For the general prejudice against the 'military', cf. *Or*. 47 *passim*; Harmand (1955), 165ff.

14 On fees, cf. *Or*. 3.6 with note *ad loc.*, *Or*. 31.19ff.

claim the same treatment from them, too? And what is my habit? Those who wish to do so, pay; those who refuse, do not. And how few are those who wish to pay, how many those who do not! For the poor man, his poverty, for the well-to-do his wealth is the reason for his failure to pay, for the well-to-do thinks that he is conferring a favour by becoming a pupil. Nobody can come anywhere near the care and rectitude that I display towards you. So if this present crime is discovered to be the work of any of you, then it is the most obvious thing in the world that I am foully wronged, for I have got evil in return for good.

(10) But now I must show that my conduct towards my assistant teachers has been beyond reproach.[15] The old professor from Ascalon[16] always used to harry them, causing them to fear a thrashing and even administering it. As soon as he made his appearance, every one of them had to jump up from their chairs, stream towards him at the double and escort him, and only return to their seats at a sign from him; they could not look him in the face, but with bowed head they had to acknowledge his pre-eminence. In consequence no one would attend anyone else's lessons but all that time had to attend him and his lectures. I leave aside mention of his new-fangled sort of tribute of students,[17] and the way the slave whom he employed on his pupils exacted this tribute, and how the assistant masters trembled when there was any deficiency in these payments. (11) When he died, the successor to his position, also from Palestine,[18] could have enjoyed the same privileges, but his qualities possibly did not approach those of his predecessor. He barely knew most of them, even to their names, and kept apart from the other teachers and held his classes in various odd corners. (12) I have behaved like neither of them: I have avoided seeking to dominate them, as the first did, and my qualities are totally dissimilar from the second. I am on terms of intimacy with all, claiming no especial prerogative on any issue, but associating with them on an equal footing. They can laugh and joke and poke fun. Sometimes I give them the lead in this, sometimes I follow theirs. And if I am told that they have students with them with

15 On assistant teachers, cf. Wolf (1952), 61ff.

16 Ulpianus (cf. *RE* XII, 2487), the sophist whom Libanius was attending when he experienced his 'conversion' to study (*Or.* 1.8), not Aedesius, as Foerster (note *ad loc.*) suggests.

17 Ulpianus, a veritable martinet, demanded a cut from the fees paid to the assistants by students.

18 Zenobius of Elusa, Libanius' predecessor, *Or.* 1.96, 104ff., *BLZG* 315.

beards[19] on their chins, my reaction is not one of offence; I have refrained both from annoyance and from touting for extras. I have not sought to remedy the sale of my family estate by the acquisition of other property,[20] and when I see some of them exchanging poverty for riches, I have rejoiced with them in their good fortune without feeling any personal resentment. **(13)** Not even when some of them put on airs and become haughty in consequence of their friendship with the governors have I lost my temper and sought revenge, but despite my recognition that such an attitude was deplorable, I none the less saw fit to endure it. And though pupil after pupil every day attached themselves to different teachers, thus breaking the rule laid down,[21] for all my annoyance at their numbers, I held my peace so as not to be annoyed, and steeled myself against any fresh departure from the norm. In this matter I could reveal my attitude at greater length, but I think that what I have said is enough. So if any teacher knows how that piece of magic practice found its way into this place, he would be unable to claim that he was revenging himself on me.

(14) Since I have so conducted myself towards every one, I thought that, upon this manifestation, the city would be stirred like the waves in Homer,[22] and that all would urge one another to make inquiry into the matter, for however hard it might be to discover the truth, their good intentions at least should have been demonstrated. As it is, so far from displaying such anger and adopting a fitting attitude to such a heinous crime, they have shown themselves hardly any different from men asleep. Not a single one of them set up an outcry or smote his thigh or raised his hand to heaven.[23] Yet they might have been excused for some mistake here and for laying hands on passers-by, however innocent of the charge they might have been. **(15)** However, when it is thought that

19 Mss. read γένεια ('chins'). Foerster reads Cobet's conjecture (γύναια = women) wrongly. Students left the *didaskalos* to study rhetoric under the sophist about the age of fourteen. The maximum age limit for a student as laid down by imperial edict was twenty, an age as well suited to whiskers as to women. The point is not so much the amatory adventures of these mature students as their backwardness. They were still in the elementary stage of their education, and paying their fees still to the elementary teachers.

20 For the personal fortune of Libanius cf. Petit (1955), Appendix 3, pp. 407ff.

21 Refers to the situation in *Or.* 43 (*q.v.*), although Wolf (1952), 48 does not accept this reference. Here Libanius hints strongly that one of the teachers in Antioch was the person responsible.

22 Homer, *Il.* 4.422f.

23 Common in Homer (e.g. *Il.* 12.162, etc.; *Od.* 13.198) as a gesture of exasperation.

a driver or a horse had been so spell-bound,[24] everything is in turmoil, as though it were the ruin of the city; yet I am treated with scant concern in the matter. The report of my sufferings has soon passed: it is regarded either as nothing out of the way that I am laid low, or as a very good thing that I should not be of the same frame of mind as before, and that I should not look forward to rhetoric and declamation and my former pursuits, but to my death, my funeral and a tomb, and that I should resent any mention of the baths or any invitation to dine.[25] This is the reward that I have got from the present inhabitants of the city.

---

24 For magic to fix the winner in chariot racing, cf. Amm. Marc. 28.1.27.

25 His depression is described in identical terms in *Or.* 1.246, a passage written at about the same time as this speech.

ORATION 34:
AGAINST THE SLANDERS OF THE PEDAGOGUE

INTRODUCTION

This speech appeared in the aftermath of the Riots of the Statues in Antioch of February A.D. 387 (for which see Libanius, *Orations* 19–23; Jo. Chrys. *Hom. de Statuis* (Migne, *PG* 49)). These had followed directly upon a sudden demand by the imperial authorities for an extraordinary levy of taxation, which had proved the last straw for a long-suffering civilian population. Protests arose immediately but, without warning and, according to Libanius, by the intervention of evil spirits, protest degenerated into mass violence. The portraits and statues of the imperial family were stoned and demolished by the rioting commons in a spontaneous outburst of mob frenzy – an enormity which gave a name to the whole incident. The authorities, taken completely by surprise, reacted vigorously. Martial law was imposed; arrests and executions followed, and the popular frenzy was immediately transformed into popular panic, with a mass exodus of civilians of all classes ensuing, fearful that the military would be let loose upon them in reprisal for their treason. In the event Antioch was lucky. A commission of enquiry with summary powers was despatched, and Antioch was stripped of civil and metropolitan status; local administration and amenities – baths, entertainments, markets and distribution – were closed, and the exodus continued with great distress among the refugees in the countryside, as dire rumours of the wrath to come gained ground. The leaders of the Christian community attempted to maintain morale in the city, the Bishop posting off to Constantinople to intercede with the Emperor for the city, and John Chrysostom remaining to comfort the remnant of his flock with a score of Homilies, while amongst the pagans Libanius and some of the more influential used their eloquence to bombard the commissioners with pleas and petitions for moderation and clemency. In this they were successful. The first punishments exacted, the two commissioners showed commendable thoroughness in their investigations and openness to petitions, and their report was conveyed to the Emperor with all speed by Caesarius, the civil investigator, while the military commissioner

Ellebichus kept order in Antioch. Their recommendations for clemency were heeded, and on Palm Sunday (so Chrysostom) the imperial despatch granting pardon was received in Antioch, to universal relief, the Bishop himself returning in triumph on Easter Day.

The whole episode had lasted thirty-four days (so Libanius, below §6), and Antioch could then struggle back to some semblance of normality as civic life and amenities were restored and refugees trickled back. Christians could and did claim numerous converts because of the staunchness which their leaders had shown in the emergency, while Libanius could congratulate himself on the success of the oratory he had deployed on behalf of his community.

Yet such success masked growing insecurity. In consequence of his permanent settlement in Antioch in A.D. 354 he had, more and more as time went on, removed himself from direct access to the corridors of power that he had once enjoyed, as death and age reduced the scope and influence of his tried and trusted friends and contemporaries. He risked being marginalized and classed as out-dated, despite the undoubted increase of his professional prestige as evidenced by his status as *honoratus*. He had long acknowledged the reduced importance of his Greek studies *vis-à-vis* Latin and law (*Or.* 1.154). He had withstood personal criticisms of his deportment, as in *Oration* 2, or general carpings about his ill success as a teacher, as in *Oration* 62, but these had been from individuals of his own social class. Now, however, he was to experience the insults of a pedagogue, a mere employee of a lower social status operating on the fringe of the educational system, who took it upon himself to criticize his conduct in the normal day-to-day workings of his school with allegations of time-wasting, favouritism, lack of direction and deficiencies in curriculum. Comments of this kind from a pedagogue who so refused to accept his proper place in the system ran counter to all academic tradition.

The allegations of time-wasting, which go so far as to include Libanius' absence due to ill-health, are countered by the recital of the voluntary absenteeism of the complainant in and, more important, after the thirty-four days of the emergency, coupled with the justification of the convention of days off, whether as reward for the whole school for a successful declamation by a student of merit (§4), or, in the case of days of mourning, as a necessary part of a student's education in his social duties (§22), or, in the attendance at the public declamations of the professor, as an integral part of his education as being models of what he should attain (§26f.). Favouritism is dismissed by the recital of the virtues and abilities of his prize pupil (§3) as compared with the deficiency and lack of progress of the delinquent complainant (§§6, 15f.), while Libanius is at his most eloquent in his rebuttal of any criticism of his curriculum and in his assertion of the value of the teacher acting as model for his pupils in the practice of declamation, arguments which in themselves are denials of any lack of direction on his part.

In no other speech is there such detailed information about the day-to-day routine of classwork in his school. Teaching is normally given to sets of ten or so (§15). Advanced composition is to be preceded by detailed study and appreciation of a text (§16), and individual tuition for laggards delegated to an assistant and supervised by Libanius himself. Vacation study is essential to consolidate past progress and to prepare for the work to come in the following session. Individual students, as reward for their progress, are to be encouraged to deliver set declamations of their own (§3), and to give demonstrations of their capacities (§27), not only for their own advancement but for that of their fellows, the whole being a mix of individual competitiveness and group sharing and co-operation. Standardized the system may have been: inhumane it was not, but ingrained in it and essential to it was the respect for educational convention that our pedagogue so blatantly ignores.

In all probability the precise timing for this speech is to be found in the interval between the return to normality following the ending of the emergency at Easter A.D. 387 and the ending of the school session in the midsummer of that year. First, Libanius' language in referring to the crisis has an immediacy reminiscent of his comments on the refugees in *Oration* 23, the only one of his speeches on the Statues at all contemporaneous with the events. Equally graphic and detailed is the narration of the circumstances which occasioned the pedagogue's original complaint. The appropriate time for a student to show his paces in declamation is likely to be at the end of a scholastic session, and of the one in which three months of teaching time have allegedly been wasted. Moreover, despite the pedagogue's complaints of inordinate concentration upon the study of Homer and Demosthenes, he does not mention the Latin teacher or the studies in Latin which are to appear frequently in later sessions. Our pedagogue is thus likely to have been the first and lowliest, but not the least hurtful, of the critics who, like Thrasydaeus (*Or.* 32) and Eustathius (*Or.* 54), took issue with him for various reasons in the year following the riots.

Accessible editions of the text are those of Reiske (II, 266–83), and of

Foerster (III, 88–206). For a translation in French, see Festugière (1959), 476–83.

AGAINST THE SLANDERS OF THE PEDAGOGUE[1]

(1) It is no more right to regard at fault people who have insulted me than it is you, my pupils,[2] since you have so easily tolerated this insult. They deserve reproof for their actions, but you would deserve it for feeling no pain at their behaviour, and you join the ranks of those who commend them, simply by not punishing them. If you say that you know nothing about it, the very fact that you know nothing of such things is dreadful: if you do know and you do not think them dreadful, how can you avoid the appearance of disloyalty? (2) Now, if it had been due to any negligence on my part that this impertinent pedagogue had said such things, in my shame at hearing the truth and in my belief that I myself had provided the occasion for such remarks, I would hold my peace, for I would not be able to accuse him: his accusations would be just. As it is, I know no other man alive who has been so shamelessly traduced. And I am ready to demonstrate this, for, while those who know the pleasure I derive from my work understand me well enough, there is a risk that some of those who do not thoroughly understand my attitude towards my students in class, may be deceived. Hence it would be as well for me to describe the circumstances which gave rise to the insult I have received.

(3) One of my pupils delivered a declamation with preliminaries.[3] He was fifteen years old, an orphan, and a quite exceptional student. He in particular had overcome all unseemly pleasures, and he could, if he so wished, relate the success of his ancestors as revealed both in the civil service and in military commands.[4] However, the lad's chief credential

---

1 *Or.* 34, ed. Foerster (III, 88–206); *Or.* 32, ed. Reiske (II, 266–83).

2 This address to his students took place in the *Bouleuterion* (City-Hall complex) where friends among the curial intelligentsia could foregather and observe the students' progress.

3 This pupil delivered a declamation consisting of a discourse (*agon*) following an introduction (*proagon*), the terms being those of the Athenian stage, as is also *chorus* of §18.

4 The imperial service from Diocletian onwards was sharply distinguished into civil and military. The *officiales*, civil servants (Greek, στρατιῶται = soldiers) served in their various departments with uniform denoting rank; cf. *RE* XVII, 2047ff. (*s.v. Officium*). The term here used for military commands (*hegemonia*) had in the early Empire been used for both provincial and military commands, *praetors* and *propraetors*.

was his modesty which was beyond the reach even of the evil-mouthed. Someone else might have added to this his readiness and fairness in paying his dues and his regard for any payment he made as being but a trifle. **(4)** Commendation of the delivery of the declamation consisted chiefly of making no addition at the end of it – in fact, there is a long-established custom to this effect, and nobody, no student, no attendant has dared criticize that. So off he went amid applause. Then I had to do my piece, namely to add nothing further after the speech made by my student. So I sat talking with some people, friends of mine, and somehow the conversation drifted to the time when I put a stop to Phila-grius' rage,[5] when he started to have the bakers flogged in full view of all. **(5)** My friends had retired to bathe before their meal when my slave ran up and told me that some rascally attendant, pedagogue of a student who was just such another, was at the doors shouting that the lad had been robbed of three months of tuition. His remarks were intended to upset the custom and to rob the declaimer of his long-established due, for, in my opinion, he begrudged the lad who had just finished his declamation his renown. But it was far better to emulate him in what he did and to gain the same reward as he did, than not to be able to do so and yet try to denigrate him for it.

(6) However, I must make clear that he was a liar. He says that three months have been wasted. How so, dog-face?[6] Our late tribulations lasted for thirty-four days, and when our troubles were resolved by the Emperor's despatch,[7] there was nothing to fear and classes could recommence. In fact, you personally were one of those who made the most of the opportunity – or, more accurately, if you did not but, fearful of a terror that was past, you lay skulking and having a good time on your estate, that is your fault, not mine. In good sailing weather, if people rob

---

5 Philagrius (*BLZG* 237(ii); *PLRE* 693(2)) was an old correspondent of Libanius who had taken part in Julian's Persian expedition of A.D. 363. He was appointed *Comes Orientis* (Count of the East), with headquarters in Antioch, in A.D. 382 at the beginning of a famine that was to last for another two years. To overcome the shortage of bread he resorted to the time-honoured method of publicly flogging the bakers, which Libanius by his protests succeeded in stopping, thereby strengthening his claim to be a patron of the working class and actually restoring the bread supply for a time. Cf. *Or.* 1. 206ff.; *Or.* 29.6f.

6 A classical insult (Homer, *Il.* 1.225), and so to Libanius' liking; cf. *Or.* 3.35.

7 The imperial despatch ending the emergency reached Antioch on Palm Sunday (Jo. Chrys. *Hom. de Stat.* 21 (Migne, *PG* 49.211ff.)). The riots therefore broke out in early February, just about at the start of Lent.

themselves of the chance to sail, it is the fault of those who do not sail, not of the sea which invites them. If you had come to my lessons and done what learners do, how have you lost the profit of three months? **(7)** Indeed, the very length of your absence you have not lost through me or my negligence: it is the punishment of your own shortcomings. Just come out and prove that I ever made any alarming statements fore-casting armed force, expropriations, massacres and arrests, or that I said that any sensible person should seek safety in flight. If I have never said any such thing, and if you are the ones to persuade yourselves of this, then obviously you should blame yourselves, and with justification. If villains had attacked you either *en route* to or already arrived on your estate, as happened often enough when panic-stricken refugees by their own troubles made things better for brigands, – well, if you both lay dead at the hands of those mass murderers, must I be the one to pay the price for the lives of the pair of you? Must the lad's father have to come and demand it of me? **(8)** If he had done so, to any sensible person he would have seemed mad, and so do you when you talk to me about those wasted months. It could not be said, either, that while not recom-mending you to leave, I commended you when you had done so. To think of all the anger I vented! The protests I made! The times I exclaimed that such a departure was suicidal, sheer madness, a dread of unreal disasters and a reckless acceptance of very real ones![8] This pair, like scores of others, probably heard all this, but despite that they thought they knew better. **(9)** And by their very own actions they testify to the fact that I never said that they should depart. Having readied themselves to go to their estate and with their minds made up, they cleared off, using every trick to avoid attention. They acted without prior notice of their intention, for they were afraid that they would hear words that would restrain them – words that in themselves could possibly persuade them.

(10) Although they are themselves responsible for their absence from class, they have the cheek to cast the blame for their own decisions upon me who protested at their removal of themselves from my lessons, – just like someone who deliberately goes to a waterless place, and then goes to a fountain upon which he had turned his back for some days, and reproaches the springs with the tale of all the days he had not drunk from them; they might reply, 'Well! From us, anyway, water kept on

---

8 A topic developed at more length in *Or.* 23, the oration nearest in time to the events.

flowing, and we would never refuse anyone who wanted to drink it.' **(11)** Good Heavens! If someone left the part of the world that basks in sunlight, went into the Cimmerian gloom,[9] stayed there for some months, then returned to the place he had deliberately left and blamed any Tom, Dick or Harry who had nothing to do with the business, would not he be a humbug? You are the one who robbed yourself of the light: then you should be the one for you to punish.

(12) Now, that they went there out of a desire for idleness while pretending an eagerness to get down to work is obvious from their neglect of any activity conducive to the memorization of classical literature,[10] and also from the fact that the lad returned well-fed and with plenty of flesh on him. More confirmation still is that his return occurred well after that of the majority of his fellows. By his speed of departure and his slowness of return he confesses, without a word said, his pleasure in the one and his resentment of the other.

(13) If you had any regard for study, you should take a look at me. I stayed. You could have done the same, too, if it had occurred to you that I had a better appreciation of my duty, if for no other reason, then because of my advanced age, – for we know how much our leading poet[11] attributes to that. As it is, you have dubbed me suicidal, yourselves perspicacious, and by revelling your time away on your estate, you have damaged your education.[12] Why! When you did finally condescend to return, how could you accuse me here of having, despite your eagerness for my lessons, refused to allow you to participate in them? **(14)** I never stopped my efforts of help in that respect, even though the numbers of my pupils were reduced in size to a mere dozen, and then to seven. I went to the schoolroom even for such a handful, and did so no more reluctantly than before. My treatment of those few was exactly the same as it had been with a larger number, and I made no alteration in my teaching routine. In fact, the stayers-on got quite a good name for themselves from having stayed on. You too could have been one of those if you had wanted to be. As things are, you have spent so many days in

9 In Homer (*Od.* 11.14) a people living in perpetual darkness beyond the Ocean. This becomes a proverbial expression. For Herodotus and the later geographers, however, they become real people located around the Crimea.

10 In theory, then as now, a good part of the long vacation is to be spent in revision of and preparation for academic work in term-time; cf. *Ep.* 894.2.

11 Homer, referring to Nestor; cf. *Il.* 1.257ff., 2.370ff. Libanius was now aged 73.

12 'Education', lit. 'the (studies) of the Muses'.

toping, and now you have come back full of eagerness for study and
expect your insulting remarks about me to count for more than all that
time.

(15) 'Yes,' comes the reply, 'for we have spent days without end
debating upon Homer and Demosthenes.'[13] The reason for this, though,
is to be found in the curriculum, not in me. You had completed part of it
– and I make no mention of the time it took you – and you could not
possibly proceed to more advanced composition straightaway: you had
to go through a text prior to that, and not to do so alone but along with
another nine or so students, in any case not much less.[14] (16) To set a
precedent for a single scatter-brain would be utterly ridiculous and
would prejudice the whole programme. So a different teacher from
myself conducted the reading, and did so under my direction. And this
teacher was so good at it that you never uttered a word of complaint:
you even expressed admiration for him, for all your ability in speaking
ill.[15] So, while you got that from him, I personally corrected your exercises and set things to right, and you had two of us instead of one. There
was no case of doing nothing in this; you gained two for the price of one.

(17) If you talk to me about my gout,[16] you should complain against
Fortune, not against me. For surely you will not go on to say that I
wanted to be ill, to pass day and night groaning with pain, and spending
more time with my doctors than with my books. My teaching was not as
burdensome as the distressing and enforced experiences I underwent,
which caused more pain than the pain they sought to cure. I have resorted
to many shifts to cure my gout, but they have produced nothing substan-
tial – merely hopes. (18) So, instead of sympathizing with me, do you
accuse me of neglect? Is fate to be held unaccountable, and I responsible
for what I am not? This is tantamount to reproaching a dead man for
not being able to do anything because he is no longer alive. But on his
behalf the Fates and their decrees could be adduced: it was because of
them that he had to die, and any activity on the part of the dead would

13 As part of their exercises the students had to practise rebuttals of statements of
Homer and Demosthenes, the models for poets and orators.

14 Libanius, for teaching purposes, evidently grouped his students into groups of ten or
so. Quintilian also recommends that pupils be divided into classes (1.2.23).

15 A *double entendre*, (i) verbal abuse or disparagement of others, (ii) inability to speak
well or personal incompetence.

16 Libanius' gout or arthritis had recurred in full force at New Year A.D. 386 after a
remission of 16 years, cf. *Or.* 1.243.

be out of the question. If I were captured by brigands and lay in chains, you would not accuse me of not performing my job of teaching the young, but, now that I am held by a far more painful – and, I might say, more powerful – bond, do you expect me to supervise students? Do you expect the very man who cannot move a step to be able to dance?[17] **(19)** A soldier, eager for combat and for the fray, yet suddenly stricken down with illness, sees his commander vexed but not putting him on a charge, and no one is so irrational as to prosecute such a man for desertion. And I? If, under the same compulsion, I have abandoned any of my usual practices, am I to have someone haling me into court? What sick man was ever found guilty simply because he was sick? None, save any who brought the sickness on himself! There are reasons enough for a man to fall sick. Even in gymnastic competitions we have often seen athletes fall sick and not even able to strip, and being greeted by the spectators with pity, not with blame, and the same when they returned home, by their own people. Their case would be described as one of bad luck, not of bad conduct. **(20)** And, moreover, in the home city of this pair it has not passed unnoticed that I have been stricken with such an affliction, and that through it I have had to take to my bed every year for some days without uttering a word, for it is near enough to our own and there is much coming and going between one and the other. So, why did you not go to other professors who were not ill? If you did come prepared to put up even with this, why do you not put up with it now that you have come? Plenty of people before you have done so, and plenty do now – in fact, all except you. Are you the solitary devotee of lessons? Are all the rest, so many of them, motivated by the desire for something different? **(21)** You will not admit this openly, but you confess it by your actions. I wonder what you would do if my affliction, so quickly over, had lasted as long as it often has done, for, instead of three weeks' duration, I have, by grace of the gods, been bed-bound for only a third of that time. What would you do then in a time-scale like that, when this is how you behave in one so much shorter?

(22) He even complains of the marks of respect I accord to the dead, whether they be friends of mine, or notables, or both, or neither but yet having some claim through their kinsfolk. He is not ashamed to commence hostilities against those no longer capable of causing pain to anyone but who are now subject to a far different lot. I would have been

17 'Dance' masks another *double entendre*, (i) literal, (ii) figuratively = 'school'.

very proud personally to have instituted such a rule, but, since others have been beforehand in that, its maintenance is a noble thing, to follow the mourners, and not to be outdone by the governors, whom I know to observe this practice tirelessly right up to the day of their death, even if funerals follow straight one after another. **(23)** And nobody is so senseless or graceless as to complain of such a show of respect. Some of the teachers even act as bearers, with their own hands lifting up those laid low by fate, while those who could not do so, by not[18] engaging in teaching class, paid their respects to the funerals, for they thought it of the utmost importance to instruct their pupils in the deference due to the dead. **(24)** But this fellow carps at this as a waste of time, accuses me for not breaking a rule of such antiquity, and bids us regard nothing as less deserving of respect than the dead. Yet what would you expect to happen to your own father, if he were to die while you were away at school? If he were to be of those accorded such tokens of respect, why will you deprive everyone else of them? If he were not, what would be the fitting punishment for you for that? **(25)** Besides, he would not dare to say either that this place has not produced many gifted orators. Some of them have shone in the courts of law, others in the dispensation of it, and yet others in the services rendered to their native cities. And each and every one of them has shown this ability while respecting this custom. If it is possible both to gain fame while maintaining the custom and in no way to be harmed as regards one's education, and if it is possible for them both to go hand in hand, what justifiable excuse is there for insulting the dead?

(26) But what makes one choke with rage is that they count the days devoted to professorial declamations among those wasted. How, you filthy beast, how can eloquence harm eloquence? How can anyone who produces a model which should be imitated be at fault as regards eloquence? I maintain that, while silence on the teacher's part is detrimental to his pupils, the flow of the teacher's words is an encouragement to them to be able to do the same. We have even seen physical trainers too, I am sure, teaching the art of wrestling in their schools with personal exhibitions, and also archers shooting their arrows for the instruction of their pupils, – anyway, we know that Apollo produced many archers in this way. **(27)** So, too, if anyone wishes to produce orators, let him provide himself as a model to his young aspirants, and if he refuses to

---

18 'Not' of the Mss. wrongly omitted by Foerster upon Reiske's suggestion.

deliver a speech, let the student avoid him like the plague and cleave to the one who is both composer and deliverer of speeches, and try to get himself ready for producing the like. Moreover, if among those still under instruction there is engendered an urge to declaim, let them have their lecture room, and let no one believe that this redounds to their credit only, but rather to that of all who drink of the same cup. **(28)** And when he has finished let no one go to the teacher and say that nothing has been done. Something salutary has been done: the better ones have improved in their critical faculty, the not-so-bad in their approach to their work, those deficient in any way in their ambition to equal the others. However if, after the assembly is dismissed, there are those who crowd around their teachers, sit them willy-nilly on their chairs and give them no time to breathe, these are insolent, denigrating the speaker with their cries that he has been boring.

(29) I have not compromised my principles, nor will I do so, nor will I fear the slanders of a wretched pedagogue. The cowards among you I hope to see, at long last, plucking up courage and recognizing themselves for what they are, and you too, my lads, hating those who have given me offence – something which, even if now present in your souls, this wretch with his insults would expel. This fellow, for whom the student's father thanks his lucky stars, as being a wall and a barrier stronger than any chamber of Danae,[19] – he is amenable to any who treat him kindly. If the lad is invited to lunch, he lets him go; if to dinner, he sends him off, giving the host the bonus of not accompanying him to the meal. **(30)** And, for all this behaviour, this nonchalance, these favours, he still thinks fit to terrorize the teachers; he confronts them with a hostile glare, thinks of nothing as good enough, everything as less than he deserves, looks for means to upset people, giving them pain on his entrance, pleasure on his departure. He denigrates the teacher currently employed and lavishes his praise on another, and by the threat of transferring the student elsewhere, he reduces to slavery the teacher who is afraid of that happening. **(31)** No! it is certainly not the lad's father and namesake who had occasioned such a speech as this. He was not a bad

19 For the pedagogue's duty of protecting his charge both in conduct and in morals, cf. *Or.* 58.7. Danae, daughter of Acrisius, legendary king of Argos, was cooped up in a brazen tower in consequence of an oracle foretelling that her son would be responsible for Acrisius' death. Zeus, however, visited her in a shower of gold, and Perseus, the result of this union, duly killed his grandfather, accidentally.

lad himself, nor did he have such a pedagogue as this one, but a decent, prudent and sensible man who protected his charge and kept him away from all improprieties, one who did not disturb the order of things and did not arrogate to himself anything beyond that allowed by convention, one, in fact, who knew just what the difference is between being a teacher and a pedagogue.

ORATION 42: FOR THALASSIUS

INTRODUCTION

After the riots of A.D. 387 the relations between Libanius and the *principales*, the leaders of the *curia* in Antioch, worsened rapidly. The reason for this is ultimately the long-established imperial policy of enforced recruitment to the *curia* and its application by the leaders in Antioch in so far as it affected his professional position and associates and also his bastard son Cimon, whose status had been legitimized (*Or.* 1.195f.), and who thus became a potential recruit. Between A.D. 387 and Cimon's death in A.D. 391 a series of attempts to recruit Libanius' closest associates were made by the *principales*, all of which were resisted by him with a sustained and single-minded ferocity.

The breaking point came by accident in the summer of A.D. 387 when, in consequence of nominations for an embassy, for which Libanius had been made responsible by the military commissioner Ellebichus, still in charge of Antioch, the *principalis* Thrasydaeus conceived a bitter hostility towards him, impugning his sophistic immunity, claiming Cimon for curial service, and alleging treason against Libanius himself as a secret supporter of the usurper Maximus (*Or.* 32; *Or.* 1.257f.). This last charge was to hang over him for a full year. He is not finally cleared until the receipt of the decision of the prefect Tatianus (*Ep.* 846) later in A.D. 388.

Another member of this same embassy was Libanius' assistant Eusebius (*PLRE* 305(24)), 'the sophist', who was only induced to participate on the firm undertaking that this would not prejudice the sophistic immunity which he already enjoyed. Needless to say, the curials tried to double-cross him, and claimed him for curial duties, on the grounds that he had, by this service as ambassador and despite this agreement, relinquished that immunity. Libanius took up the cudgels on Eusebius' behalf with orations (*Or.* 32) and voluminous correspondence, and Eusebius succeeded in fending off persistent attempts to recruit him. However, his position was not to be secure for the two years following this embassy, despite, or perhaps because of, the enthusiastic support of Libanius, who in A.D. 388 extended his criticisms of the *principales* in

Orations 48 and 49, in which he roundly accused them of a lack of even-handedness in their treatment of recruits and deliberate victimization of their fellow decurions of lower degree.

In the meantime, more friction arose in A.D. 389 following the death of his old friend Olympius, who paid him the doubtful honour of naming him principal legatee in preference to his own brother Miccalus (*Or*. 63; *Or*. 1.275ff.). This involved him in more than the usual testamentary litigation attendant on such questions of inheritance, and generated much ill-will against him, since because of his existing immunity the council was deprived of a source of much-needed revenue.

It was therefore not surprising that the councillors should continue in their efforts to curb Libanius and his clique. The obvious targets were his son Cimon, whose status had long been known to be a source of anxiety to him (*Or*. 1.145, 195f.), and yet others of his professional associates, of whom the most prominent was his secretary Thalassius. They could well afford to wait for Cimon, for, in view of his father's age and uncertain health, he would in no too distant time become available to them. Thalassius, however, was ripe for the picking. He had been long resident in Antioch, was well known in upper-class circles, certainly enough to have upset some people, and he did not have Eusebius' advantage of the possession of sophistic immunity from curial obligations. As Libanius admits, his fortune was adequate, and indeed he had already had a foretaste of what might come in A.D. 389 when the governor Eustathius had requisitioned a ship of his for the corn supply (*sitegia, Or*. 54.47). As the pressures against him mounted, his attempts to evade the dubious honour of curial status, with all the ruinously expensive obligations it involved, became more desperate, and in A.D. 390 he went to the extreme by applying for membership of the Senate in Constantinople, despite the mass of legislation designed to prevent such evasion.

His manner of approach is outlined in this oration. He had never held any office which guaranteed senatorial rank, so that his chosen method was to be that of co-optation. He therefore submitted his application, with details of his financial standing, to the appropriate imperial bureau, and received the diploma conferring upon him the status of *vir clarissimus*, the lowest grade of senator. This, however, was provisional only upon acceptance by the Senate itself, which, as it was evidently entitled to do, formed itself into a court of enquiry to investigate his credentials, under the presidency of the urban prefect of the city (*PVC*), Proclus. Should he survive this scrutiny, his position as *vir clarissimus* would be confirmed, he would proceed to undertake the praetorship which involved the payment of the *summa honoraria*, a lump sum proportionate to his fortune, and he would thereafter be free from impressment by the *curia* and the constant drain upon his resources which the performance of the liturgies involved. Here, however, things went wrong. Three of the most influential senators, Proclus, the prefect in charge of the session, Optatus, himself to become *PVC* inside the next decade, and an unnamed military man who can only be Ellebichus, heretofore a steady supporter of Libanius, combined in opposition to Thalassius' candidature on the grounds of his lowly origins and the 'sordid' source of his income, ownership of a sword factory, no less, and personal failings towards them, and they carried the Senate with them. Despite the testimony of witnesses presented by Thalassius with the blessing of Libanius, he was black-balled.

Libanius' reaction was to try again for a review of the case. By midsummer A.D. 390 he sent a string of letters to acquaintances at court, whom he numbered among his friends (*Epp.* 922–30, 932, 936–7), including the three chief opponents, asking them to use their influence to secure a change of mind. This too was unsuccessful: Thalassius' application was steadfastly refused, and probably for the reason that Libanius nowhere mentions, that Thalassius was in fact liable to curial obligations.

The final episode in this story comes later in this same year with the composition of the present oration, written ostensibly to the Emperor in explanation of Thalassius' course of action and extolling his merits as a teacher and philosopher – there are strange echoes here of the arguments of the *Demegoria Constantii*, whereby the Emperor Constantius had presented the philosopher Themistius for membership of the Senate a generation before. This is combined with some of his choicest invective in character assassination of the three chief opponents, and concludes by commending to the Emperor an alternative means whereby Thalassius might obtain senatorial status. The method of co-optation being ruled out, the Emperor himself should appoint him direct to an official post which would automatically confer upon him the right of entry. Since in later letters (*Epp.* 1031, 1057, 1059 of A.D. 392 and *Ep.* 1103 of A.D. 393), Thalassius is mentioned as being still with Libanius in Antioch, this ploy was clearly unsuccessful, if indeed the oration reached or even was intended to reach the imperial court.

The very viciousness of the sentiments and language has caused doubts as to his intentions. Seeck ((1897–1921), 250) for this reason

could not believe that the oration belonged to Proclus' lifetime but this
ignores Optatus, who was *PVC* in A.D. 404–5, well after the time when
Libanius had, presumably, died. Sievers ((1868), 160) would put it in the
class of 'Flugschrift', designed to attract attention from interested
parties at court, in the manner enunciated at the end of *Oration* 2. It is
more likely to have been a composition designed to relieve Libanius' feelings, a safety-valve whereby he might spit out his spite against fair-
weather friends at court, and restricted only to his closest friends and
associates, in the same way as the additions to the original *Autobiography* had been. In any case, he would not be likely to allow untoward
publicity on his part to hinder the efforts of Cimon to escape the *curia*,
which he had already put in train.

It remains a pungent commentary upon the hazards besetting those
members of the teaching profession who were not lucky enough to have
obtained sophistic immunity from curial obligations and upon the desperate shifts to which they had recourse to escape such burdens. Moreover,
as regards Libanius himself and his public relations, nothing is so striking
or so distasteful as the difference in tone between the public professions
of friendship, verging on sycophancy, towards high-ranking officials
like Proclus and Ellebichus, and the vilification of them in such secret
compositions as this should they happen to cross him.

Available editions are those of Reiske (with some difficulty), and of
Foerster (III, 305–33). The information it contains is central to P. Petit's
article, 'Les Sénateurs de Constantinople dans l'oeuvre de Libanios',
Antiquité Classique. 26 (1957), 347–82.

FOR THALASSIUS[1]

(1) I have come, Sire, to support a friend who has been insulted and
prevented from obtaining a position he might reasonably have obtained
in preference to many who have done so, in respect for the claims of
friendship and at the same time fearful that you should condemn me for
my silence. For you might reflect what my attitude to other people
would be if I showed remissness about such as him. **(2)** I myself am well
aware nor is anyone else ignorant of the fact that a single individual
who has grown old in teaching the young is no match for a senate which

---

1 *Or*. 42 Foerster (III, 305–33), Reiske (II, 388–419). For Thalassius, cf. *PLRE* 888(4),
BLZG 291(iv).

resents not being thought superior to the pattern of what it should be. Had it been any other emperor to listen to my arguments and assess their merits, I would have been afraid that, for all the justice of my claims, I would fail before the title of the senate, and the more important would win the day. But since the decision today will be given by one who has earned the favour of the gods by his respect for truth[2] and by his disregard for all else in legal matters and his concentration upon truth alone, I have high hopes that now too the judge will be true to himself and, if he finds the senate in the wrong, that he will not shrink from pronouncing the simple verdict, that they are in the wrong.

(3) But let me recapitulate a little, so that you may know that I had good reason to make Thalassius my friend and that their action lacks any decent excuse.

A love of eloquence possessed me from the very start, Sire, and having spent no little time as a pupil, I was induced by men of repute to allow them to share in my attainments, and I obeyed. Disregarding everything else, so much so as to relinquish my family's position,[3] and with a name for composing speeches that were not bad, I became terribly attached to the task, with Maximus to look after my declamations.[4] He died, and my orations required someone to take his place, and Fortune granted me Thalassius here, who has been so badly treated by the senate. He was, in general, far better than his predecessor, in his regard for his trust, his love of eloquence, his goodwill towards me, and, moreover, his control of his appetite and sexual desires. (4) His reward for this was to spend his life in these pursuits and for all our city to know that his time was devoted to them. As for financial reward, he has neither the need nor the desire, since he has landed property that is enough for him.[5] There are plenty of people whom the vastness of their

2 Any possible offence which might be given to a devoutly Christian emperor like Theodosius by the pagan terms hinting at his name is removed by the compliment to his rectitude.

3 A self-effacing summary of his deliberate and consistent adherence to a sophistic career, as outlined in *Or*. 1, in preference to assuming the curial position to which he belonged by birth. He generally presents this as a personal sacrifice (e.g. *Orr*. 36.12; 58.15), but the present argument is the more desirable in an oration ostensibly intended for an emperor so committed to a policy of curial recruitment and repression of evasion of curial duties, in view of the tenacity with which he clung on to his own sophistic immunity and sought to protect his family with it, although being an owner by inheritance of curial land.

4 Maximus, his secretary in A.D. 364, had died in A.D. 380; cf. *Or*. 1.184, 'who held my flock together by his services and toils'.

5 Cf. §37, below.

wealth does not check, but he even goes to considerable expense on these orations of mine, by often getting copies of them, and the causes for this are many. **(5)** However, as I have said, Thalassius was for me a gift of Fortune, and freed me of the fear I felt consequent upon Maximus' death, but he drew down upon himself, in his efforts to relieve my life of irritations, the attentions of those who begrudge success to their neighbours. They began to egg each other on, and drivelled away; they abused both of us before the more pliable of the governors, and obviously would, if they could, misuse us, just as improperly.[6] **(6)** At this juncture, a man who seemed sensible enough advised him to become a member of the senate and in this way reduce his traducers to impotence. We were not afraid of any justified accusation, but the ability of certain persons to ride rough-shod over those who did not have this capacity caused us alarm. So Thalassius followed the normal procedure in this.[7] He obtained a commendation with your signature and forwarded it to the senate for its confirmation. Straight away then Optatus[8] leapt to his feet and, raising hands up to heaven, exclaimed 'Great heavens above! Thalassius a member of our senate!'

(7) And what's wrong with that, Optatus? His mother was a free woman, his father a free man, his upbringing, though not opulent, was respectable. As things are, indeed, by the gods' will he has property: he has not diminished it by dicing, drinking or sex, but he has continually helped those of his friends in need and supported those who work for him on the produce from the land: he believes that gods exist and observe happenings on earth, and he behaves as one of such convictions should do. He has turned his back on marriage and all sexual activity, and thinks that in an old man like me he has a son, and he finds it far more pleasant not to indulge in those sexual activities than in the pleasures of other kinds of intercourse. **(8)** Horses, chariots, the stage, racing drivers and all such things have been cast aside, and while not voicing disapproval of any who delight in such pursuits, he regards

6 Improperly, by attempting to break Libanius' immunity; also, but not improperly, by impressing his son, Cimon, for curial duties, and by claiming Thalassius who, despite his position as a teacher, was not immune from them. The governor is Eustathius (cf. *Or.* 54).

7 The procedure is defined in *Cod. Th.* 6.2.13. Thalassius conforms to it precisely, but to no avail (cf. §48, below). Here he receives the diploma of the clarissimate, the lowest and most numerous section of the senatorial order, and forwards his application to the *censuales*.

8 *PLRE* 649(1); *BLZG* 226(ii).

others as proper to himself. No one has ever seen him litigating over a piece of silver or gold, or trying to wring a banker's neck, or setting up a hue and cry after any defendants, or beating up their slaves, even when they have done him wrong.[9] **(9)** He has been held in the greatest reverence by the students in his charge, and by those who employ their eloquence in the courts of law. He is respected by our city council and also by those who expect to be honoured because of offices they have held.[10] No parent has been so ignorant of the man as not to pray for his own sons to follow in Thalassius' footsteps rather than in those of their father. Indeed, Sire, you may easily realize that he has gained the name of philosopher,[11] and you are not unaware of the kind of activities by which a man may acquire the title.

(10) So this man should not be repulsed when he voluntarily seeks admission to the senate: he should be drafted in even against his wishes, and should be thought of as one more likely to give rather than to take, to honour rather than to be honoured, to make them greater rather than to be made so himself. Reflect, Sire, what the senate would be like – I am not speaking from the point of view of its wealth, but of its morals – if all its members were like him. We know that Sparta also was an object of admiration on the part of wealthy cities, though as a community she remained poor, in obedience to the god's command.[12] So I concede that all members of the senate are richer than Thalassius, but I deny that there is any more righteous than he.

(11) So it is a man like this that Optatus rejects. And what is he, himself? Whose superior is he? Whose inferior is he not? What recommendation can he make for himself? As soon as he began to learn his letters, out of dislike for them he absconded and sought refuge, lurking in some farmyard. Nobody tried to find him: his parents thanked the gods for casting him out. His nurse lamented, indeed, but her lament was that the parents had no lament for their son. The farmer who came across him, picked him up and brought him back home, they even sent

9 An interesting example of the amusements and behaviour unbefitting a gentleman includes litigiousness together with the examination of the slaves of the opposing parties.

10 The *honorati*.

11 This and the arguments of §10 were the criteria used by Constantius in recommending Themistius for co-optation into the Senate, cf. *Demegoria Constantii* (Themist. *Orationes* pp. 22ff., ed. Dindorf). Thalassius is, apparently, the unnamed philosopher of *Or.* 40.22, to whom Eumolpius (*cons. Syr.* A.D. 384) had recourse.

12 Cf. Tyrtaeus, fr. 3, Plut. *Lyc.* 6.

away empty-handed, for they thought that he had done them a hateful deed by once again bringing back a plague that had passed from them.[13] **(12)** He saw that his elder brother was doted upon because of his devotion to what was right and proper, and that prayers were offered to the gods on his behalf, and though still a boy, he had the nerve to communicate with some sorcerers and to seek his brother's death, telling them that their reward would come from the actual death of his brother. He thus corrected his inability to pay by his promise to pay. Caught in the act in such plots, he got the assistance of the victim of his plots, who gave this concession to the claims of nature, and so he was released. And shortly after, such are the tricks of fortune, this saviour of the would-be murderer and his parents all died. **(13)** And this fellow, with never a tear, buried his parents and got control of the estate. He shunned education and associated with the worst riff-raff, and from them learned to lose all sense of shame. He began to attack his elders, men who had learned how to blush and think it wrong to engage in conflict with a fellow like him, who is unversed in no vulgarity of word or deed, who shrinks from no other form of impropriety, a mere muck-stirrer.[14] With all this as his passport to disgrace, he ruined the majority of them, and has made himself an object of fear by reason of his assaults. He ought to have been expelled long ago, but he slams the door upon his betters, and exults in his power, though by rights he should be submerged by it.

(14) 'Yes! You see, he was indeed a great help to the Egyptians. They practically worship the months of his governorship.' Why, in their account they bury the period of governorship, and if they resurrect it, they hold it as an abomination. A sea of such disasters, they say, overwhelmed Egypt, with the wrong-doers ruling the roost, their victims betrayed, the market in a state of slump,[15] the populace neglected, and oratory driven into exile. **(15)** They were bound to expect all this, after

13 An abusive parody of the Oedipus legend colours the account of this domestic tragedy.

14 An Aristophanic insult, cf. *Equ.* 309.

15 Optatus was *praefectus Augustalis* in A.D. 384, a period when the Antiochene famine of A.D. 382–5 evidently had its counterpart in Alexandria. His offence is mentioned in *Or.* 28.5, where Libanius acquits him of all the charges levelled against him except the flogging of decurions (which was banned in *Cod. Th.* 12.1.85). He was not a Christian, as Reiske thought (cf. Socr. *H.E.* 6.18), and his activities were confined to the forcible recruitment to the *curia*, which evidently caused the flight of the teachers.

the wrongs done to Ptolemaeus.[16] Optatus tore him away from the very images, under whose eyes he lived a life that proceeded by prayer, libation, sacrifice and books: he was an old man now, and the whole course of time was cognizant of these virtues that were his, but for all that Optatus snatched him away from the temples, transferred him into court, had him strung up and his ribs run over with heavy hands, looking for a confession to what had never taken place, practically drinking his blood and with no reverence either for his grey hairs. Yet, at dinner parties perhaps, certainly not at lessons, for he never attended lessons, he was told how Achilles welcomed Priam,[17] father of the man who had killed the one dearest to him. But he, resenting it that the philosopher was not his tool, actually used his old age as the basis of his insults. **(16)** At this, Sire, everyone was upset at the subversion of the laws, while those whose life was spent in literature, whereby the attainment of divine philosophy may be secured, went hot-foot over the borders of Egypt, for it was impossible to escape his wrath if found within them. And the teachers of the arts that uplift and bless mankind – something in which Alexandria excels all other cities[18] – took their leave, concealing these accomplishments, since they had this precedent to spur them on, and students began to miss their teachers.

(17) And yet, even had he improved the city in other respects, and still had defiled it in this one alone, he would deserve to be punished most severely both by it and you. As it is, he has extended his harmful activity universally. At any rate, arrest followed office, and an inability to go where he liked. Control over this lay with those who had his person in their custody: it was according to their whim that he walked or stayed still, did or did not eat, slept or did not. I personally saw this and tried to offer what assistance I could by interceding with his escort,[19] not because I thought him any good, but because somehow I

16 *PLRE* 753(3). A pagan, probably a neo-Platonist philosopher and decurion of Alexandria. Optatus' treatment of him was certainly excessive, if he had him flogged as a recalcitrant decurion despite his advanced age.

17 Homer, *Il.* 24.513ff.

18 Such commendations of Alexandria are rare in Libanius. Here it is due entirely to its position as a centre of neo-Platonist philosophy. For its reputation as a centre of learning, cf. Amm. Marc. 22.16.17f.

19 Optatus travelled under escort from Egypt to Constantinople by land, so passing through Antioch as here mentioned. Sea voyages for such a purpose were hazardous and unusual.

quickly succumb to feelings of pity. **(18)** Well, he reached the capital. Everywhere it was thought that he deserved to be put to death, both for the acts he had committed and the lies he had contrived against others, but yet he found allies in plenty among the enemies of Clearchus, who were well aware that he would like this fellow put down. So he escaped by the influence of some people, though he deserved to be put to death and only remained alive to become a nuisance to Clearchus.[20] **(19)** So, he avoided the sword that loomed so close, and though everyone thought that he would spend his life indoors, keep his mouth shut and abate his insolence towards his superiors, by the very fact of his preservation he became the more insufferable. He took a delight in hounding the cream of the senate, thinking that he would, in consequence, become a man of mark without any justification, just like Thersites at Troy.[21]

(20) My point is that you should free the senate of him, not make it his slave, for I know of no other term to describe the present situation. When what he decides becomes mandatory for it, what other term is there for it? As it is, he is the biggest rascal of them all and yet wants to be their leader, and says that he is, and has them conceding it: he puts on an air of gravity, censure and reproof, and flaunts before the simpletons that Gorgon's eye of his,[22] that threatens to pop out of his head.

(21) Why, he made some mention of manufacturing swords, dubbed Thalassius a sword-maker, and so tried to get his expulsion. But Thalassius never made a sword in his life, never learned the craft or had it – nor did his father either. He had slaves to do this job, just as Demosthenes, Demosthenes' father, did;[23] and nothing stopped Demosthenes, son of Demosthenes from having slaves of this sort, and from championing the cause of Greece, rescuing its cities, pitting himself against Philip's strength and success, and being responsible for his state enjoying crowns and addresses. I could mention some Athenians who reached power, who were not just owners of slaves engaged in manufacture, but who actually came from manufacture themselves.

20 Clearchus, prefect of the city of Constantinople (*PVC*) and consul, A.D. 384, which was when his influence was at its peak. Nothing is heard of him thereafter; cf. *PLRE* 211(1), *BLZG* 108(i).

21 Homer, *Il.* 2.214.

22 As Hector did, ibid. 8.348f.

23 Plut. *Dem.* 3, Libanius, *Vita Dem.* Co-optation into the senate of people who plied such 'sordid' trades was forbidden, cf. *Codex Justinianus* 12.1.6, of A.D. 385.

(22) But let us leave aside the Athenian democracy, if you please, and the Pnyx, the speaker's platform and Solon,[24] and investigate the present position. Would anyone dare state that the senate in its entirety consisted of men of four-square decent ancestry, of people whose fathers and fore-fathers had held office, acted as envoys, performed civic services, and gone through the careers that can confer distinction? Let Optatus induce the senate to accept an investigation like this! But he won't! The whole basis of the senate is such as to prevent this, for everyone who offered himself for membership was seeking to oblige its founder, and new additions thereafter have never ceased to retain something of the same characteristics. Not that I blame them! They are often better than those with a pedigree.[25]

(23) And if I must put a name to some of them,[26] other people may perhaps speak with more authority about present members – for naturally, I believe, anyone present on the scene has true knowledge of these facts – yet as regards previous members, land and sea are filled with their story and I will relate what is shouted aloud and what nobody needs to learn, because he knows it already. Tychamenes, from Crete, the minister of works,[27] was a coppersmith's son: yet everybody knows the power Tychamenes wielded in the senate. Ablabius was native of the same island. Originally he was under the underlings of the governor of Crete: he set sail from there, and on his voyage he prayed the gods in the sea for a few pence but, when he arrived in town, he began to rule the ruler, and whenever he entered the senate-house, he was like a god

24 The Pnyx was the area of Athens where assemblies of the people were held: the speakers addressed them from the *bema*. Solon was by universal tradition, regardless of the later claims for Cleisthenes, held to be the founder of democracy.

25 Unlike the decurions of Antioch, and Libanius himself, who belong to a long-established institution and could boast of long tradition and pedigree, the Senate of Constantinople was established within living memory and, according to Libanius, largely composed of upstarts of little culture (cf. *Or.* 1.76), and the enrolments by Themistius in A.D. 358 at Constantius' orders had done little to improve it. For Libanius, its conceit was out of all proportion to its parvenu status and lack of tradition, although he was admittedly always critical of the new capital and its institutions.

26 For a similar list of upstarts, cf. *Or.* 62.11.

27 The nature of this office is uncertain. *PLRE* 927 notes that he appears first in what seems to be chronological order in a list of dignitaries of the reign of Constantine and his son who had reached this position through the newly organized post of *notarius*. It is suggested that he flourished under Constantine, and that the duty was that of general superintendence of the construction of the new capital.

among men.[28] **(24)** And what of Philippus?[29] and Datianus?[30] Philippus'
father made sausages, Datianus' was a bath-attendant, looking after the
bathers' clothes. Who were Taurus'[31] parents? or Elpidius'?[32] or Domi-
tianus'?[33] He was unjustly put to death by lynching and the rope, but he
too was son of a man who made his living by his hands. Dulcitius too
was a member of the senate. He collected gold just like Midas: he used
to commiserate with collectors of silver; and he left his father behind in
the laundry, for he was the finest fuller in Phrygia, and he became a
member of the senate.[34] He rose to be governor of Phoenicia, and of
Ionia, and nobody rose to say, 'Good grief! We've got a laundry
walking in. Far better for the senate to be done away with!'

(25) And for all these, whom I have mentioned, the door to the senate
was unlocked simply by their skill in this shorthand.[35] Thalassius, too,
has this accomplishment, as well as certain qualifications in education
by attendance on me. At any rate, many people saw many others eager
to receive his commendation of declamations, because of his ability to
assess the merits and demerits of style. Yet this guardian of the senate
has not a hint of a qualification like this. So enter the lists, where
eloquence is needed, and contend with this fellow who is unworthy of
the senate. Thus you will know what it is for the likes of you to have
insulted the likes of him, for all your victories in the senate are due to
your ranting and raving and your accomplishment in dicing. **(26)** Well,
and what actually is this fellow's family tree? Is he from one of the
founding families and legislators of Rome, or of those who won subject
peoples or protected those already won?[36] Not he! There was an

---

28 *PLRE* 3(4), Eunap. *V.S.* 463f., Zos. 2.40. Constantine put the young Constantius in
his charge. The 'underlings' were the *officiales* on the staff of the governor of Crete.

29 Flavius Philippus, praetorian prefect and consul, A.D. 348, *Or.* 1.69; *notarius, Or.*
62.11; cf. *BLZG* 237(i), *PLRE* 696(7).

30 Cf. *Or.* 62.10, and often in the correspondence, especially *Epp.* 1148, 1260. Consul,
A.D. 358; cf. *BLZG* 113, *PLRE* 243(1).

31 Praetorian prefect (Italy) and consul, A.D. 361. *PLRE* 879(3).

32 Cf. *Or.* 37.3, 11, and in the correspondence. Praetorian prefect (Orient) A.D. 360/1. cf.
BLZG 168(i), *PLRE* 414(4), *s.v.* Helpidius.

33 Praetorian prefect (Orient), lynched in Antioch A.D. 354; cf. Amm. Marc. 14.7.9.

34 For his career, cf. *BLZG* 125(iii), *PLRE* 274(5). His greed for gold and his country of
origin combine in the cynical reference to Midas.

35 For shorthand, cf. *Or.* 31.28.

36 In the fourth century, snobbery encouraged the notables at Rome to assume for themselves and their families some connection with the founding fathers. A similar snobbishness

Optatus,[37] school teacher, who taught Licinius' son[38] for the price of a couple of loaves and the rest of the rations linked with them. He happened to go on a trip to Paphlagonia, and he lodged with an innkeeper with a pretty daughter who was barmaid. He fell in love with her good looks, and asked her to marry him, and won her and got her. Well, while Licinius was emperor, he had no advantage from his marriage; but when Licinius' power passed to another, then all of a sudden the woman's husband became great, renowned, successful, a consul.[39] And because of him, people in the theatre had to take wing and fly with the birds.[40] **(27)** The woman had two brothers, decent enough people – let me give credit where credit is due – but sons of the father I have mentioned. They upped and left their birthplace, and hurried to town to share their brother-in-law's success. And that they did, and nobody brought any objection against them because of their father and his inn-keeping, for they were decent, respectable people who knew how to enjoy their success. Optatus here, the son of one of them, refused to take a leaf out of his father's book, and turned out to be a hound, and not a decent fellow. It would be much better, I'm sure, for his family to have the chance of telling all and sundry that he really was his father's son.

(28) And for you to understand the reason for his present behaviour, and that he puts on airs not from any wish to support the senate, I will give a brief account of this business too.

There is a fellow called Sabinianus,[41] who acts as ponce for good-

---

permeates all sections of upper-class society, as can be seen in the claims made by Libanius himself for his family in Antioch.

37 Consul, A.D. 334, and the first of Constantine's new patriciate (so Zos. 2.40). Cf. *BLZG* 226(i), *PLRE* 650(3).

38 Licinius was the last of Constantine's rivals as Augustus, a position he held from A.D. 308 until his defeat in A.D. 324. His son Licinianus was Caesar, A.D. 317–24. Cf. *PLRE* 509(4).

39 Here Reiske, not unreasonably, saw an innuendo, that Optatus' rise to favour came in consequence of his complaisance towards misconduct on the part of his wife, who had been, of course, a barmaid.

40 Reiske interpreted this as referring to the extravagance of Optatus' consular games. A more likely reference, however, is to Aristophanes' *Birds*, where honest men do well to steer clear of him.

41 *PLRE* 790(5). Note that Silvanus also (*Or.* 38.8) reached a position of some prominence in Antioch, according to Libanius, by providing such services. For pederasty centred around the schoolroom, see the long discussion in Festugière (1959).

looking young fellows. Time brought him to this; while ever he was a beardless lad, he required the services of ponces himself. Though he provided his services to many persons in many cities, he expended his efforts for no one so much as Optatus here, bringing grief on fathers, sons and mothers. **(29)** This task of his took him through our city too, and he had the impudence to visit my class of students, and was observed to make overtures to some of them, to buttonhole them, get into conversation with one of them up against a pillar and to behave even more improperly. He was seen and sent packing, and told that he must learn to behave himself and, if he couldn't, to go on the prowl elsewhere. Even among us he was not without aids and abettors, but he went to Optatus and, though he had not experienced anything very serious, he exaggerated the business in his relation of it, and set him, since he required his accomplishments, at loggerheads with Thalassius here in particular, through whose agency I had administered the reproof on my students' account. And Optatus continually sought means whereby he could defend the fellow, and upon the opportunity presenting itself, he did defend him, making due return for those fine favours, and at the same time working up his enthusiasm for more to come if he realized that he would not be wasting his efforts on an ingrate.

(30) And to vouch for the truth of this, I will provide witnesses whom you could not disbelieve, some for his remarks before this insult, some for those after it, some who knew what was going to happen, some who knew of his delight at its occurrence. Did ever Hector take such pride at the killing of Patroclus,[42] or Achilles at the killing of Hector,[43] as this ponce did, when his excess of joy induced him to say things better left unsaid? At any rate, he laughed and jumped for joy; he embraced and kissed his particular intimates, and exclaimed, 'This is my doing. What is done because of me may properly be regarded and described as my doing.' **(31)** So how grateful should the senate be to Optatus here for his behaviour towards us, when it is due to a quite different reason? Patroclus was not the reason for the captive women's laments: they did that because of their own troubles.[44] Indeed, if Optatus had any real regard for the senate, he would surely have Sabinianus erased from its number. One such as he is more of a disgrace to the senate than all those who cry

---

42 Homer, *Il.* 16.530ff.
43 Ibid. 22.330ff.
44 Ibid. 19.301f. This became proverbial, cf. *Corp. Par. Gr.* (Diogen. 7.47).

out in Syriac for the customers who needed them for mending their wooden bowls.[45]

(32) 'I'm the senate's watch-dog,'[46] he declares. Then why not bite those you ought to bite – the wicked. There are plenty of kinds of wickedness, but no one would include in them the ownership of slaves skilled in making swords, whereby you can protect your own country and add to what you have.

(33) So much with regard to Optatus. But as for Proclus,[47] my wish is to commend him even now, but in view of the serious and wanton insults he has employed against Thalassius and me, whatever my wish might be, I am bound to say that he has treated me badly. He sat in judgement and, for all that he should judge his cases without anyone bawling, disturbing and causing confusion to people, but rather from the standpoint of truth, he immediately diverged towards all this, and the judge became one of the oppressors in his refusal to listen to the laws which place him who will deliver the verdict as impartial to each side. (34) Optatus declared that Thalassius should not be enrolled, and abused him into the bargain. Just wait for Thalassius' advocates to speak on his behalf, or else become his advocate yourself by requiring proofs, the one thing that lends any weight to an accusation. But you refuse to take either course: then be quiet. As things are, he has transferred himself into the ranks of the witnesses and, worse still, has put Optatus into the shade in what he says. Optatus' complaint was only to do with swords. Proclus, however, said that he deserved to be put to death, and that, during his tenure of his third governorship here,[48] he had been very

45 The only explicit reference in Libanius to Syriac speakers, for him the lowest of the low.

46 Borrowed from Demosthenes, c. Aristog. 1.40.

47 For Proclus, cf. Or. 1.212, 222; Or. 10, when he was Comes Orientis based in Antioch, A.D. 384; Orr. 26.30; 27.30, 39ff.; 29.10 (where he is called by the insulting nickname Kokkos – 'pillock' – a sure sign that these orations were never widely published). He appears often in the correspondence of A.D. 388–92, when he was prefect of the city of Constantinople (PVC); cf. BLZG 248(iii), PLRE 746(6), s.v. Proculus. As such, he presided over meetings of the Senate, and was therefore in charge of this examination of Thalassius' credentials for entry. Nothing is more disconcerting than the difference in tone between Libanius' attitude towards him in the orations which remained suppressed and for private consumption, and that in the correspondence which reached a wider public. This has a parallel in his dealings with the Son of Gaison (§45 below). Libanius' relations with Proclus are examined in detail by Martin (1988), 205–11.

48 He had been governor of Palestine and of Phoenicia before arriving as Comes in Antioch in A.D. 383, cf. Or. 10.3.

eager to arrest him and have him executed; he had been upset that he had saved himself by decamping. (35) And what was the place or time of this, Proclus? What province is aware of it? What city or household? What man, boy, elder, or woman? What slave or free man? Why! Legal proceedings should precede punishment, and they could not occur without someone to initiate them. So where are these proceedings, and their initiator? What panic caused him to decamp? What accuser caused this panic? What injury caused the accusation? Who ever had cause to grieve for anyone because of him? Who ever suffered any deterioration in his fortunes? Who ever took him to court because he expected trouble from him? (36) In his silence, Sire, you have confirmation of the fact that his statement, 'He scarce escaped my onset', is mere boasting. He regards Achilles' words[49] as appropriate to himself, you see! Well! what onset? when and where did it happen? Wasn't Thalassius with me all the time, night and day? Wasn't he at my side at the delivery of my orations, and before and after it? Did not everyone, who loved my oratory and wanted to get and keep it, make his approach to him, negotiate with him, and feel grateful to him, if he succeeded in getting it, and be put out if he did not? Most important, he accompanied me on my frequent visits to you and, when I was admitted, he took his seat in the ante-room, and that was the only thing that separated us. You had people to inform you of every detail, so many indeed as to trample all over each other; you knew where Thalassius was seated, yet you neither showed resentment nor arrested him, nor yet did you threaten to do the sort of thing you have not done. (37) Well, after that you lay sick here in Antioch; he was in Samosata,[50] on the estate of which his outstanding merit had made him owner. He settled matters there to his satisfaction and returned here, you still lying sick. He gave no grounds for suspicion, nor did you suspect him. At this juncture you began to lavish unparalleled honours on me, the intimate associate of this wicked sorcerer, and to nobody had you any word to say against him, whether great or small.[51] So how can

---

49 Homer, *Il.* 9.355.

50 Thalassius' place of origin.

51 These statements should be compared with his account of his relations with Proclus as given in *Or.* 10. These first visits were evidently the formal monthly audiences made by Libanius in his capacity as sophist of the city and before his elevation to honorary office in A.D. 383. The emphatic denials of their occurrence in *Or.* 1.212 and 222f. are merely wishful thinking, evidence that the feud was a one-sided affair, mostly conducted by Libanius himself. The ante-room, separated from the audience-chamber proper by a lattice-

you say that he has escaped you, when he was in the same city, at your doorstep – close to your carriage? Moreover, I would not have been unaware of your feelings, for I too had friends who were your confidants, and Thalassius would have found out and put himself out of the reach of trouble. If it is obvious that he never took himself off elsewhere and vanished, your behaviour is an insult to him.

(38) 'I was afraid of the senate,' he explains, 'in case it should appear that I was one of those who oppose it and belittle its prerogatives.' Leaving aside the point that, however great the anger of the senate, he had no justification for resenting Thalassius because of its lack of devotion to the gods,[52] what I would like to know, Sire, is what complaint could the senate have against him, if he had kept quiet? Under what compulsion did he say what he has now said? Who would not have assumed him to be unacquainted with Thalassius? What stopped him from simply stating that he was unacquainted with him? Who would have proved him a liar, if he had said so? (39) How much more honourable to have muzzled Optatus and refuted his insults by referring to Thalassius' friendship with me! Anyway, however much Proclus might have wanted to appear in agreement with Optatus' view of Thalassius, he should have stuck to the same story and confined his remarks to the matter of the swords. He would have insulted him even with such a lying tale, but not nearly so much as now. And by insulting him he did not exclude me, either, since I have such a high regard for Thalassius. (40) Look at the sort of fellow you promote to office, Sire! He is uneducated in either language, and cannot claim knowledge of law to compensate for eloquence, for he has none of that, either.[53] He has reached man's estate through a life of pleasure, extravagance and drunkenness, and could never be induced to regard solecism as a sin. (41) It wouldn't

---

worked trellised barrier, was where the attendants waited while their superiors were admitted to the inner sanctum. They could, however, hear and see the proceedings inside, and likewise could be observed from within.

52 A covert hint of religious discrimination against Thalassius, a known pagan, by the bulk of the Senate, now mainly Christian. Proclus and Optatus, however, were themselves pagan.

53 This is strong stuff, considering that Proclus was son of an old and influential friend, the praetorian prefect (Orient) Tatianus, and was himself prefect of the city and pagan by religion. As often in Libanius' orations, alleged educational deficiencies are presented as a cardinal sin – indicating perhaps that such orations were restricted to the very select literary côterie of his own cronies.

be so bad if, despite his misuse of the language, he otherwise respected what was right and proper, but what plague has done away with so many Phoenicians as he? For Palestine he made himself worse than any plague. His tenure of office over a group of provinces[54] was more grievous than any kind of warfare. Alas, for the blood that dyed the ground! for the swords that pierced throats! For the graves that were added to those already existing! Alas, for the floggings that cause death incessantly; for the floggings that the Sun-god has seen over all his daily course![55] Alas, for the exiles, and the imprisonments! For the afflictions, both present and expected, that oppress or inspire dread! Alas, for eloquence dishonoured, and for the honours attached to ignorance! Alas, for dishonest favours! Alas, for the cities transformed into what they should never be! For the harm in what is undone and for the harm in what is done![56] **(42)** No one, says Demosthenes, could possibly recount the evils of his period of office.[57] Thus, when it was over, you could have seen the people who had got rid of him making holiday,[58] and on his entry his future subjects going into mourning. There is this much support for those who deny the existence of gods, for, 'If they existed,' they say, 'they would look after the world; and if they looked after the world, he would not be governor.' When he doesn't obtain this from you, in his claims to overreach the people in office, he makes a present of it to himself. Phoenicia knows this well enough, and would testify to it, if she could get a god to go bail for the time to come.[59]

(43) So let him govern, if you like; but let him be punished for his insults to Thalassius and to me, when he revealed the distinction he accorded me in the matter of my portrait for what it was, and showed that its intention was something different from what he

---

54 The *Comes Orientis* is regularly described as 'governor of the nations', i.e. the south-eastern provinces bordering on Mesopotamia.

55 Libanius constantly refers to his brutality as *Comes*, but Zosimus at least regards him as a good and popular governor. The reference to the Sun-god is all the more sour since he, as governor of Phoenicia, is known to have celebrated his pagan cult at Heliopolis, cf. *PLRE* 746(6). The string of lamentations following is reminiscent of those in the Lament upon Julian (*Or.* 17).

56 Possibly refers to Proclus' enlargement of the Plethron, criticized in *Or.* 10.

57 Demosth. *de Fals. Leg.* 65.

58 He left Antioch in disgrace previous to the Olympia of A.D. 384, cf. *Or.* 1.221f.

59 Cf. Demosth. *de Cherson.* 49.

claimed.[60] Actions can be judged by the consequences. Had any thought of distinction been the reason for presenting the portrait, he would have kept Optatus under control, but this was not the reason for it, and so conduct far worse than that of Optatus provided a natural sequel to Optatus. **(44)** And leaving aside his lies in the senate, the matter of the portrait, if considered in isolation, would confer no distinction either. He set it up, but he set up others before it, and of people such as no other man perhaps would have done. Even had he had my portrait done first, and then proceeded to the others, it would not have been much of an honour. But what honour is it for him to proceed from them to mine? Still, grant that paint and canvas confer distinction. Didn't the general publication of my oration confer a greater?[61] So he gained a favour, and let him be punished. It will be enough for me if you decide that the fellow is guilty of such misconduct.

(45) There is also a third person whom I can accuse, Sire, the son of Gaison.[62] After being as poor as a church mouse,[63] he became rich and came into so much money that he could build mansions of gold to vie with those of stone, and on these marble halls, too, his expenditure was so ostentatious that the business looks like madness. He had received

60 The portrait of Libanius set up by Proclus in the City Hall is clearly in official recognition of his elevation to the prefecture in A.D. 383. Libanius, however, takes umbrage because the unveiling of his portrait at this ceremony does not take precedence over others.

61 He delivered an address of thanks for this ceremonial unveiling, here adding that this conferred a greater distinction than he had received. Cf. Foerster, fr. 39 (XI, 632).

62 Gaison was the barbarian military commander of Magnentius who in A.D. 350 murdered the Emperor Constans. Here 'the son of Gaison' is a pseudonym for a real historical personage, devised as an insult, with its connotations of a treacherous barbarian regicide, in the same way that Kokkos had disguised the identity of Proclus in his orations of A.D. 384–5 (see note 47). The only one of his 'friends' at court whom Libanius approached on Thalassius' behalf on this occasion in A.D. 390 to have the qualifications of barbarian origin, military command, and senatorial status, then resident in Constantinople is Ellebichus, the military commissioner after the riots of A.D. 387 (*Ep.* 925). The other fourteen, who include both Proclus (*Ep.* 922) and Optatus (*Ep.* 923), are all civilian dignitaries. Elsewhere, Libanius has commended him in most flattering terms in his speeches, and in his correspondence (*Ep.* 898) has praised his building of a mansion and baths in Antioch. In view of the way he vilifies Proclus when he crosses him, it comes as no surprise that Libanius here vilifies Ellebichus for the 'insult' of not supporting him in this matter of Thalassius' application for senatorial membership. This is yet another indication of the very restricted publication of this speech.

63 Lit. 'after Arcadia and its poverty'. Arcadia was proverbially poor: 'acorn eaters', Herod. 1.66; cf. Paus. 8.1.6.

from me every mark of honour,[64] but to no purpose, for where he could, if he wished, have honoured me, he refused to do so, and he personally has become one of those who have injured me, since he states that any witnesses who may support me should be prosecuted by the senate. He even tried to propose that they should be brought before the house and be punished. **(46)** One of them had already crossed the straits, on urgent business, and was in Chalcedon; another, also under pressure of business, was down at the harbour about to do the same. Yet a third was still in the senate-house, and though he was greeted with black looks, he spoke sincerely and truthfully, that in giving evidence about the great merits of Thalassius' associate (myself, that is), he would be doing nothing wrong. Then, Sire, consider this statement as belonging to the absent pair also. Then all three state, 'Son of Gaison, we testify that Thalassius is a fit and proper person, for we see him to be as a son to a man who eschews the wicked.' **(47)** What will cause these witnesses to deserve punishment? If I too am wicked, the witnesses have no grounds for argument: if I am not, they have plenty. They could have presented arguments even more convincing than this, and if they had divided up their commendations between them, each could have spoken at length, so many grounds for commendation has Thalassius' career provided. Indeed, I expected the son of Gaison not to release the witness he possessed, but to recall those who had sailed away, and not just to give me that favour, but this besides, to summon Thalassius and examine him in person, and then, if he found him of good character, to enrol him,[65] and if he turned out to be a rogue, to have him punished for his criminal desire to enter the senate. As matters stand, they have made us the target for irresponsible abuse, and have acted as our enemies could wish by their unproven allegations.

(48) Moreover, Sire, although it is your ambition to increase the numbers of the senate, they don't perceive your intention and try to prevent this. People who would like to enter are deterred by fear of similar treatment, for, though it is an impossibility for a man to have no

64 He had delivered a panegyric on him in A.D. 385, *Or.* 1.232, and the mini-panegyric after the riots, *Or.* 22.

65 The vocabulary used by Libanius to describe this senatorial investigation is consistently that of the Attic law courts, despite his earlier rejection of appeal to Athenian precedent in §22. Thus Proclus is *dikastes* (§33) and Thalassius here presents his *dokimasia*. Significantly for Libanius, Thalassius had already given a full demonstration of his worth – he had delivered an oration of his own in Constantinople (*Ep.* 929).

enemy, if they anticipate that something like this will happen to them at the hands of their ill-wishers, they will not subject themselves to their enemies, but remain in their present position. But Thalassius, before reaching the senate, in spirit already performed public services and was eager to make financial sacrifice, in this behaving exactly contrary to the rest.[66] What we see them using every means to avoid, we can see him pursuing with the utmost zeal. Thus it was devotion that took him to the senate, and no expectation that his expenditure was a source of profit.[67] **(49)** But Optatus, O Zeus of Counsel, treats your devotee to a reception like this. And as for him, if the god had given the response that in a time of universal woe the vilest man alive should be sacrificed, he would certainly be the one to be put to death, since if the depths of degradation deserve to be honoured, he would win the crown. He, indeed, adduces the hatred aroused by reason of his wife as a serious indication of the city's dislike. But he hates her because he is hated, and he is hated for defiling the god of wedlock by his lusts, for enriching himself with her dowry, and for employing his riches against her from whom his riches come. **(50)** She has a twofold cause for lamentation – the girls and the boys because of whom he has failed to become the father of more offspring. When he saw her lying prostrate on the ground and in greater distress than at the death of her children, how do you think did he stop her and raise her up? Not by uttering words of consolation – not he! – nor by telling her that he would behave himself, nor yet that he would do away with himself, unless she ceased her weeping: he whetted his sword and made at her, and it was fear that fetched her to her feet. When he turns his own household into something like this, do you think that he will be responsible for any good to the senate? No! I would say that, to take Homer's words,[68] even a cobbler who lives with his wife

---

66 Cf. *Demegoria Constantii* (Themist. *Or*. pp. 24f., ed. Dindorf). As Petit observes ('Les Senateurs de Constantinople', *Ant. Class.* 26 (1957), 364, note 1) Themistius had made no such financial contribution, since he was exempted from the praetorship but had taken up residence as citizen in Constantinople. Here Libanius attributes to Thalassius his desire to have performed such citizen service and his actual willingness to undertake the financial obligations of the praetorship.

67 Cf. §6 with note *ad loc*. By the terms of *Cod. Th.* 6.2.13 of A.D. 383, the candidate must accept the *nomen senatorium* and undertake the expenses of the praetorship, which would give him the profit of curial immunity.

68 Homer, *Od.* 6.192ff.

has more virtue and is more worthy to be a member of the senate than such a plague as this fellow.

(51) Well, then, I may be asked, since there are but three who made these remarks, how comes it that you level your reproaches against the whole senate? Simply because, while these were the ones to speak out, the rest kept quiet; they abused us, and the rest did not contradict them; they slandered us, and the rest did not resent it; they attacked us, and the rest did not budge; they ejected us, and the rest did not try to retain us; they committed an act of aggression, and the rest failed to support us. So, by this silence, the conduct of the three becomes that of the whole. **(52)** In cases of fire, for instance, if anyone can put it out and refuses to do so, he commits arson. If he can rescue a child from the jaws of a hound and yet refuses, he throws it to them, and if a city can send reinforcements to a city under attack and does not do so, it collaborates in enslaving it. And if a doctor allowed an illness to get control of the patient could he really avoid blame? In general, anyone with abilities to prevent anything untoward that remain quiescent and neglect the potential damage, with no attempt to restrain it, acts in collusion with the guilty parties. For instance, I regard the Argives, who remained immobile while the Persians captured and demolished Athens,[69] as part and parcel of those who demolished it. Why did they not behave as the Spartans did?[70]

(53) Then it is with good reason, Sire, that we believe that we have been insulted by the whole body, and, on a proper view of the matter, you will find that even our complaint expresses our respect for it, for by our very disappointment we show how highly we regard the senate. Had we despised it, we could have cited Hippoclides[71] and said not a word of what you have now heard.

(54) Then console the injured party, Sire – an act that is part of the practice and custom whereby you have for so many people transformed their lamentations into rejoicings. Tell the senate that they would be better not to treat the affair in this manner, but in one more correct, more just and more prudent, and one less likely to inflict disgrace upon this devotee of the senate. So they perhaps will cure their own ills, but you, Sire, may confidently employ his abilities upon governmental

69 In 480 B.C.; Herod. 7.148–52.
70 In the Marathon campaign of 490 B.C.; Herod. 6.120; Plato, *Menex.* 240.
71 'Hippoclides don't care!', Herod. 6.129.

posts, whether you wish to entrust to him control of a single province or of several.[72] For you will find him, in matters both great and small, of such quality that you will think that your administration has lost something in times past.

72 The alternative here suggested is the direct appointment by the Emperor to a provincial governorship. This would automatically ensure Thalassius' entry into the Senate, and remove any risk of being black-balled such as was inherent in the method of co-optation. Thalassius would thereafter be *honoratus* and exempt from any curial pressures. The suggestion proved fruitless: Thalassius is still in Antioch in A.D. 392–3 (*Epp.* 1031; 1059; 1103).

ORATION 58:
TO HIS STUDENTS ON THE CARPETING

INTRODUCTION

This oration certainly belongs to the last years of Libanius' career. The Latin rhetor who is here alleged to be the person ultimately responsible for this outrage to the pedagogue had no official standing in Antioch until A.D. 388, as is clear from the sequence of events in the *Autobiography*. The institution of such a teacher is there attributed to the unnamed Christian *Comes Orientis* who entered office after the riots of A.D. 387 (*Or.* 1.255), and is also noted as being roughly contemporaneous with the quarrel with Thrasydaeus and Eusebius' success in the embassy to Court in A.D. 388 (ibid. 257; cf. *Or.* 32 *passim*). The internal evidence of this oration indicates that it follows at some interval after these events, for the sophistic in-fighting which inevitably resulted from such officially approved competition was clearly not a development of the immediate past (cf. §22; especially the implications of 'often caused transfers'). Indeed a date not before A.D. 390 may be assumed with some confidence from §16, which was rightly interpreted by Sievers as a reference to the disgrace of the *consularis* Eustathius in A.D. 389 (Sievers (1868), 191; cf. *Or.* 1.274).

The speech is yet another example of the oratory of reproof. The occasion for it is the misconduct of certain students, his own among them, acting in support of the Latin rhetor, towards a pedagogue who had remained loyal in his support of Libanius and his educational programme. Their offence had been that they had got him and tossed him up and down on a carpet – a well-known form of hooliganism in Rome (*sagatio*, cf. Suet. *Otho* 2), not unlike the practice of 'bumping' recorded in English public schools until comparatively recent times. Since the attendants and the teachers worked so closely together upon the students' behalf, the pedagogues in a body here protest against such indiscipline to Libanius as sophist of the city. They are supported by this oration, not only upon the point of principle, that it is bad in any educational system for students to treat so contumaciously the persons into whose care they are entrusted, but also upon that of self-interest, since the victim had been strenuous on behalf of Libanius himself. The warmth of such support makes §§6–14 of the speech a *locus classicus* for the representation of the ideal pedagogue. Conversely, *Oration* 34 contains some of the severest strictures against those pedagogues who arrogate to themselves the right to criticize the conduct and content of the traditional Greek teaching, and especially that of Libanius himself.

Accessible editions are those of Reiske (with difficulty) and of Foerster. For a French translation, with notes, cf. Festugière (1959), 467–75.

TO HIS STUDENTS ON THE CARPETING[1]

(1) Now too, I feel, I have need of the same remedies as I have used previously, since my students have again been visited by a distemper far more serious than some have suffered before. And, as for the actual cure, I could wish you to be like those other sufferers, with the same treatment producing the same results at this time too. This treatment consists of words of admonition and the assurance that self-control is better than a life of misconduct. In fact, I have refrained from trying to impose correction by beatings and floggings, for I have observed that these often have the opposite effect,[2] and, in my belief that the benefits accruing from advice are more advantageous and more corrective, I have resorted to this course. (2) So, since circumstances have given me ample opportunity of demonstrating this with people who are no longer merely minor offenders, I have not thought it proper to reject this method of correcting you[3] and to cast around for some other, for you, I believe, will refuse to be seen inferior to those who, by their obedience, won me renown and the pleasure resulting therefrom.

(3) The correct thing, then, was for you, by your personal actions, to reduce somewhat the troubles with which the eloquence of Greece finds itself faced in these critical times, and to withstand to the best of your ability the force of the gale.[4] In fact, by your misconduct, you add to its

1 *Or.* 58 Foerster (IV, 175–200); *Or.* 59 Reiske (III, 252–71).

2 Cf. *Or.* 2.20. Libanius at an earlier date had resorted to the corporal punishment usual in the schools (e.g. *Ep.* 1330), but, even so, not to punishment for punishment's sake (e.g. *Ep.* 1184, *Or.* 62.6). His reluctance to punish increased as he grew older, with the realization that it did little good.

3 The oration is thus another of his favourite forms of address to his pupils – that of reproof (*epitimesis*, as explicitly stated in §§4, 39). So also *Or.* 36.3.

4 For his repeated complaints about the decline of the Greek education, cf. *Or.* 1.214, 234; *Or.* 43.4ff. See Petit (1955), 358ff., Walden (1912), 119ff.

tribulations and increase its difficulties, just like sailors who, in a surging sea when the ship is buffeted by the waves, instead of trying with all their might to save the boat, aggravate the danger and the panic by their own actions. It is misguided of you, then, to fail to defend the position of this type of study in its time of trouble and distress and instead to initiate practices which will cause it to deteriorate further. **(4)** It would be cause for reproof, then, as being harmful to me, for you to attack even any of the others, that is, any of those outside the Muses' holy ground.[5] No craftsman should be misused by a student whose life is spent in education; but let the lad be at peace with them and let him not deprive himself of the praises of those who make a living by their hands.[6] Rather he should induce the tongues of such people to praise him and, so far from abusing any such person, he should endure it, even if any such abuse be directed against him by any one of them, thus revealing the vast difference that exists between the street-corner boy and the student who has been deemed worthy of initiation into the rites of Hermes. **(5)** This would be the counsel of perfection, but if you cannot be wholly perfect, confine your imperfection to abusing goldsmiths, assaulting cobblers, hitting carpenters, kicking weavers, frog-marching hawkers and threatening oil-sellers. None of this is creditable, nor is it worthy of the shrines you attend each day, but let your misconduct stay outside of them and let it not dare cross the threshold. But imagine also this piece of impropriety – not intolerable, maybe – but suppose one student falls upon another and attacks him, either with bare hands or using his book-cover[7] instead of a stone. Even though

5 The profession of rhetoric embodies the real religion of Libanius, e.g. *Orr.* 3.35; 62.8ff. Festugière (1959), 91ff. The religious terminology is all-pervasive ('sanctuary of the Muses', 'rites of Hermes'; his school is 'a temple of Hermes' (§19)).

6 For his solicitude for the working classes, cf. *Orr.* 1.205ff.; 2.6; 36.4, and especially the orations concerning Icarius (*Orr.* 26–9). From a more materialistic point of view such misconduct jeopardizes any pretensions to patronage that these higher-class youngsters may entertain for the future.

7 *Pera, Ep.* 376.4 – the leather schoolbag or satchel to carry the papyrus rolls of school books. These were carried to school by a slave because of their weight (cf. §19), but when school was dismissed they became ideal weapons in schoolboy rough-and-tumbles, as schoolbags still are. It may be remarked that the shape of the roll itself determined the need for a professorial chair. The teacher could only develop his text when seated to read from the roll. An over-eager student who buttonholes his teacher for the explanation of a textual point from a book when out of doors was a nuisance, as Libanius himself discovered (*Or.* 1.8).

wounds may occur as a result, I could still derive consolation from the examples I have heard and seen.[8] **(6)** However, the present incident is unprecedented and has never before occurred in a school. You have made war upon the pedagogues[9] whom it was the custom for you to respect. You have either assaulted or threatened them, and you have degraded a profession that has had a proud tradition, for its members have been overwhelmed by the humiliation they have experienced or by their anticipation of a similar experience.

(7) This is not the way they were treated when I was a schoolboy. They enjoyed a prestige second only to that of the teachers, and in this the students followed the lead of the teachers, who personally accorded to the pedagogues honours that were right and proper. For great, truly great, are the services they render their charges – the compulsion required by study and, far more important, the habit of self-control. They are the guardians of youth in its flower, its protections and its defence: they repel unsavoury admirers, send them packing and keep them at a distance: they forbid association with them and frustrate their advances like dogs that bay at wolves.[10] **(8)** This is something a son could not get from a father, nor a pupil from his teacher. The parent who puts the man in charge of his son is engaged upon other activities – the administration of the city, the care of his estates and the slaves, both male and female, that are on them, and often some such business occurs which causes him to spend the entire day in the city square. The attendant, however, has this single job only – to concern himself with his charge and his charge's welfare. At nightfall the father can lie asleep, and besides spend part of the day at it, if he likes; but the attendant brings himself and the lad to the light of the lamp, and first of all, he wakens himself up, and then he goes to the boy and outdoes the crowing cocks, for he rouses him with his

8 For student fights, which could escalate into pitched battles, especially at Athens, cf. *Or.* 1.19ff. (these he had both heard of and seen, but without actually taking part), Eunap. *V.S.* 483ff., Himerius, *Or.* 69 (ed. Colonna). His attitude is ambivalent. He always deplores the use of physical violence, but equally, as in *Or.* 3.22f., he deplores the latter-day absence of such support from his own pupils.

9 The personal attendant appointed by the parent to supervise the upbringing of his son in every sense save that of formal teaching, which remained the preserve first of the *didaskalos* and then of the sophist. He could be most influential in a teacher's relations with his pupils and their parents, whether working in harmony with him, as here, or against him, as in *Or.* 34.

10 The possibility of pederasty, though rarely fully developed since a criminal charge was involved, is always hinted at as a threat to his pupils' welfare by Libanius, cf. §30.

hand.[11] **(9)** Even the teacher's activity falls short of all this. His acquaintance with the lad extends to midday: thereafter he does not see him, associate with him or perform his task upon him. In fact, the learning that he himself imparts to the boy is preserved for him by the attendant, and the method of such preservation is for the attendants to apply pressure, shout at them, produce the cane and wield the strap, drive the lesson into their memories by tasks to this end, some painful, some, as a result of practice, troublesome no more. **(10)** Moreover, although this has nothing to do with formal education, in times of illness they either vie with the mothers or else outdo them – to say nothing of the nurses – for the womenfolk, when they have exhausted themselves in vain, get themselves a rest, but the attendants sit at the bedside, give the patients whatever they need, and proffer their services as they are told or else even before they are told. And if the lad dies, the laments of the attendants are no less than those of the parents, and their grief is more enduring: the parents merely give way to what is natural, but the pedagogues, even though free from such a tie, none the less go into mourning. **(11)** Some I know have even made homes for themselves at the tombstones of their charges, and speak to them from close at hand, applying their lips to the slab, and some of them never left the place until quite a long time afterwards, while others have actually died there. In fact, I know of one case when the father died and the attendant became the rightful guardian to the boy and relieved him of all consciousness of his orphan condition. **(12)** A more able sophist than I, if he let himself go on this theme, would have much to say, and you should respect all this and regard the pedagogues as something precious, and prevent anyone else from insulting them rather than be yourselves guilty of this misconduct. **(13)** What surprises me is that the legislators, who have had such regard for parents that they punish those children who neglect them, have not deemed pedagogues also worthy of the same legislation.[12] I personally used to support my own attendant, a cripple, both here and abroad,[13] just as if there were laws in plenty ordained for the benefit of pedagogues, and even if I expended no money on the others, I still treated them with other marks of esteem. **(14)** My wish was that you too should be, and should be seen

---

11 The school day begins at crack of dawn and ends at midday, cf. *Ep.* 25.7 (where his pupils keep the neighbours awake by performing their practice recitals in the early hours).

12 Such legislation was attributed to Solon, cf. Demosth. *c. Timocr.* 105.

13 I.e., while he was abroad studying in Athens, A.D. 336–9.

to be, people of this sort. But look what happens now! It is the exact reverse: you misuse them. You assault them, insult them, and introduce into the haunts of the Muses practices devised by the amusement of wastrels; and though you should consider outsiders too[14] as good for nothing if they play such tricks, you have brought their malpractices into the holy ground of learning and have yourselves participated in their performance.

(15) Now I will be asked 'Are all pedagogues good, then? Do they all deserve to be respected? Is there none that is a rascal and fit to be punished?' For my part, even about people in other jobs I could not say that all are paragons and guilty of no fault, great or small. Both among governors and governed, among the city councillors and the commons, among judges and advocates, in towns and in the countryside, even among the shepherds who hold converse with their sheep – in every one of these it is possible to find something amiss. But it is not permitted that a gang of ten or a dozen persons should collect together and beat them up, or even take it out of them with words of abuse. You have either to prosecute wrongdoers according to the form of law or keep silent. (16) Hence, quite often a man sits in judgement, though he is guilty on more than one count, and he even puts to death people who have done the same as he, but no one assaults him, or ejects him from his judgement seat, hurls him to the ground and kicks at his head: he will lodge a charge against him, have him brought to justice and see him punished, or if he does not, he will keep his hands to himself. This is what we saw recently in the case of governors who had taken bribes: an accuser presented himself, witnesses were called to testify to the means by which the money found its way to his quarters, and it was brought to light: then, since there was no longer room for denial, the money was reclaimed and the machinery of the law took its course.[15]

(17) So your course of action should have been the same – indictment, prosecution, conviction. If you had proved your case, no one would have words of blame for you, but for those who were guilty, and so obviously so that concealment was impossible. As it is, you failed to take this course, and you arrogate to yourselves to ride rough-shod over your

---

14 These are probably students of disciplines other than his own, i.e., of the Latin rhetor.

15 Sievers ((1868), 191) plausibly identifies this rogue governor with Eustathius, *consularis* of Syria, who was found guilty of extortion and disgraced after leaving office in A.D. 389. See *Or.* 1.271–4, *Or.* 44, *Or.* 54 *passim*.

pedagogues: you cannot possibly deny your misconduct, especially after assaulting them in a most brutal manner. I don't know where this practice originated from, for it to be introduced here for the first time. **(18)** The manner of it is for a carpet to be stretched out on the ground, and for it to be held at each edge by people, many or few, as its size dictates. The prospective victim of this outrage is put in the middle of it, and they toss him up as high as they can[16] – high enough, in all conscience – amid shrieks of laughter. And laughter is provoked among the bystanders, too, for the dizziness of the victim ensures this, and his cries as he is tossed up, and his cries as he comes down. Sometimes he lands in the carpet when it is held high, and he is all right, but at times he misses it and lands on the ground, and off he goes with injuries to his person, so that the outrage is not without physical danger; and the worst of it is that this, too, is a source of laughter.

(19) So this practice, which passes everything for insolence, should, if possible, have been banned from the whole Roman empire,[17] but, failing that, it should never have been introduced into a place of learning, especially when I am in charge of it, for under me, even if this scandalous conduct existed already, it should have been brought to a stop. But as things are, good heavens! It did not exist before, but it has come into being, and not against the slaves who follow you with your books,[18] but against members of an honourable profession who are necessary for the performance of the teachers' task. **(20)** And in consequence the victim takes to his heels and makes off, or, if incapable of so doing, he stays reluctantly, and lives skulking somewhere, and as a result of his experience he is unable to utter a word or look anyone, whether friend or foe, in the eye. The business is so rankly degrading that anyone who has experienced this carpeting is an object of ridicule not merely when people look at him but when they hear him mentioned, for the hearers engrave the incident in their memory. Such are the weapons with which you have attacked the pedagogues, and in giving them a drubbing, you thereby do harm to the teachers, whether they be unaware of the outrage or, if aware of it, they make light of it.

16 Latin, *sagatio*, originally a military practice, Suet. *Otho* 2, Martial 1.4.8.

17 A recognition of Rome as the civilizing power, a comparatively rare admission for Libanius, but in this instance double-edged, considering the Roman origins of a practice he regarded as barbaric and that it was now used for the Latin rhetor's benefit.

18 Cf. §5, above, *Or.* 25.50, Philostr. *V.S.* 2.27.7.

(21) 'The reason,' I am told, 'is that this pedagogue was guilty of malicious behaviour towards one of the teachers of Latin,[19] and the person
against whom his malice was directed said so.' But it is not yet a proof
of malice that A charges B of malice towards him. Surely what is required
is the proof that he has wronged him in such and such a particular way.
So let the complainant reply – or else do it yourselves for him. Did he
turn any of his friends into an enemy? Did he, when people were praising
him, utter any remarks to the contrary, at variance with these commendations? Did he prevent the attendance of any would-be pupils? And did
he cause the defection of any existing ones? **(22)** 'He wanted to do so,'
will be the reply, 'but he could not.' But his story is that the accusation is
false – he wanted no such thing; but he gave this impression because of
his regard for my eloquence, for he forced his students to admire it and
not to attach more importance to Latin letters than to my own. But the
Latin teacher wanted his subject to become superior to mine and he has
often caused pupils to transfer from Greek literature to Latin, and so he
was demanding satisfaction for the welfare of his students, if, in fact,
such welfare consists in the conjunction of first- and second-rate subjects
and not in the suppression of the first-rate for the second-rate.[20]

(23) 'Well, he asked for what he got.' Then the teacher should have
been satisfied with the normal punishment, namely to persuade the
parent and have him dismissed from his supervision of the young, and,
failing that, to keep quiet. But instead of adopting this procedure that
any ordinary person might be expected to take, he enjoined upon you an
improper course of action, the probable consequences of which will be
as discreditable for you as they are pleasing to him. **(24)** At any rate,
from that day to this the city has been full of the tale of the carpeting,
and people pity both the victim and his tormentors, but you more than
him since your behaviour has been of such a kind as this. Thus, if you
were sensible, you ought to have regarded the person who demanded
this of you as your foe. For why did he require of you something he did

19 It is clear from this passage that some, if not all, of the students of Libanius did not
attend his Greek lessons only, but also studied part of the Latin curriculum, as was only to
be expected. Some Latin had been taught at private level before the institution of an official
chair in A.D. 388. Indeed, soon after his arrival in Antioch Libanius is found inviting Latin
teachers to work under him (*Epp.* 534; 539), and now, 30 years later, there are evidently
several Latin teachers, the professor being the African of *Or.* 38.6. What irks Libanius is
not the existence of Latin teachers but their pretensions to primacy over his own system.

20 Cf. *Or.* 3.24. The Greek system is for him superior to the Latin.

not require of himself? If there was nothing wrong in this carpeting, he should have ordered his own pupils at the top of his voice to put the pedagogue on the carpet so as to suffer the treatment that followed. If, however, he condemned the practice as wrong, then he was at fault in introducing you to practices in which he thought it improper for himself to be seen to participate. **(25)** You have made of yourselves instruments for the performance of an action which he was reluctant to perform, and you were not ashamed. The victim of the outrage was just one man, and by the grace of heaven he was not killed, but the alarm has affected all the pedagogues alike, for in the occurrence lies the threat of the extension of the outrage to them all. So don't be surprised that, although only one has had a taste of carpeting, they have banded together with mutual support and set up a cry of protest.[21] Their common fear has provoked this meeting: their idea is that it is better for them not to have this experience than to have it and lament it.

(26) Well, they could, if they had so wished, have approached the governor, but they thought it enough to approach me and to summon me to judge the issue – which is more than you did. This, it appears, was unworthy of your standing! I quenched the flame by my words, but you – you turned up your noses at the dictum of Sophocles[22] and at argument and persuasion, and you jumped to do the deed, and puffed up still further with insolence in consequence of this carpeting, you made off, and next day came into school, when you ought to have been sitting in some dark corner, reproaching yourselves for your misconduct, and doing as all wrong-doers do, blaming fortune instead of yourselves.

(27) 'Oh, yes!' you will tell me, 'only one man was our victim. We have maintained all due respect for the others.' So you did for him, before you treated him so; but for all that, he has been vilely misused. And the fact that he had not experienced it before did not prevent him from experiencing it then. Everyone of those who have not had a taste of carpeting reflects that past immunity is no guarantee for the future, and that the past holds no assurance for what is to come, but that, if anyone ever

21 The pedagogues hold a protest meeting and appeal *en masse* to Libanius as sophist of the city to stop the misconduct of his own pupils. They do not approach the governors, who are for the most part presented in the *Autobiography* as hostile to him. It was, for instance, an unnamed *Comes*, a Christian, who had instituted this Latin chair, and even tried to weaken Libanius' hold on the chair of Greek.

22 Sophocles, *Philoctetes* 97f., 'Now, when I come to the proof, I see that words, not deeds, are masters among men.'

loses his temper, there will soon be many such occurrences. You vented your insolence on a single individual without touching the rest. Does that mean, then, that you have not assaulted the man you assaulted? And by the same argument, is a man who has killed a single individual no murderer, because he has not killed everybody? And I suppose he could not properly be punished for murder because people are still alive! **(28)** No! In my opinion we inflict punishment for two reasons, to assist both those who have and those who have not yet been victims of injustice, as consolation to the first and protection for the second.[23] So while ever the pedagogues see one of their number subjected to such victimization, they live in constant fear of similar treatment, and the fear itself is part of the victimization, the future victim being, as it were, one who has already experienced it.

(29) 'Oh, but look here! Teacher told us to do it.' You are not yet talking about the 'boss', then! Yet even for slaves, if they do wrong under orders, it is not enough for them to blame the boss and tell all they would have had to put up with if they disobeyed. They are punished for their obedience, and they are taught that they must not obey the boss in everything, not even if his behaviour, when in a temper, is harsher than the penalties of the law. **(30)** 'Teacher told us!' Then you should have told this fine teacher, 'We will do what we ought, if you tell us, but not everything. We shall not do anything wrong. We shall not beat our parents, nor yet overthrow altars, when people tell us to, nor yet kill any enemies of theirs.' It could happen, I suppose, that a teacher is smitten with admiration for a handsome pupil and bids him grant favours as he requests. Are we then to grant him this favour, too? That would be scandalous. In fact, as soon as a teacher makes any improper request of a pupil, he loses the right to control him, for this control arose from the pupil's welfare, and if he harms him, he would be his enemy, and the custom is to cause your enemy pain, not pleasure. So, in this case too, the teacher could not reasonably have expected obedience from you when he bade you perform actions which result in the whole body of pedagogues loathing you and the well-behaved students avoiding you.

(31) Every place in the city is full of this story, that certain persons,

23 For Libanius the theory of punishment is confined to the deterrent and the retributive. Any notion of a reformative element is reserved for the process of reproof (*epitimesis*), and is therefore outside the sphere of punishment, which remains corporal.

who desire to strip the students of their pedagogues' protection so that they can indulge themselves to their hearts' content, when unable to find any other means, introduced this practice of carpeting, so that the pedagogues might realize that they had either to keep away from any handsome pupils or, if they persisted in their duty, to be involved in this nasty business of carpeting. **(32)** And how do you think your fathers will feel, if they hear talk of this? Happy and smiling, as fathers would be at the receipt of good tidings? No! Unhappy are the parents of whom you are the sons. Won't they rather moan and groan at the thought of the sons they have sired? Moreover, if you are responsible for such grief and tears in your parents, have you no fear for the wrath of the gods? Or have you but slight regard for this matter, too? In that case, high are the hopes you will live with!

(33) Another thing! It is the habit of students after leaving school to recount in their reunions the things they used to do when at school. Are you going to tell them, then, of what you have just done and brag about it? No, you won't show such self-dislike. You will try to keep it dark and, should someone else mention it, you will be annoyed. Isn't it better, then, not to have done something which you will be ashamed of having done?

(34) Well, isn't a student right to try to please his teacher? Of course he is. So when you behave like this, isn't it inevitable that I should feel despondent? Obviously! And here, even if some imprecation does not follow, grief, even though silently expressed, has the same effect. We must believe that the Furies have the same regard for pedagogues as for parents.[24]

(35) Tell me! Have you, who behaved so, no pedagogues? You have? Then, if you have no respect for them, you are part of an impious crew. If you do respect them, why do you persecute those who belong to other people? What your pedagogues are to you, these are to them, and they bring me profit, just as yours do.[25] And if it were a breach of the rules for your people to receive a beating from someone else, then the rules

24 Refers to Orestes, harried by the Furies after the killing of his mother Clytemnestra.

25 Sc., by recommending Libanius as teacher of their charges. For a pedagogue to be subjected to forcible persuasion for the benefit of the Latin rhetor will result in a loss of pupils, and so of fees, to Libanius. The word 'impious' is not uncommonly used by him to denote Christians. It may well be so used here.

have been broken now, when pedagogues in charge of others are assaulted by you.

(36) This assault and the fear of the like can cause a reduction in the numbers of my flock. By reserving his admiration for a school where he will not suffer this experience and by reporting ill of my own, he will advise parents to send their sons there, and a pedagogue would be pretty plausible in pretending that he liked my system but that he attached more importance to his student's well-being. So instead of the punishment which you should seek of the gods on my account, you are seeking a punishment that damages me.

(37) But leave me out of it, if you like. Let us have another look at your victim who has taken the tossing. He will not make his living here at the same job, for he will not do the job for shame at showing himself before people who saw his misfortunes, and in the place where they occurred; and wherever he goes, he will find the tale of the outrage he has suffered already current. Worst of all for a pedagogue, the fear he exercised upon his charges will be removed. If he finds them idling their time away, he will find them staring him out and bringing the carpet forward. So who will give him his daily bread? He won't be able to turn even to wool-working,[26] for he knows nothing of it. All that is left is a life of beggary and tears. Ought you, then, to be responsible for bringing such a fate on any man alive? Have you no fear of the wrath or the power of the deities who hate such goings-on?

(38) Besides, those who have not yet reached the peak of their ability in their studies would naturally want to enjoy the reputation of good behaviour, and they don't want those who have this ability to damage the reputation it brings by the ill-repute of misconduct like this. Then don't bless the hearts of those who are ill-disposed to me because of envy. I have been told that they revel in the tale of the carpeting, and that they put the blame on me and on my leniency. 'If only he knew how to administer a proper thrashing,' they say, 'this misbehaviour would not happen.' However, I would prefer my students well-disciplined as a result of argument than as a result of the lash, and because of respect rather than because of a beating.[27]

(39) Some of you may say, perhaps, that to reprove you all is unjustified, since you were not all involved in the incident of the carpeting. But,

26 Women's work.
27 Cf. note 2 above.

in my opinion, those who failed to prevent the deed are as guilty as the participants in it, since they are far more numerous than the perpetrators of it, for anyone who had the power, but not the will to put a stop to it, connived in the act. Either you ought not to have allowed it or, by condemning what occurred, you ought to have kept yourselves clear of this brutality. But you did neither, and the result is that, however much you may desire not to be regarded as accessories to the carpeting, this is impossible.

(40) So this address must be considered as due not so much to me, its composer, as to yourselves, who have imposed the need for it. I pray the gods that your souls have been touched by what I have had to say and are the better for it.

ORATION 3:
TO HIS STUDENTS ABOUT HIS SPEECH

INTRODUCTION

This speech was composed by Libanius in his old age (§5), more precisely at some little time after the riots of A.D. 387 (§29) and the institution of an officially appointed Latin rhetor in A.D. 388 (§24). It may be noted that a situation analogous to the fruitless invitation to his declamation, so tartly described in §11ff., is to be found in his later correspondence described with even more bitter irony (*Ep.* 1075 of early A.D. 393).

At first sight this is merely another example of the oratory of reproof (*epitimesis*), a recognized and accepted genre of which Libanius is by temperament and technique a past master. Addressed to his students who have complained of being deprived of their customary declamation from him, it purports to be the vehicle by which his refusal to deliver any such speech is confirmed, with reasons for his attitude – their indiscipline and inattentiveness in lectures and their disloyalty to their teacher. There is, however, a double paradox in this, first in the method of his approach, and second in the content of what he has to say – paradox being undoubtedly one of the most potent instruments for winning the attention of an audience. First, by this profession of refusal to deliver such an oration as they have required, he does in fact deliver one, and secondly, by this manipulation of the content, he has transformed them from being complainants to being themselves the recipients of complaint. He was not the first sophist to take this line. Aelius Aristides, the second-century sophist whom he had taken as his model in so many of his orations, had also composed an oration against critics who complained that he did not give enough declamations, similarly mounting a counter attack. Hence Libanius could claim good classical precedent, as the scribe of Ms. D (Martin) makes clear when he gives this oration the same title as Aristides had chosen. However, by this transformation of rôle he has also transformed the material, bringing it down from the stylistic elevation of the traditional declamation to the day-to-day experience of schoolroom conditions familiar to pupils and teachers alike, however exaggeratedly expressed, and he has simultaneously maintained the pure form of the oratory of reproof as enunciated in the text-books.

The paradoxes and this tacit appeal to the precedent of Aristides make it probable that this speech begins as a *jeu d'ésprit*, designed not merely to reprove his wayward students but first to gain their attention by entertaining them. This tone is set by the deliberate perversion by *double entendre* of the Homeric citation (§6; Homer, *Od.* 15.373), where the Homeric *aidoiois* masculine ('respectable men') becomes neuter ('sexual organs'). Every schoolboy was well enough drilled in Homer to recognize the citation and had wit enough to appreciate the risqué pun, which has the hallmarks of a school joke. This tone is supported by the choice of vocabulary in the following sections (11ff.), where members of his audience find themselves unflatteringly described as mincing in like brides or tightrope walkers and engaging in the various misdemeanours with which they were evidently familiar, the recital of which makes the passage a *locus classicus* for schoolboy misconduct. Having thus secured their full attention with this racy recital of their sins of omission, he then proceeds in more serious vein to their sins of commission and his justification of his attitude on what was evidently for them a special occasion in the school year.

What exactly this occasion was has, owing to long-standing textual corruption, long been a matter of debate. However, Martin's restoration of the correct reading from minor manuscripts has made it clear that this was to be the special speech given by him to mark the closure of the academic year before the summer long vacation. It was clearly the custom for the sophist to deliver open declamations during the autumn and spring, and to round off the session with a final address, on an occasion analogous to the modern school speech day (§9). The misconduct of his students on these earlier occasions had induced him to take this drastic step while simultaneously devising the means to circumvent it.

Available editions are those of Reiske and Foerster and, more recently, the Budé edition by J. Martin (1988). Translations are, into French, by Festugière (1959), 446–52, and much better, by Martin (1988), 83–101, and into German, by Wolf (1967), 143–153.

On Libanius' declamations, see now Russell (1996).

TO HIS STUDENTS ABOUT HIS SPEECH[1]

(1) No one could blame you, in your desire for renown,[2] for demanding your usual discourse, but I think it a reasonable[3] course for me to stay silent. When you hear why, you will pardon me, and quite likely against those who have caused this constraint you will call upon those gods whose special delight is in the composition and delivery of oratory.[4] **(2)** Yet I am surprised that you have not pondered to yourselves what it is that has caused the reversal of this my normal practice, and then, having pondered, you have not perceived the cause, and then, having perceived, instead of keeping quiet or opposing at least those responsible for this state of things, you have the hardihood to talk to me about a speech. **(3)** So, then, if you have neither sought nor found, and are unaware of the actions of those who injure me, you too cannot avoid some responsibility for these same injuries, if you are asleep when you should be wide awake, and are in a state of ignorance when you should know every one of my intimates, especially when your time is spent in the same place and when you meet and talk with one another every day,[5] and it might be expected that you each have as much acquaintance with your neighbour as with yourselves. This would imply not so much minding your own business as complete neglect of me.

(4) Shall I begin my remarks to you on the assumption that you know nothing of the matter, though who could believe that? Now, if because of my silence I were convicted of idleness and negligence, I would be ashamed and regard it as the failing of some rascally slave, for whom the idea of a high day and holiday is to lie abed, hardly stirring a muscle. **(5)** As it is, everyone knows how much my friends blame me for my labours in my old age, when I find it more than honey sweet always to be engaged on my compositions and welding an oration together, and how the worst part of my arthritis is that it

---

1 The variant title in Ms. Laurentianus LVII 44 (*La*, Foerster; *D*, Martin), 'Against those who complained that he did not give declamations', points to Aristides, *Oration* 51 (ed. Dindorf), translated by Behr, *P. Aelius Aristides The Complete Works*, II, 166–72, Leiden 1981.

2 I.e., that gained by their support of their teacher.

3 There is a pun on two different meanings of the Greek *logos*.

4 Hermes and the Muses, as often.

5 In the school, rather than (as Reiske) in hostel accommodation provided by the rhetor. For similar complaints of culpable neglect by his students cf. *Orr.* 34.1; 36.14.

keeps me from writing.[6] Why is it then that I have refused to maintain the custom, even though I have many orations to hand to do so, and why, though they are there, do I not deliver them?

(6) You may perhaps think that I am going to speak of the injustice I suffer in connection with my fees.[7] It is indeed reason enough for anyone to lose his temper and to make him keep silent, that a lad should get money from his father to pay his professor, and then divert it to drink, dicing or amorous adventures[8] – adventures which at times are more brazen than is lawful; and then that he, enveloping his shamelessness about himself,[9] should burst into the classroom, with shouting, threats and assault, and treat everyone else like dirt, and expect the fact of his own arrival to be counted as the professor's reward. (7) However, for a poor student there is both forgiveness and criticism, for should he offer no payment, it is because he cannot, whereas if he joins company with the rest and behaves as badly as they do, how can that be tolerated? (8) One or two are even more insolent in their behaviour than these, for they hope by this means to hide the fact that they have paid no fee, and then, falling under the influence of the others, they waste their time at school on such fine toadying as this, and some don't even know what their professor looks like while others do him all the harm they can in the end.

(9) Any one else, then, would have given this also as a reason for not delivering an oration, not hesitating to proclaim that he was getting his

---

6 Arthritis or gout, which had plagued him from A.D. 355 to 370 and, after a remission of 16 years, had resumed in full force in A.D. 386 (*Or.* 1.243).

7 Libanius consistently refused to exact fees from his pupils, though well aware of the disadvantages of this attitude; cf. *Orr.* 62.19f.; 36.9; 43.6. As professor he drew an official stipend from the community, which was supplemented by fees and presents. His assistants could rely only on these last, which were often slow in coming; cf. *Or.* 31 (*passim*), Petit (1956), 144. Themistius also did not insist on payment (*Or.* 23.349c-d, ed. Dindorf). Augustine mentions avoidance by pupils of paying teachers' fees (*Conf.* 5.12.22).

8 As noted in the Introduction above, a deliberate misinterpretation of Homer, *Od.* 15.373. Probably a smutty joke current in the schools.

9 Textually corrupt. Mss. read ἀναίδεσας or ἀναίδευσας, obviously by confusion with the following ἀναίδειαν. All editors before Martin read ὀνειδίσας, which is a nonsense conjecture. Martin reads ἀνακαλέσας, but it is hard to see why such a sensible word should have become corrupted into the mss. reading. I have translated ἀναδήσας, a conjecture which maintains the confusion of sight and sound with ἀναίδειαν, and is likely to have confused the scribe, being unusual and a more startling variant of ἀναδησάμενος, in keeping with the tone of the passage.

own back on such people for not making payment in full. However, I have long been used to taking no fee, and perhaps by doing so I penalize both the non-payer and the non-recipient – but there it is! It has been a long-standing concession on these lines! No! The question of the money is not the reason why I refuse to end this year's session with a speech.[10]

(10) Then what is, if that isn't? Just this – that I do not see all my students in love with my declamations or even knowing what my job is. They gave me a fine demonstration of this last spring and winter, when I delivered orations on both occasions.[11] **(11)** Just consider. I tell my slave to invite the students to a lecture. Off he runs and does my bidding, but they don't match his speed, though it should be even outdone by their own: some of them dilly-dally over popular songs, or horse-play, or joking, and if ever they do condescend to put in an appearance, when the onlookers object to their slowness on such occasions, they mince along like brides or, with more truth perhaps, like tight-rope walkers,[12] both before and after entering the door, so that they annoy those already seated and awaiting the arrival of such idle young good-for-nothings. **(12)** That is what happens before the speech; but when I am speaking and developing any theme, there is much nodding of heads to one another about drivers, actors, horses, dancers[13] or some fight that has happened or is due to happen. **(13)** What is more, some stand there with arms folded like graven images, or fidget with their noses with either hand, or sit stock still, though there is so much to excite them, or they force an excited listener to sit down, or count the number of the newcomers, or content themselves with looking at the leaves[14] or

10 Martin's reading, following the Mss. JKL is undoubtedly correct – τῆτες for received τῆδε, κατακλεισθῆναι for received κατακλυσθῆναι, which could only be justified as an exaggeratedly strained metaphor, 'being deluged by oratory'! This reading proves that this year's session ended with a speech day.

11 I.e. the orations publicly delivered in his rôle as sophist of the city during the course of the session. His students were expected to support him with attendance and applause.

12 Cf. Lucian, *Rhetorum praeceptor* 9.

13 These were the entertainments which he had given up on his conversion to study at the age of 14, and at which he looked askance all his life (*Or.* 1.5). For students as fans of chariot drivers in the hippodrome, cf. *Or.* 35.13ff. The only legal form of fighting in the arena at this time were *venationes* – man against beast. Gladiatorial combats had been repeatedly banned over the past half-century. For mime he had no good word at all. It was an immoral and indecent form of entertainment.

14 Not (as Festugière (1959), 511) leaves of a book, but of the trees which the inattentive can see in the outside court of the *Bouleuterion* from the lecture room.

chattering about anything that comes into their heads – anything rather than attend to the speaker. **(14)** And the horse-play, too! – spoiling genuine applause with the slow hand-clap,[15] preventing the utterance of an approving cheer, walking through the middle of the whole theatre and diverting as many as they can away from the speech, sometimes by a faked message, sometimes by an invitation to bathe before dinner – yes! There are people who waste their money even on things like that! You wretched students, there is no more profit in it for you, any more than for absentees, nor for the speaker, at least as far as you are concerned, when he fails to get the one real reward for declamations.[16]

(15) And no one could say that I am lying and bringing a baseless charge now, implying that otherwise at the actual time of the occurrence I would have lost my temper at once and used words of anger against the offenders. You know that that is what I have often done, and that I have not seldom called to somebody and told him to get hold of an idler by the scruff of the neck and throw him out, and if that didn't occur, it was because of people who pleaded for him.

(16) What I have just described, then, is proof of your misbehaviour towards me. And the sign that they refused to pay attention when they did come to listen to me is surely the fact that they took away with them inside their heads not a word of what I had spoken. **(17)** In the days of the students who preceded you here the opposite was the case. Every one would go away having memorized a different passage: they would then meet and try to fit them together and reconstruct the whole oration, and they would be annoyed at anything, little though it might be, that escaped them, and their one aim for three or four days afterwards was to repeat the speech[17] to their fathers at home, and for a much longer time here. **(18)** But you are off back to your songs again – you know them off by heart well enough – and to oblivion you consign Demosthenes,[18] peroration and introduction alike, and if somebody asks you whether I

---

15 Mock applause, such as Libanius himself had done with Bemarchius, *Or*. 1.41.

16 Genuine applause, cf. *Or*. 25.50, 'The sophist needs applause, and to win such reward he devotes himself to his oratory'.

17 For examples of such feats of memorization, cf. *Or*. 1.56, 88.

18 Demosthenes here refers to both Libanius himself, who as author of the *Hypotheses* was noted as a specialist in Demosthenes' oratory, and to Demosthenes as the subject matter of his declamations. His prologues on such themes had been particularly well received, cf. *Or*. 1.55, 88.

have made a speech and what it was about, he will receive the answer 'Yes' to the first question, but still not hear what it was about.

(19) 'Ah, yes!' I will be told, 'but I have fallen off and my lectures now are not as good as they used to be.' But that is not what people here say, whether young or old, whether they are still engaged in the legal profession,[19] or after that arduous career have passed on to one of office. No single detail of a speech of mine allows them to sit even a moment unmoved: you can hear them exclaiming that I have excelled myself, that I was good before, but there is a little bit extra in my speeches now, and old age is no impediment. **(20)** So you cannot seek refuge in comments like that, for their praise is testimony to my superiority and debars you from casting aspersions upon my oratory. Surely you would not claim to be better judges of oratory than they are, and yet you blatantly insult them too by your unresponsiveness when their emotions are aroused. Even if you were blind, as far as oratory goes, you should use them as your guides and share in their enthusiasm.[20]

(21) The truth is that you have not the mentality of students who realize what the term 'professor' implies, for whom in their actions on their professors' behalf it is creditable even to overstep the mark. Anyway, whoever describes them in this instance as 'possessed' is no foe but a friend, and bestows upon them high praise, not reproof.[21] **(22)** Many other people far and wide besides myself have seen such students treating these teachers either with the same respect as they do their fathers or with even more, and their fathers fully aware and approving of what they do, even though they see on their sons' bodies the evidence of the battles they fight on their teachers' behalf, scars on head, face, hands and on every limb. In men of such a disposition this affection is so great and strong that it grows old with them. **(23)** Who of you could say

---

19 *Syndikein* is the career of advocate, which is one of the recognized paths to office in the imperial administration and so to immunity from curial liturgies. Syndics would be expert critics of Libanius' oratory.

20 Cf. *Or.* 1.88, for the rapturous reception of his declamations.

21 Cf. *Or.* 34.31. Students were expected to support their teacher through thick and thin, and to take part in the fierce gang fighting between rival schools. Libanius himself had been shanghaied on his arrival at Athens in A.D. 336 and forcibly enrolled as a pupil of Diophantus (Eunap. *Vit. Lib.* 2), and so felt himself absolved of the need to give any such physical support to his professor (*Or.* 1.17ff.), but he had been brought up in such a tradition and regarded such support by his students as a laudable and valuable aim in all but exceptional cases such as his own (*Or.* 58.5).

that he has performed any such service on my behalf? What fight, what danger, what fisticuffs have you encountered? Indeed, by what word, what utterance, threat or glance have you taken my part? **(24)** You have abandoned your loyalty to your professor and have become part of the following of other chairs and titles,[22] and there instead you pay the dues you owe, and by so doing, you wrong me and support them with word and deed and favours of every kind: you thrust the second-rate forward to occupy pride of place, and you plume yourselves on the desertions you have caused among my students, and on the increased prestige of the man to whom you have attached yourselves – prestige won at the cost of damage to the rest. **(25)** So far from undertaking any task on my behalf, you would not even remember me in your prayers. And even that is not enough for you: you have even cursed me before now. **(26)** How have I come to be convinced of that? Why, by two sure tokens, by your annoyance at my success and your delight at my distress. Isn't that your attitude both when I get new students and when my students sail away to other places?[23] Is this, then, good reason for me to deliver a speech?

(27) 'Then are they all malicious?' it will be asked. 'Have you not one decent, genuine pupil?'[24] Yes, but you can count them on the fingers of your hands, while the bad are legion. Under these circumstances it is more logical not to deliver my speech because of the many than to deliver it because of the few. If it had been possible to oblige these on their own, it would have been my dearest wish, but it is impossible, and so the decent students must put up with it, if I cannot grant the favour I would like to do. **(28)** But shall I be giving these rascals yet another chance of behaving like this, because of whom I have had to endure such dreadful complaints about hooliganism among my students, and – upon my word! – have had to listen to such remarks from people whose chief delight is to be able to criticize me? I could not say whether their

---

22 Although in-fighting between schools of the rival teachers had always been the norm, in Antioch it had become more vicious with the installation of an official chair of Latin in A.D. 388 (cf. *Or.* 1.255), whereby the truancy and desertions already deplored at an earlier date had increased (cf. *Or.* 43 *passim*). Libanius naturally regards alternative studies like Latin and law as second-rate and inferior to his sophistic education with its impeccable Hellenic literary background. His pupils and their parents did not always agree. Cf. *Orr.* 36.8; 58.22.

23 To Rome or Berytus, for the study of law.

24 For the same argumentations cf. *Orr.* 35.30; 58.15.

accusations are true, but in any case everyone ought to have taken the utmost care and not given the ghost of a chance for complaint.[25]

(29) There was great necessity for the frequent orations which have become the source of criticism. I had to give our generous emperor his due from us,[26] and your fathers had to realize that I was at my task and not reduced to silence, overwhelmed by the vastness of our troubles. **(30)** Now, however, I see no good reason for a declamation. Indeed there is this point too. If I don't invite those I used to invite, I would offend people I should not: if, however, I do invite them, I would make them better acquainted with your short-comings, and they would not keep quiet about them upon leaving. So why should I broadcast more widely what goes on here?

(31) 'Yet some of those, also,' it may be objected, 'asked for the speech, as well as the better sort.' True! They asked, but they asked only with their tongue; in their hearts they wanted none of it. I am not such a fool as to think of nonsense of this sort as more effective than a long period of time and so much trouble.

(32) 'Well, how will you behave towards this group,' it is asked, 'if any of the gods gives you another year's lease of life?' If there is any improve-ment – and everything lies in the lap of fortune – I shall follow the lead of events: if things stay as they are now, I shall behave exactly as I do now, and devise some other method by which the decent students may derive some advantage.

(33) Then you will be surprised that I choose to live in such trouble and despondency when it is in my power to be rid of pupils like these. But what am I to do? Am I to send them packing, and reduce my numbers? What greater pleasure than that could I give to 'Priam and his brood'?[27] They keep their eyes on me, desiring only to see me in charge of a handful and with my command dwindling. But I have seen even a general commanding an infamous army steeling himself to endure and

25 Hooliganism of the pupils out of school discredits the teachers who are held respon-sible for it. Cf. *Or.* 38.12. It is not impossible that this passage refers to the circumstances of *Or.* 58.

26 Theodosius, referring to his clemency after the riots of A.D. 387. For Libanius' conduct at that time cf. *Or.* 34.6 and notes. This passage gives the lie to his claim (*Or.* 1.253) that his oratory on that occasion was well received, a mark of his growing unpopu-larity since.

27 Homer, *Il.* 1.255 – the speech of Nestor on the occasion of the quarrel between Achilles and Agamemnon.

taking precautions that they should not fall into the hands of the foe. **(34)**
It is also a characteristic of mine to be reluctant to settle old scores, and I
have been schooled to endure rather than to hit back. But most important, I am on friendly terms with their parents and their home towns.[28] I
am therefore afraid that, if they hear of their expulsion, they will mourn
for them as though for the dead, or even more, since they consider
disgrace worse than death, and they are aware that such a disgrace as
this is worse than any that the courts can inflict. **(35)** Legal disgrace, in
fact, can be removed, but this must remain for ever and accompany a
man from his boyhood to his grave; it must ruin all opportunity of free
social intercourse at every stage of his life, for he will be met with
remarks like these. 'Shameless wretch with the eyes of a dog,[29] were you
not expelled from the sacred rites of oratory for defiling the haunt of the
Muses?' **(36)** My desire is to spare his father, mother, home town and
unborn children upon whom this disgrace must inevitably fall, and so I
have not resorted to that, but have adopted this alternative counsel, a
counsel which, I am convinced, is right.

(37) It is in your power to ensure that nothing of this kind recurs. If
you improve – and that is easy, if you so wish – then you will see the fulfil-
ment of all obligations on my side also, and you will see me extending to
you an invitation to such an oration rather than being urged by you to
give it.

---

28 It is essential for the teacher to remain on good terms with the parents, so as to maintain student numbers and the efficacy of his teaching by such harmony, cf. *Or.* 62.32.

29 Homer, *Il.* 1.225. Scholastic insubordination is for Libanius tantamount to impiety,
since oratory and religion are inseparable.

INDEX OF PERSONS AND PLACES IN THE TEXT

References are to speech number and section of the translation; entries are arranged in the order in which the speeches appear in this volume.

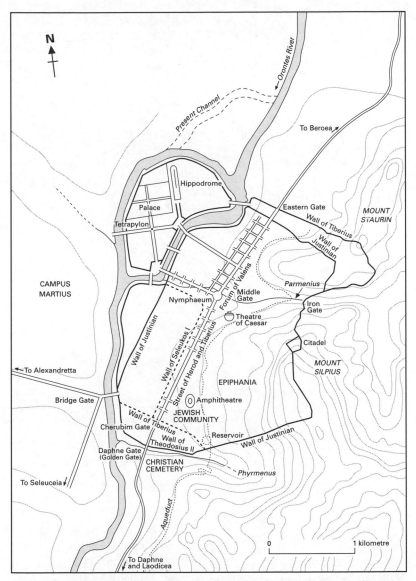

Antioch in late antiquity (based on *The Chronicle of John Malalas*, trans. Elizabeth Jeffreys, Michael Jeffreys and Roger Scott, Byzantina Australiensia 4, Melbourne 1986, 309; and G. Downey, *A History of Antioch in Syria*, Princeton 1961, Plate 11).